LONG RUN TO FREEDOM:
SPORT, CULTURES AND IDENTITIES IN SOUTH AFRICA

Global sport is a mélange of diverse
contexts, networks, and social processes.
This series seeks to enhance our
understanding of global sport through
the publication of critically informed,
interdisciplinary scholarship in history,
cultural studies, political economy,
international relations, and management.

LONG RUN TO FREEDOM:
SPORT, CULTURES AND IDENTITIES IN SOUTH AFRICA

JOHN NAURIGHT

FITNESS INFORMATION TECHNOLOGY
A Division of the International Center for Performance Excellence
262 Coliseum, WVU-CPASS ▪ PO Box 6116
Morgantown, WV 26506-6116

Library of Congress Card Catalog Number: 2010921219
ISBN: 978-1-935412-04-5

Production Editor: Matt Brann
Cover Design: Scott Lohr, 40 West Studios
Cover Photo: South Africa president Nelson Mandela congratulates South African rugby team captain François Pienaar before handing him the William Webb trophy after South Africa's victory over New Zealand in the final of the 1995 Rugby World Cup at Ellis Park in Johannesburg. Photo courtesy of Jean-Pierre Muller/AFP/Getty Images.
Printed by: Thomson-Shore, Inc.

10 9 8 7 6 5 4 3 2 1

Fitness Information Technology
A Division of the International Center for Performance Excellence
West Virginia University
262 Coliseum, WVU-CPASS
PO Box 6116
Morgantown, WV 26506-6116
800.477.4348 (toll free)
304.293.6888 (phone)
304.293.6658 (fax)
Email: fitcustomerservice@mail.wvu.edu
Website: www.fitinfotech.com

CONTENTS

For Jenni, Ashley, Lauren, Shiloh, and Spike and to the memory of Dennis Brutus and the memory and honor of all the South African men and women who have fought for a level playing field.

— JN

LIST OF ABBREVIATIONS

ABM	American Board Mission
ADC	Aide-de-camp
ANC	African National Congress
AWB	Afrikaner Resistance Movement
BMSC	Bantu Men's Social Centre
BSC	Bantu Sports Club
CABTA	Citzen's All Black Tour Association
CSRU	City and Suburban Rugby Union
DDAFA	Durban and District African Football Association
DSR	Department of Sport and Recreation
FA	Football Association
FAK	Federasie van Afrikaanse Kultuurverinigings
FASA	Football Association of South Africa
FIFA	Federation of International Football Associations
FNB	First National Bank
GAA	Gaelic Athletic Association
GWCRFU	Griqualand West Colonial Rugby Football Union
IAAF	International Amateur Athletic Federation
ICC	Imperial (later International) Cricket Council
ICU	Industrial and Commercial Worker's Union
IOC	International Olympics Committee
IRB	International Rugby Board
JAFA	Johannesburg African Football Association
JBFA	Johannesburg Bantu Football Association
JCC	Johannesburg City Council
MCC	Marylebone Cricket Club
NEAD	Johannesburg Non-European Affairs Department
NGK	Dutch Reformed Church
NNFA	Natal Native Football Association
NOCSA	National Olympic Committee of South Africa
NP	National Party

NSC	National Sports Congress/National Sports Council
NPSL	National Professional Soccer League
NSL	National Soccer League
NZRFU	New Zealand Rugby Football Union
PAC	Pan African Congress
PFP	Progressive Federal Party
RDP	Reconstruction and Development Programme
RWC	Rugby World Cup
SAACB	South African African Cricket Board
SAAFA	South African African Football Association
SABC	South African Broadcasting Corporation
SACA	South African Cricket Association
SACB	South African Cricket Board
SACBOC	South African Cricket Board of Control
SACCB	South African Coloured Cricket Board
SACOS	South African Council of Sport
SACRFB	South African Coloured Rugby Football Board
SACU	South African Cricket Union
SADF	South African Defense Force
SAIRR	South African Institute of Race Relations
SANROC	South African Non-Racial Olympic Committee
SAOCGA	South African Olympic and Commonwealth Games Association
SAONGA	South African Olympic and National Games Association
SANZAR	South African New Zealand Australian Rugby
SARB	South African Rugby Board
SARFU	South African Rugby Football Union
SARU	South African Rugby Union
SASA	South African Sports Association
SASF	South African Soccer Federation
SASF-PL	South African Soccer Federation Professional League
SCSA	Supreme Council for Sport in Africa
TRFU	Transvaal Rugby Football Union
UCBSA	United Cricket Board of South Africa
UDF	United Democratic Front
WDNFA	Witwatersrand District Native Football Association
WPCC	Western Province Cricket Club
WPCRU	Western Province Coloured Rugby Union

PREFACE

Two major international events in 2009 and 2010 have prompted me to revisit the book I wrote on sport in South Africa in the mid-1990s. The first was the release of the movie *Invictus* directed by Clint Eastwood, which stars Morgan Freeman as Nelson Mandela and Matt Damon as South African national rugby team captain François Pienaar. *Invictus* recounts the story of the 1995 Rugby World Cup, which was a pivotal event in the shaping of the last two chapters of this book and in the beginnings of forming a new national identity in post-apartheid South Africa. The second is the FIFA World Cup of soccer being held in Africa for the first time in 2010, which will be hosted by South Africa. I hope that readers of this book will gain insights into how both of these sports and the other major South African team sport of cricket have shaped identities in South Africa. It may be a cliché to allege that one country is more "sports mad" than another, and whether South Africa is relatively sporty or not, it is clear that sport plays a central role in broader social identification, in political calculations (President Mandela and the 1995 Rugby World Cup or President Jacob Zuma on stage with FIFA President Sepp Blatter at the World Cup final draw in Cape Town), and in economic development strategies in ways that touch the lives of virtually every South African either directly or indirectly. Millions of South Africans play sports formally or informally, and many millions more follow the fortunes of their national teams and leading sports figures.

Sport, Cultures and Identities in South Africa was written at a time when the future of sport in South Africa was uncertain, despite the momentary euphoria surrounding the 1995 World Cup victory, and in which histories of sport there largely ignored over 85 percent of the population. During my work on the book, South Africa was in the process of transformation from an apartheid society to one in which all adults had the vote and the government worked hard to ensure the future for all of the population, rather than a privileged few. Several key events in society and in sport suggested that the future would be more positive than the past, although the challenges were great. Most notable among these were the election of Nelson Mandela as

President in 1994, the successful hosting of the 1995 Rugby World Cup, in which the South African team won in dramatic fashion over arch-rivals New Zealand, and the South African victory in the African Cup of Nations soccer tournament a year later (football for those readers outside the USA), which was moved to South Africa at the eleventh hour. Almost overnight anything seemed possible, although the harsh legacy of apartheid meant that day to day life would take many more years to change for most South Africans.

The successes of South Africa, not just on the field but in the operation of these events, suggested to some that there were greater opportunities for South Africa in the world of global sporting events. Strong bids were organized for the right to host the 2004 Summer Olympic Games and for the 2006 FIFA World Cup in soccer, the two golden prizes in global sport. Although both of these bids failed, the latter in dramatic fashion by one vote (coincidentally cast by an elderly New Zealander), they suggested that South Africa should be taken seriously as a possible host by FIFA and the International Olympic Committee for their marquee events, particularly as each wants to demonstrate that their organization is the most universal one on Earth (both have more affiliated national governing bodies than the United Nations has total members). Indeed, FIFA and its President Sepp Blatter were impressed enough to alter their process for tournament location selection. As a result, South Africa won the right to host the 2010 World Cup, as FIFA ensured that its tournament rotated across the continents. So, in 2010 the sporting world focused on Africa. Much is riding on the success of this event, not only for South Africa but for all African nations as they look to the future.

The question on many minds within South Africa is what will the legacy of the 2010 World Cup be? This will take many years to fully ascertain. Hosting a mega-event is a risky business. We know from recent global sporting events that there can be long-term benefits—the revitalization and modernization of Barcelona, Spain, and the reclamation of an entire wasteland area of Sydney, Australia, which is now a public park full of world class sporting facilities, stand out as examples. But, there can be long-term difficulties—half empty soccer stadiums in Japan, long-term debt in Montreal, Canada, and failures to meet long-term projected tourism targets. With upwards of half of the population unemployed and increasing infrastructural needs from basic electricity, clean water, and housing to public education, South Africa risked more than many other nations. Some question whether a corporatized event run by a multi-national sporting organization that controls so many aspects of the World Cup can really serve the long-term needs of so many South Africans. Others argue that without the World Cup the funds that are flowing into the South African economy would take many more years to materialize. Both sides are wise to be cautious in their long-term predictions.

What is hoped, and what the publication of a new edition of this book is meant to do, is that a fuller understanding of the history of sport in South Africa and of South African society in general will generate a long-term interest in the future of the country within the international community. In the lead up to the World Cup and in its aftermath, I hope that a reading of *Long Run to Freedom: Sport, Cultures and Identities* in South Africa will give those turning an eye to the country for the first time a sense of the role that sport has played, and continues to play, in the most developed country in sub-Saharan Africa. The first edition was well received and has been used widely but, sadly, is now difficult to find in print. So, I am excited that Fitness Information Technology has agreed to release a new edition of the book, particularly as I am told it is still the most widely used overview of sport in South Africa.

This book does not claim to be a full A-Z history of all sports in South Africa, as that is far too vast an undertaking for a single volume. Rather, I situate sport within the wider social, political, and economic development of South Africa over the past 150 years, with particular focus on the three main team sports played there by men: association football, cricket, and rugby union football. These are also the most commercialized of the local sports. Additionally, the main ethnic groups in South Africa and their sporting histories are examined in this volume with examples from local, regional, and national levels.

Sport was divided in many ways during the eras of segregation and apartheid. Whites, those South Africans fully descended from the peoples of Europe, played in their own competitions, while Blacks, all of those not fully descended from Europeans, had a number of competitions. At different points in time, black South Africans played in non-racial or mixed competitions in which all blacks could play. At others, Africans, those people fully descended from the peoples of Africa, played in their own leagues, and "Coloureds" and "Indians" played in theirs. Although not really accepted as a racial term in other parts of the world, in South Africa, "Coloured" was an official racial category that encompassed mixed-race people as well as the descendants of slaves brought from southeast Asia to the Cape colony in the seventeenth century, many of whom were Muslim and who have retained their Muslim faith. It may be surprising to outsiders but even within the Coloured community competitions in the Western Cape before 1960 were divided between ones that banned Muslims and ones that were primarily, though not exclusively, Muslim. The reasons for this are explored within these pages. In the latter part of the nineteenth century, indentured servants were brought into the Natal colony (present day KwaZulu-Natal) to work on the sugar plantations there. Many stayed in South Africa, some temporarily, such as Gandhi, others permanently. Some are Hindi, some Tamil, and some Sikh. Whites were also divided between the original settlers who were Dutch (first appearing at Cape Town in 1652) with a smattering of French Huguenots who arrived soon after and English-speaking whites who began to arrive in 1820. In the latter part of the nineteenth century, a nationalist and language movement emerged within the former group who labeled themselves Afrikaners and their language Afrikaans. During the twentieth century, Afrikaner men took to rugby and largely shaped it as their game, although English-speaking whites also played. Cricket, on the other hand, was almost exclusively a game for English-speaking whites within white South Africa.

Thus South Africa was a society that was divided in many ways: legally, linguistically, culturally socially, and, indeed, in sports. For example, all the main groupings listed above played association football and cricket in significant enough numbers and all but Indian South Africans played rugby union as well. Despite this history, relative isolation meant that certain sports became aligned with certain social groups. Rugby became a game for whites that symbolized masculinity and struggle, particularly for Afrikaners, while soccer was viewed less positively. For black South Africans, however, soccer symbolized a freedom of expression often denied them in wider society and indeed within other team sports. Collective will is required for success in rugby union, and although collective will is important in soccer, individual flair can carry the day. Thus, stylistic play came to be prized by black soccer fans and was taken up by many black players. Black soccer players achieved a celebrity status within black communities that could only be matched by the top echelon of African National Congress leaders, many of whom spent much of their early careers in sports administration. As a result, association soccer came to be the dominant game for African, Indian, and many Coloured South Africans. The dichotomy appears simple: rugby was a white man's game while soccer was a black man's game. Many believed this to be true, although the histories of both sports clearly demonstrate that the reality was less clear-cut. A significant number of whites played soccer, and an equally significant number of blacks played rugby. In summer, cricket was the largest sport across the major racial groups and, although segregated as well, was less attached to the black/white divide than the two main soccer codes. For women, netball was by far the largest sport, and very few women played the main men's team sports before at least the 1990s. Women's sports sadly remained at the margins in a society that was not only divided by race but also prescribed strong gender boundaries.

Although South Africa has, since the arrival of Europeans in 1652, had a segregated society, the election of the National Party to power in 1948, at a time when former colonial powers were moving towards granting independence to their colonies after World War II, placed South Africa at odds with the rest of the world. The National Party ran on a platform of apartheid, which planned for the total separation of society spatially and socially. All geographic space in the country would be assigned to a particular racial group. Indeed, to make this happen, vibrant multi-racial communities such as Sophiatown in Johannesburg and District Six in Cape Town were razed, and residents were removed farther away from the central city to new racially designated areas, while the formerly black dominated areas were declared for whites only. Sophiatown was even renamed Triompf, which is Afrikaans for triumph or victory.

Apartheid laws extended segregationist policies and included such edicts as the Group Areas Act (dividing the country into racial residential areas), the Mixed Marriages Act (banning inter-racial marriage), the Suppression of Communism Act (meant to limit political dissent, and communism was defined more broadly than even in the USA of the 1950s), and the Universities Act (which made South Africa's universities for whites only in 1959). These were meant to order society racially and to protect distinct communities. These appeared in rapid succession after the National Party consolidated their position in the 1953 election.

The Western world largely went along with what was happening in South Africa due to several key factors. Chief among these were that South Africa held the largest supply of strategic minerals used in nuclear weapons outside of the Soviet Union and that South Africa was a settler society within the British Commonwealth of nations. All of this began to unravel by the early 1960s. The Sharpeville Massacre, where 69 black South Africans were murdered by the South African police who overreacted to a protest, made the world turn a sharper, more critical eye on South Africa, as did the arrest, trial, and imprisonment of Nelson Mandela shortly thereafter.

In sports, it was the tradition that whites-only teams represented South Africa in international competitions and that whites-only national associations were recognized by international sporting organizations, which were white dominated at the time these associations were granted official status. As former Asian and African colonies became independent nations and gained voting rights in international sports federations, the power began to shift slightly away from the imperial old boys' network based in Europe, North America, and Australasia that had hitherto governed world sport. As long as South Africa remained a country in which blacks were denied an equal vote and equal access to national sporting teams, opposition to South Africa was bound to increase in this changing world context. Indeed, sport emerged at the vanguard of international pressure on South Africa and became a key element in the anti-apartheid movement. As a result, South Africa was denied participation in the 1964 and 1968 Olympic Games and was finally expelled from the Olympic Movement in 1970. The government argued that the expulsion was part of a global communist plot against South Africa, but this could not be alleged in the same way when formerly close sporting allies such as Australia, New Zealand, and the United Kingdom began to limit South African participation in international rugby and cricket.

This was the legacy of sport in South Africa that shaped its sporting history into the 1990s when the first edition of this book was written. I had the benefit of examining sport in the first few years of "unity" in the post-apartheid era, although the bulk of my concern was with sport in the eras of segregation and apartheid. Indeed, it was not yet clear whether events such as the 1995 World Cup would be transformative or would merely create temporary diversion from the widespread societal problems that the newly reformed nation faced. Supporters have argued for the former, while detractors have pursued the latter. As is often the case, the reality lies somewhere in the middle. *Invictus* quite rightly portrays the 1995 World Cup as a powerful moment in the attempts to build a new South Africa centered on the impressive personalities of President Mandela and national team captain Pienaar. Having been in South Africa at the time, I can confess that the feel good factor the movie attempts to capture was genuinely felt throughout society at the time. It is a feeling that South Africans have tapped into from time to time but never to the levels achieved during the 1995 tournament. South Africa also won the 2007 Rugby World Cup to widespread acclaim, but this was outside of South Africa and thus more removed from people's daily lives than when it was in their midst.

There have been new events and a number of historical studies of South African sports that have appeared since the publication of the first edition.[1] These have enhanced, but not altered, my general thinking about sport in South Africa. Thus, I stand by the general arguments made in the first edition of the book with a few minor caveats based on my own further research and that of others since the book first appeared. In the rest of the preface, I refer to their insights and bring out a few of my own that have emerged since the book was first published.

What we know about the role of sport in South African society has been enriched by several studies of single sports that were published after *Sport, Cultures and Identities in South Africa*. Of particular importance are books that have focused on single sports, such as the excellent history of soccer by Peter Alegi, entitled *Laduma! Soccer, Politics and Society in South Africa* (2004); the study of rugby by Black and Nauright, *Rugby and the South African Nation* (1998); and the examination of cricket by Merrett and Murray entitled *Springbok Cricket* (2004). All three focus on the role of politics and race in South Africa's major male team sports. Black and Nauright focus on the role of rugby as a South African cultural activity and then how its centrality to white culture in particular made rugby boycotts highly powerful, particularly when pressure was applied by their archrival, New Zealand. Murray and Merrett highlight the domestic and international politics that affected cricket in South Africa and beyond, accessing previously unavailable archival sources for the significant period of the 1960s. Douglas Booth's *The Race Game* (1998), which appeared about the same time as the first edition of this book, focuses attention on the broader role of politics in the struggle for non-racial sport in South Africa, covering material from soccer, rugby, and cricket and other sports in the best single volume dealing with politics and sport during the apartheid era.

Alegi's work is the starting point for a thorough understanding of the history of soccer in South Africa from a political and social history perspective up to the early 1970s. His book encompasses archival and interview material to examine soccer on a scale not yet achieved by any other historian of soccer in South Africa. What Alegi highlights, and I discuss in this text, is the role that soccer played both for African communities as a whole and for the development of political skills, as many future politicians began their careers as soccer administrators. As with Coloured rugby in Cape Town, soccer culture in Johannesburg encompassed gangsterism, fame, and stardom beyond the confines of everyday life, and indeed, soccer playing and supporting became outlets for what Alegi calls a "rowdy masculinity." We are now learning more fully about the ways in which sports provided outlets from the emasculation and impoverishment felt by many black South Africans during the eras of segregation and apartheid. Overcrowded facilities and lack of resources for quality infrastructure meant that black sporting cultures developed in ways that were different from the white experience of sport in cleaner and more modern sporting facilities. Although sports facilities improved during the 1980s, particularly with the building of the Soccer City stadium in Soweto, at the time of President Mandela's election and the unification of sporting structures in South Africa that occurred during the early 1990s, the experiences of black and white sports players and fans were vastly different. These differences have not been fully resolved; however, professional sporting competitions in soccer, rugby, and cricket in particular are now spaces where class differences, as much as race, are becoming evident as access is based primarily on the ability to pay more so than to specific communities. Other sports are emerging; however, they have not captured the national imagination in ways that the main men's team sports have.

We are still awaiting broad histories of netball, track and field, swimming, and other sports that have been played for a long time and by various groups within South Africa. So although there have been positive additions to our historical knowledge of sport in South Africa in the past decade, there is still much work for historians of sport in South Africa to do. In this book, I offer a framework for which these studies might approach histories of individual sports, as well as for a broader history of all sport in South Africa, but my primary goal is to develop an understanding of the role that sports have played in the development of South Africa as a nation and in the cultural meanings and identities that have been attached to sport. Sports are part of the heart and soul of South African identities and in the development of pride in a new multi-cultural South Africa. There is still a long way to go, but so far things have moved in a generally positive direction.

BEYOND 1995 AND THE ROLE OF THE 2010 FIFA WORLD CUP

After the 1995 World Cup victory, South Africans were motivated across all sectors to work for the development and future of the country. Politically, President Mandela gained additional popularity, especially with white South Africans. His successor, Thabo Mbeki, sought to further Mandela's and the African National Congress' (ANC) policies to continue improving the lives of South Africans while at the same time encouraging international investment and economic growth. Indeed, just before becoming President, then Deputy President Mbeki quoted from this book in a 1999 speech in which he sought to increase investment in sports sponsorship.[2] Unfortunately, Mbeki did not have the international or national cache or charisma that Mandela had and was eventually maneuvered out from within his own party in favor of Jacob Zuma. The ANC, post-Mandela, has struggled to convert itself from a liberation movement to a governing party, and opposition that was contained in Mandela's government of national unity has slowly emerged, particularly in the Western Cape and KwaZulu-Natal regions where opposition parties have won control of provincial governments on occasion since 1994.

In sport, South Africa won the 1996 African Nations Cup tournament, which it hosted as a last-minute replacement. The tournament built on the 1995 Rugby World Cup in maintaining good will for the nation via the country's sporting teams. The South African cricket team has been ranked in the top two or three nations for virtually the entire period since 1995, despite the shocking revelations of match-fixing by the late former national captain Hansie Cronje. Indeed, after the Truth and Reconciliation Commission, "Hansiegate," as it was called, was the highest profile public enquiry held in post-apartheid South Africa. Cronje tragically died in a plane crash not long after his banning from cricket and in true post-apartheid fashion was at least partly rehabilitated in reputation by none other than Mandela himself.[3]

With the ending of apartheid and the political and cultural baggage that was attached to the major team sports in South Africa, other sports sought to capitalize by presenting themselves as less tied to old identities and structures. The Australian Football League undertook a program to develop Aussie Rules in South Africa with some success, while Major League Baseball (MLB) established its "Pitch, Hit, and Run" program there in the 1990s. Since that time, seven South Africans have signed professional baseball contracts in the USA, three with the Kansas City Royals, now perhaps the best known MLB team in the country.[4] The National Basketball Association (NBA) set up its African "Basketball without Borders" program in Johannesburg, ostensibly to promote basketball and development in Africa but also clearly to market the NBA in South Africa, which is easily the biggest media and money market for the League in Africa for the foreseeable future.[5] The NBA is not alone; soccer academies are appearing around the country, and the Dutch soccer giant Ajax Amsterdam set up Ajax Cape Town, one of the leading soccer clubs in South Africa. With the soccer world tuned into South Africa since 2000, the interest in investing in players and media presence by foreign clubs increased dramatically.

Although other sports have had some successes in the New South Africa, the traditional sports of soccer, rugby, and cricket for men and netball for women have remained strong and are widely followed. Soccer is still the undisputed king of sports among black South Africans and has pockets of strong support in white South Africa. Cricket remains popular across all sectors of society, and rugby, although still followed more intensely by whites, is also generally supported. Rugby was reinvigorated with the 2007 World Cup win by the Springboks and the subsequent 2009 Tri-Nations Championship.

Since the ending of apartheid, South Africa has embarked on major campaigns to lure large-scale events to South Africa in the hopes of promoting infrastructural development and enhancing tourism. Using what Swart and Bob call the "seductive discourse of development," South Africa has sought to use its position as the only relatively developed nation in sub-Saharan Africa to lure global events that had previously ignored the continent.[6] As I have mentioned, the 1995 Rugby World Cup and 1996 Africa Cup of Nations tournaments were well run and put South Africa on the international mega-events map. As a result of planning and organization of these events, Cape Town was viewed as a creditable candidate for the right to host the 2004 Summer Olympic Games. The bid was actually initiated by businessman Raymond Ackerman in 1990 while negotiations for "unity" in sports and politics were in process. By 1993 the bid was in motion prior to Mandela being elected in 1994 or any major event being hosted in the country since the end of apartheid. Ackerman was maneuvered out in 1995, and a public-private partnership with strong government support officially proposed the bid to the IOC in December 1995. Although 11 cities initially bid, only five were allowed as finalists by the IOC: Cape Town, Athens, Buenos Aires, Rome, and Stockholm. Cape Town survived to the third round of voting but lost out to Athens and Rome, the former of course winning the right to host on the final ballot. The Cape Town bid presented itself as "a bid for Africa" and, if successful, as a launching pad for an African renaissance. This theme reappeared in discourses surrounding the 2006 FIFA World Cup bid, which resulted in South Africa winning the right to host the World Cup in 2010. As Swart and Bob rightly argue, the Cape Town bid was premature, yet it was important in establishing South Africa as a destination that could handle an event as large as the Olympics or the soccer World Cup.

Despite the rush of attention and the increase in scholarship on sport in South Africa, the wider world, particularly North America, knows little about South African sport and South African society in general. International media raised concerns about security in the lead up to the FIFA World Cup with little reference to South Africa's successful experiences of hosting major international events up to that time. Nor do many outsiders fully appreciate the nuances and differences between countries in Africa the way they do about European countries. Few non-Europeans would mistake or conflate France and Germany or England and Italy, yet there is little understanding that South Africa is different from Nigeria or Kenya in ways that are perhaps even more striking than between the European nations just mentioned. South Africa has many problems common to developing countries but also has highly developed industrial and technological sectors, has a well developed tourism infrastructure, and was viewed as safe enough to host the Indian Premier League 20/20 professional cricket competition in 2009 when security concerns on the Indian subcontinent threatened the competition.

South Africa still faces many challenges. Unemployment and poverty are far too high. Sporting opportunities have not been extended throughout society, although international development initiatives in sport and the presence of major events in the country have started to make a difference. When I completed the first edition of this book in early 1997, I was pessimistic about the future of the country, despite the momentary success of "Mandela's Boys" in the 1995 Rugby World Cup. The challenges are great, but the future is promising. If we are to understand where we need to go in South Africa in sport, we need to understand what role sport has played historically and what meanings have been attached to various sports in the country.

From segregation to apartheid to "unity" to globalization, sport has undergone many changes in South Africa; yet, as former President Mandela famously said:

> Sport has the power to change the world. It has the power to unite in a way that little else does. It speaks to youth in a language they understand. Sport can create hope where once there was only despair. It is more powerful than governments in breaking down racial barriers. It laughs in the face of all types of discrimination.

With hard work and perseverance, sport has helped lead symbolic change in how South Africans see themselves and each other. It is my hope that this book will provide readers with insights into the history and meaning of sports in South African society, whether in Cape Town, Cairo, Chicago, Cheyenne, Colchester, Chennai, or anywhere else around the world. For as much as we have differences, the South African phrase "Simunye" reminds us that "we are one."

NOTES

1. Among the most important are:
   Alegi, P. (2004). *Laduma!: Soccer, politics and society in South Africa*. Durban: University of KwaZulu-Natal Press.;
   Allen, D. (2008). South African cricket: Imperial cricketers and imperial expansion, 1850-1910. *International Journal of the History of Sport, 25*(4), 443-471.;
   Badenhorst, C. (2003). New traditions, old struggles: Organized sport for Johannesburg's Africans, 1920-90. *Sport in Society, 6*(2/3), 116-143.;
   Badenhorst, C., & Mather, C. (1997). Tribal recreation and recreational tribalism: Culture, leisure and social control on South Africa's gold mines, 1940-1950. *Journal of Southern African Studies, 23*(3), 473-489.;
   Black, D., & Nauright, J. (1998). *Rugby and the South African nation*. Manchester: Manchester University Press.;
   Booth, D. (1998). *The race game: Sport and politics in South Africa*. London: Frank Cass.;
   Booth, D., & Nauright, J. (2003). Sport, race and embodiment in South Africa. *Contours: A Journal of the African Diaspora, 1*(1), 16-36.;
   Cobley, A. (1997). *The rules of the game: Struggles in black recreation and social welfare policy in South Africa*. Westport, CT: Greenwood Press.;
   Farred, G. (2003). 'Theatre of dreams:' Mimicry and difference in Cape Flats Township. In J. Bale & M. Cronin (Eds.), *Sport and postcolonialism* (pp. 123-146). Oxford: Berg.;

Jones, D. (2001). In pursuit of empowerment: Sensei Nellie Kleinsmot, race and gender challenges in South Africa. *International Journal of the History of Sport, 18*(1), 219-236.;

Means, J., & Nauright, J. (2008). Sports development meets sports marketing in Africa: Basketball without borders and the NBA in Africa. In S. Chadwick & D. Arthur (Eds.), *Case studies in international sports marketing* (pp. 372-388). London: Butterworth-Heinemann.;

Murray, B. (2001). Politics and cricket: The D'Oliveira affair of 1968. *Journal of Southern African Studies, 27*(4), 667-684.;

Murray, B. (2002). The Sports boycott and cricket: The cancellation of the 1970 South African Tour of England. *South African Historical Journal, 46,* 219-249.;

Murray, B., & Merrett, C. (2004). *Caught behind: Race and politics in Springbok cricket.* Johannesburg: Wits University Press and Durban: University of Kwa-Zulu-Natal Press.;

Nauright, J. (2010). Africa. In S.W. Pope & J. Nauright (Eds.), *The Routledge companion to sports history* (pp. 319-329). London: Routledge.;

Nauright, J. (2005). White man's burden revisited: Race, sport and reporting the Hansie Cronje cricket crisis in South Africa and beyond. *Sport History Review, 35*(1) 61-75.;

Odendaal, A. (2003). *The story of an African game.* Cape Town: David Philip.;

Saavedra, M. (2003). Football feminine—Development of the African game: Senegal, Nigeria and South Africa. *Soccer and Society, 4*(2/3), 225-253.

2. Speech by Deputy President Thabo Mbeki at the Sponsors of Sport Dinner, April 13, 1999. Retrieved from http://www.info.gov.za/speeches/1999/990730101p1008.htm.

3. I examine the coverage of the Cronje crisis in some detail in Nauright, J. (2005). White man's burden revisited: Race, sport and reporting the Hansie Cronje cricket crisis in South Africa and beyond. *Sport History Review, 35*(1), 61-75.

4. This is discussed in Klein, A. (2006). *Growing the game: The globalization of Major League Baseball.* New Haven, CT: Yale University Press.

5. See Means, J., & Nauright, J. (2008). Sports development meets sports marketing in Africa: Basketball without borders and the NBA in Africa. In S. Chadwick & D. Arthur (Eds.), *Case studies in international sport marketing* (pp. 372-388). London: Butterworth-Heinemann.

6. Swart, K., & Bob, U. (2004). The seductive discourse of development: The Cape Town 2004 Olympic bid. *Third World Quarterly, 25*(7), 1311-1324.

INTRODUCTION

To my mind only a fool would pretend to understand comprehensively what South Africa is really about, or be objective and far sighted enough to glimpse its future course.

Breyten Breytenbach, *Return to Paradise* (1993): xviii.

As famous South African author Breyten Breytenbach suggests, South Africa is perhaps one of the most complex of modern nations and made up of so many competing cultures, identities and ideologies that close analysis is always fraught with danger. Any study will be criticized from some angle as not being inclusive enough of this or that group or issue, in particular sport and its role in identity-formation in South Africa is also a difficult topic to understand. Many believe that South Africa is a sports mad nation and few will not have heard about the boycott movements, and its segregated sports system during apartheid. A number of writers have observed that sport, along with *braais* (barbeques) and sun bathing are the main cultural activities of white South Africans. Nelson Mandela and the ANC-led government view sport as one of the key areas of reconciliation in the 'New South Africa', and as perhaps the best cultural activity through which to promote or generate a new national identity. Millions of people around the world saw Mandela in a Springbok rugby jersey as he supported South Africa in the 1995 Rugby World Cup Final in Johannesburg. While these images had contradictory meanings, given the role of Springbok rugby as a racially based sport in the old South Africa, it is clear that the change from apartheid to post-apartheid South Africa has not affected, and may even have enhanced, the significant public role that sport plays in South African society.

This book is an attempt to explain and understand the various meanings that sport, and in particular team sport, has had in the diverse communities that comprise present day South Africa. A particular concern of this book is the role that sport played in shaping group and 'national' identities. For different groups and at different times, the same sport has had numerous meanings depending on the social positioning of particular individuals, and has played an important role in popular culture for a long time. Sport has served to both unify and divide groups, it has been closely interwoven with the broader fabric of South African society and has been at the forefront of social and political change. In the late 1980s and early 1990s, sport moved ahead of negotiations between political parties, creating unity and eliminating the vestiges of apartheid. Despite that, it remained firmly entrenched within power structures generated by the 'old' South Africa and ideologies developed out of the British imperial sporting inheritance.

In 1997, whites remained the majority in the administration of rugby, cricket and netball, while blacks controlled many similar positions in soccer and the National Olympic Committee of South Africa. Even though there have been changes in the make-up of top sporting officials, and a new government dominated by the former banned opposition, the discourses surrounding elite level sports remain similar to those of the segregation and apartheid eras, but cloaked in non-racial language and under the guise of promoting a new national unity.

International elite sporting success is one of the key ways that countries can promote themselves internally, and also to the rest of the world, as successful and powerful, and South African sport must be understood within the broader processes of globalization. Nowhere is the global system more evident than in the Olympic Games run by the International Olympic Committee (IOC). It is ironical that in the campaign for Cape Town to be awarded the Summer Olympic Games of 2004, President Nelson Mandela, who gave so much of his life to fight apartheid, had meetings with President Juan Antonio Samaranch of the IOC, a former stalwart supporter of the fascist leader General Franco in Spain. As former South African Council of Sport (SACOS) leader Joe Ebrahim stated in reference to sport in 1993, 'we defeated apartheid, but we could not defeat capitalism' (Ebrahim interview, 1993). The commercialization of sport in South Africa appears to have been too great, and the links between South Africa and the global system in the 1990s are such, many argue, that the government has little choice but to support international and elite level sport, thus retaining many structures of sport that existed in the apartheid era.

This book is not meant to be a comprehensive 'history' of South African sport, as such an endeavour would require more detailed groundwork and numerous local and regional histories yet to be written. Unfortunately, South African sporting history has had fewer analysts than places such as Britain, Australia or North America, and what exists is almost all about the white minority. It is possible, however, to reconstruct much about its black sporting history from popular sources, academic studies which have begun to appear in recent years, and some historical documents that shed light on the development and role of sport in black societies. South African society has been divided by class, geography and gender as well as by race and it is therefore important to examine the range of meanings given to particular sporting and cultural activities by different groups in different places and at different times. Before discussing the broad contours of sporting development it is necessary to have a basic understanding of major processes in South African history, and these are discussed in detail in Chapter 1.

When writing about South Africa, it is impossible to overlook ethnic and racial divisions that were categorized and became part of the dividing programme of apartheid. Four main racial groups existed in the periods of segregation and apartheid which, in terms of most common usage, are: 'African'; 'Coloured' (referring to mixed-race South Africans and those who are descended from slaves brought out from parts of present day Indonesia, Malaysia and Sri Lanka, sometimes further divided into a sub-group called 'Cape Malays'); 'Indian' (descendants of those brought out from the Indian sub-continent in the late nineteenth century to work on the Natal sugar plantations); and 'white', those descended from the peoples of Europe. When the term 'black' is used, it refers to all those who are not full descendants of European peoples or who could not pass as white during the apartheid era.[1] Both Africans and whites are spread throughout the country, while the majority of Coloureds live in the Western Cape and the majority of Indians in Natal. The book will follow the general usage of these categories, though they are by no means entirely satisfactory.

The book is constructed in three main sections, with the first chapter providing a short, but very necessary, overview of South African history and the writing of social and sporting history in South Africa. The second section examines the rise of sporting cultures during the imperial and apartheid eras, concentrating on the rise of a British-influenced sporting culture among whites, the development of sport among the urban black elite, the rise of Afrikaner nationalism and its links to rugby, and the place of soccer as the dominant sport in urban black communities. The final section considers the contradictory identities that emerged through support or opposition to non-racial sport and sporting boycotts, followed by an examination of sport, culture and identities in the new South Africa as it returns to international sporting competition.

NOTE

1. During apartheid hundreds of people were reclassified by race and others applied to have their racial status changed. Some whites were reclassified 'Coloured', for example as their hair was too curly or other features were thought to be too similar to blacks.

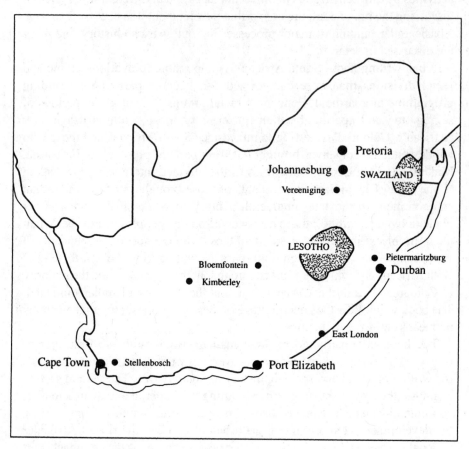

Pretoria

Johannesburg

SWAZILAND

Vereeniging

LESOTHO

Pietermaritzburg

Bloemfontein

Durban

Kimberley

East London

Cape Town   Stellenbosch   Port Elizabeth

Map of South Africa

1

THE MAKING OF MODERN SOUTH AFRICAN HISTORY AND SPORT

For white South Africans generally, sport is much more than mere escapism or an opportunity to demonstrate individual or team excellence. It is more than a religion, it is a total strategy against a total onslaught; it is the guardian of our national character; the barometer of our despair or hope.

Frederick van Zyl Slabbert, *The Last White Parliament* (1985).

The Springboks are our boys. I ask every one of you to stand behind them because they are our pride, they are my pride, they are your pride.

President Nelson Mandela, during the Rugby World Cup 1995.

These quotes vividly illustrate the significance of sport in both the old and the new South Africas. Although many sportspeople from South Africa have been successful in the international arena, until recently only a small minority were allowed to represent their country in international events. Since readmission to international sport in 1992, its athletes have won the Rugby World Cup, the Africa Nations Cup of Soccer (both hosted by South Africa), gold and silver medals in the Olympic Games, achieved success in international test and one-day cricket and reached the final of the netball World Championships. Excitement about sport among officials and business leaders culminated in Cape Town's bid for the 2004 Olympic Games, the ultimate international sporting prize in most people's estimation. In addition, there has been discussion about a bid for the 2006 World Cup of Soccer pending the outcome of the Olympic bid. In preparation for such global sports events, Greater Johannesburg will host the All-Africa Games in 1999. Sport is being promoted as a unifier for a new 'Rainbow Nation' that is, at least on a discursive level, inclusive of all people. Despite the rush to forgive the past and to move to the future, the development of sport cannot be readily separated from its history.

This chapter explores social divisions in South Africa, brought on by invasion, conquest, settlement, capitalism and racially- and gender-based social ideologies, that have shaped the contours of modern South African society, as well as social practices such as sport. A brief historical overview is followed by an analysis of specific issues related to the creation and maintenance of social divisions and various attempts to create forms of social unity.[1] Finally, writing about sport in South Africa and internationally is discussed.

The history of the country has been characterized by continuing waves of immigration and the progressive conquest of land. The first Africans arrived in the country at least 2000 years ago, migrating down from Central Africa. These migrants only settled as far south and east as the Fish River in the eastern Cape region about 800 kilometres up the coast from Cape Town. Because of the lack of reliable rainfall, settled populations could not be sustained further east and, as a result, only small groups of hunter-gatherers lived in the area around Cape Town when Europeans first arrived in 1652. A series of battles were fought between Dutch soldiers at the Cape and local residents as the Dutch continually expanded their use of land. By the 1680s, however, the Dutch held the upper hand and settled on farms beyond Table Mountain and out to present-day Stellenbosch. White settlers enslaved some locals and imported others from Madagascar, the Indian sub-continent, Sri Lanka, Indonesia and Malaysia. White farmers pushed westward along the coast until the 1770s when they came upon the Fish River and the densely settled Xhosa people.

Many border skirmishes ensued with neither side advancing very far as neither side had the military strength to subdue the other. In the late 1700s the Cape featured in the problems of Europe, leading to a shift in power relations in favour of whites. As part of the Napoleonic wars, the British occupied Cape Town in 1795 and then permanently from 1806. In order to stabilize the frontier, the British brought settlers to the Eastern Cape region in 1820 and also provided military power to subdue the Xhosa. From this point, South African history for the next eighty years was dominated by struggles over land and for control of the vast mineral resources that were discovered in the interior. Clear tensions emerged between different groups, local white capitalizing interests and the British imperial state concerned to minimize costs of administration.

The British abolished slavery in 1834 which many Afrikaner settlers opposed. This resulted in several thousand trekking out of the area of British control in search of land where they could be in charge of their own destiny and maintain the social relations of production that they had established on their farms and in their communities, before the onset of British administrative authority. During the first three decades of the nineteenth century a widespread process of state formation took place in the interior of southern Africa. In Zulu, this process was called the *mfecane*, or the time of crushing. By the 1820s the Zulu Kingdom appeared under the leadership of Shaka, and other large states such as the Basotho and Swazi kingdoms consolidated their power, while many smaller groups were either incorporated or forced to flee to other areas of the continent. As a result of dispossession, conquest and struggle over the land, elements of an agrarian-based capitalist economy began to emerge as large-scale white-owned farms appeared in the interior between the areas controlled by African kingdoms. Many dispossessed Africans obtained work and places to live on these farms by the middle decades of the nineteenth century, while some African chiefs participated in the supply of labour in exchange for secure positions as local or regional leaders. Land struggles continued through the nineteenth century with white settlers ultimately establishing four political and geographical entities; two controlled by the British – the Cape Colony and Natal, and two Afrikaner republics – the Orange Free State and the South African Republic (Transvaal).[2]

During the nineteenth century emerging racial ideologies conditioned thinking about the different groups of people within what became present-day South Africa. Afrikaner religious and political leaders promoted the idea of an Afrikaner *Volk* that was divinely ordained to rule over southern Africa as a 'chosen-people' and be masters of Africans whom they believed God had chosen to be 'hewers of wood and drawers of water'. In other words, Afrikaners began to believe that they had Biblical justification for restricting Africans to menial and service positions. While the basic tenor of Afrikaner attitudes towards blacks appeared to be somehow timeless until the 1980s, Afrikaner history and ideologies were re-shaped many times in the late nineteenth and twentieth centuries. Much historical writing from a conservative and liberal British perspective sought to lay South Africa's racial divisions and problems at the feet of an Afrikaner pathological hatred of blacks. Such an analysis is far too simplistic and belies the fact that it was emerging capitalist relations of production that led to hardened racial attitudes in the late nineteenth and early twentieth centuries (Keegan, 1996). In the first half of the nineteenth century, British racial social philosophies began with attempts to socially uplift Africans through a 'civilizing' process based on Christianizing and 'de-tribalizing' Africans, or to make Africans more like the British. This process was based on concepts of European supremacy but towards the end of the nineteenth century such attitudes shifted as whites began to fear being swamped by blacks. In other colonial settings where whites settled in large numbers, native peoples were decimated by disease and war, but in southern Africa there were too few whites and too many densely settled Africans for whites to become a majority of the population. As a result, whites had to devise other methods for maintaining their dominant position which they believed was scientifically, religiously and culturally justified.

THE MINERAL REVOLUTION AND INDUSTRIALIZATION

During the 1870s and 1880s, South Africa underwent dramatic trans-formations brought on by the discovery of diamonds at Kimberley in 1867 and gold on the Witwatersrand in 1886. As a result, it experienced an industrial revolution and the movement of tens of thousands of people to the mines and the cities around them. In addition to thousands of immigrant miners from Britain, Australia and elsewhere, some mission-educated Africans moved into lower level administrative posts, setting themselves up as an urbanized African elite in Kimberley and Johannesburg. This group adopted many elements of British culture, including sporting practices, as Chapter 3 discusses. In addition to an African elite, thousands worked in the mines as unskilled migrant labourers. Because of the high cost of mining and the necessity of importing equipment from overseas, the only way that mine owners felt they could control their costs was through the use of large numbers of cheap African labourers. Officials and mine owners worked together to create a migrant labour system whereby the cost of reproducing the labour force would be met in rural areas, rather than by state and capital interests in the cities. Despite these attempts to keep Africans away from permanent settlement in the cities, thousands flocked to the rapidly developing cities, initially settling in urban slum areas and taking jobs in service, supportive industries and the informal economy.

The rapid expansion of the gold mining industry, and the resultant changes it brought to demographics and economics, ultimately caused a war in South Africa. Due to the gold mines being located in the South African Republic (Transvaal or present day Gauteng), an area controlled by Afrikaners, mining magnates urged the British government to assist in the securing of greater long-term profits through taking control of the area. The mine owners believed that a British administration would be more favourable to them and they resented the policies of the Republic and its president Paul Kruger. Although the causes of the South African (or Anglo-Boer) War of 1899–1902 are complex and have been hotly debated amongst historians, it is clear that the control and profitability of gold played a key part in the outbreak of war. The South African War was fought between the British Empire, its local colonies of the Cape and Natal and the two Afrikaner republics in the Orange

Free State and the Transvaal, with most blacks on the sidelines. The British sent 450,000 British and colonial troops to fight against 40,000 Afrikaners who held an advantage in knowing the territory and how to fight a bush war. In order to force an end to the war, the British captured and placed 40,000 Afrikaner women and children in concentration camps where 26,000 died. Although the way that the British won the war generated animosity and hatred amongst Afrikaners, the British government pressed for unification of the four states into one administration. As a result, English-speaking and Afrikaner leaders, along with British officials, agreed to form the Union of South Africa in 1910. The Afrikaner hatred of the British was expressed in sporting contests between schools and clubs from the different groups for many years following the war.

British officials encouraged immigration to South Africa in the early 1900s in the hopes of creating a British majority among whites. The policy failed, however, leaving Afrikaners in the majority. Although the Cape Colony had a franchise system that allowed a small number of Africans and Coloureds to vote, the 'Cape franchise' was not extended to the other colonies as recommended by the South African Native Affairs Commission of 1905. Thus, the two white groups colluded to prevent blacks from gaining greater citizenship rights in the new Union. Indeed, the Cape franchise was progressively eroded during the next four decades and blacks lost the vote. Thus 'democratic' elections were only for the 15 per cent of the people classified as 'white'.[3] While many whites initially voted along class lines, some Afrikaners determined that if others could be convinced to vote as members of one *Volk*, then they could wrest away some of the economic power held by English-speakers. In 1918 a secret society known as the Afrikaner Broederbond was founded to promote the expansion of Afrikaner political and economic interests. During the 1920s and 1930s a nationalist political, economic and social movement among Afrikaners emerged, ultimately leading to the victory of the National Party in the 1948 election and the introduction of *apartheid* or apart-ness. Although these policies entrenched division in South Africa, they built upon the existing system of segregation that had pervaded its society well before 1948.

URBANIZATION, SEGREGATION AND APARTHEID

Due to the onset of industrialization, brought on by the discovery of large deposits of diamonds and gold, South Africa underwent rapid urbanization in the late nineteenth and early twentieth centuries. The largest area of development centred around Johannesburg and the rest of the Witwatersrand gold mining area in the Transvaal. Industrial development and emerging capitalist relations of production in the rural areas drove thousands of poor whites and blacks to urban areas in the first few decades of the twentieth century. Because of the expensive and fixed costs of production, gold mines cut costs by using cheap unskilled African migrant labour. The mining industry's labour patterns and the urban development created by mining meant that whites initially predominated in Rand cities. By the turn of the twentieth century, whites increasingly viewed the city as a 'white' and 'civilized' space, a refuge from 'black' and 'barbaric' Africa. Such discursively based ideologies greatly influenced sport, and the pronouncements about sport, as it did for all activities within South Africa.

Non-mineworking Africans began to move to Rand cities in the 1890s and early 1900s as van Onselen (1982a; 1982b) demonstrates. Initially most moved to the mixed-race slum areas which developed near the city centre, similar to patterns of early black urbanization in other southern African cities. In the early 1900s, white officials demonstrated a limited tolerance for mixed-race slums, especially once the plague and other diseases became common in those areas. A ship from India brought bubonic plague to Cape Town in 1901, and its subsequent outbreak led to a series of slum clearance policies. As Swanson (1977) shows, whites in the Cape Colony developed a discourse that linked blacks and slum areas with disease, which he terms the 'sanitation syndrome'. As a result, Africans were progressively moved out of the sight of whites into specific residential 'locations'. Often these locations were situated next to refuse dumps and sewage works, areas where whites did not want to live.

The physical separation of the urban population was to have important consequences for the future development of South African society. An increasingly segregationist discourse emerged that categorized Africans as 'diseased', 'tribal', 'dirty' and 'lazy' which led to progressively hostile attitudes, largely based on white ignorance of their life and living conditions. Additionally, missionaries and officials idealized rural culture and viewed the urban African as a cultural mutant needing assistance and protection. These attitudes were by no means unique to South Africa and arose out of white European and North American concerns about the consequences of industrialized urban living on the lives of the poor in general, and blacks in particular.

By the 1920s locations, or townships, were established across the country with Africans having few places where they could own land in the urban areas. Only those few townships that pre-dated the Native Land Act of 1913 had freehold land available for blacks to buy. The 1913 Land Act limited African land ownership to 7 per cent of the country, increased in 1936 to just over 13 per cent, although Africans at the time were 75 per cent of the population. As a result of urban and rural land policies, South Africa was legislated as a spatially segregated society by the 1920s, well before the apartheid era. The Native Administration Act of 1927 gave the Governor-General the power to rule by proclamation and remove any African group or person anywhere within South Africa. Additionally, it outlawed incitement of 'feelings of hostility' between racial groups or incitement to change existing laws. The Riotous Assemblies Act of 1930 further strengthened legislation designed to prevent mass agitation against the government or the laws of the country. As a result, most political protests were illegal and mass gatherings required a police permit, or faced the possibility of being declared illegal with participants subject to arrest and imprisonment.

Fears of blacks swamping whites in the urban areas led to further segregationist policies. Indeed, the 1929 election was fought and won on the issue of the *swaart gevaar*, or 'black peril', that many whites thought would sweep them away as more Africans moved to the cities. Such fears went back at least as far as the 1870s when there was a black rape scare in Natal, though this was largely a constructed fear and not one based on substantial evidence (Etherington, 1988). In cities, fears were generated by the presence of African men walking through white areas on weekends as miners and domestic workers spent leisure time in black townships (Nauright, 1992).

As Chapters 2 and 3 show, the development and organization of cultural activities in South Africa, including sport, were conditioned by segregationist thinking. Sport was segregated by the first years of the twentieth century, with national representative teams for whites only and white only competitions organized in every sporting code. National sporting colours and the Springbok emblem were designated exclusively for whites, and in the rare cases where mixed teams were allowed to participate internationally in the 1970s and 1980s Springbok colours were not awarded. Thus in the sporting context, the South African nation referred to a whites-only nation and not one inclusive of all the people in the geographic entity 'South Africa'.

The 1930s and 1940s were marked by more rapid urbanization than in the previous decades, the rise of Afrikaner nationalism as a dominant political force in white politics, increasing attempts to 'control' the urban black population, the Second World War and, finally, the emergence of large scale black protest against poor wages, poor living conditions, segregation and racial discrimination. With the rising urban population, sporting organizations flourished in the townships of Johannesburg, Durban, Kimberley, Port Elizabeth and Vereeniging, and the working-class areas of Cape Town in particular. Soccer, also popular among the white working class at the time, was organized on city and regional levels and achieved a mass following by the end of the 1930s, particularly in Transvaal and Natal townships. By the 1940s, soccer was widely popular in most townships of the country, with rugby strong in the townships of the Eastern and Western Cape where missionaries promoted the game amongst the educated African elite. In white sport, rugby began to be Afrikanerized as that group began to play the game in ever increasing numbers, and Afrikaner nationalists appropriated rugby in their promotion of a particular ethnocentric national identity.

In an electoral upset, the reconstituted National Party (NP) led by D. F. Malan won the national election in 1948 defeating the United Party led by Jan Smuts, a general in the Boer War and long-time leading South African politician. The NP soon began to implement their policies of apartheid. While the segregation system had gone a long way towards dividing the country spatially and socially, the apartheid system went further in attempts to completely segregate society. During the 1950s and 1960s numerous new laws were passed in attempts to achieve the ultimate goal of separate development and social isolation. Through policies of forced removal, pass laws and influx controls, the government tried in vain to stem the tide of black migration to the urban areas. Many thousands of people were dumped in rural areas which the government tried to pass off as African 'homelands', based on its reconstruction of African 'tribes'.

Under the Group Areas Act of 1950, many urban areas occupied initially by black people were redesignated as areas for whites only and, during the 1950s and 1960s, this led to the demolition of old and famous townships and locations with vibrant cultures such as Sophiatown in Johannesburg, District Six in Cape Town, Cato Manor in Durban and Top Location in Vereeniging. Forced removals and segregationist policies impacted heavily on social and cultural life, and disrupted sport among blacks. Many teams were lost and competitions damaged through forced removals and local and national policies that denied black access to the best sporting facilities. A broad non-racial national identification through sport was made impossible by apartheid's focus on maintaining and creating differential group identities. Under apartheid, the state sought to coordinate and control all aspects of society.

As part of efforts to limit black opportunity, to manage popular debate and to prevent mass criticism, successive governments supported a system of censorship and tight control of the media. In addition to government policies and regulations, the majority of the print media has been owned by three main groups, making the South African media one of the most controlled and centralized. Between 1924 and 1936 private companies and local authorities controlled broadcasting. From 1927 the African Broadcasting Company operated, broadcasting in English and focused on the urban market. It was replaced in 1936 by the South African Broadcasting Corporation (SABC). The SABC's policy was to build a consensual nation among whites while it largely ignored blacks until the 1980s (Merrett, 1994b). As a result of these policies and white ownership of the media, white-dominated sports always received a disproportionate amount of sporting coverage.

While sport has received little attention from scholars working on the social and cultural history of South Africa, a vibrant literature that examined the everyday lives of disadvantaged people developed in the 1980s. A few studies began to examine sport, but not in as much detail as other social activities. Nevertheless, this literature on social and cultural history forms a necessary background from which future studies of sport must proceed.

THE WRITING OF URBAN SOCIAL AND CULTURAL HISTORY

While much of the history of white South Africans has focused on political and economic history, with a few studies of Afrikaner and poor white conditions, the study of Africans in urban areas began many decades ago with the work of anthropologists concerned with the effects of cultural contact. Much of this work appeared in the 1920s and 1930s and focused on changes in the rural areas. However, several studies of African culture in towns were also undertaken, most notably Ellen Hellmann's 1930s investigation of Rooiyard, a slumyard in New Doornfontein, Johannesburg. Hellmann (1934) examined the impact of urban conditions on cultural practices and the struggle of Africans to survive economically in town. Her work provides rich detail on the organization of urban life in slumyards during the early 1930s.

In addition to the work of anthropologists, several missionaries wrote of the experiences of Africans who came to Rand towns in the 1920s and 1930s. Most notable among these were the American Board Missionaries, Ray Phillips and J. Dexter Taylor. Phillips published two books (1930, 1938) on the situation of urban Africans and what should be done to ensure more orderly urbanization. He wanted to prevent Africans from falling into the hands of agitators and worked diligently to establish 'healthy' outlets for them during their leisure time. Phillips was instrumental in the development of recreational facilities for mineworkers and in the creation of social clubs for mission-educated urban Africans, particularly the Bantu Men's Social Centre and the Gamma Sigma Debating Clubs. His primary concern was to encourage Christian and Westernized behaviour among urban Africans and to prevent political radicalization.

In the 1940s and 1950s, communist and socialist intellectuals wrote pioneering analyses of African politics and resistance to white domination. Most significant among these was Eddie Roux's *Time Longer Than Rope* (1948) and the later study by Jack and Ray Simons (1969). Both works concentrate on black and non-racial political groups and protests against racial oppression, providing much important data on personalities and political struggles. Baruch Hirson (1989), another activist during the 1940s, recently added to this literature. Much of the early academic focus on Africans also examined national political movements and struggles against oppression (Karis and Carter, 1972–77; Gerhart, 1978; Walshe, 1971). Recent scholarship has also been influenced by contemporary events. The emergence of a radical historiography in the 1970s was sparked by the Durban strikes of 1973 and especially by the Soweto student protests in 1976.

During the 1920s and 1930s, W. M. Macmillan and C. W. de Kiewiet were the first South African historians to recognize the need to integrate the study of blacks into South African history. Unfortunately, both men went into exile and their successors turned to other topics; later researchers did not build on their insights until the late 1960s. The liberal school dominated South African English historiography until the end of the 1960s and culminated in the publication of the *Oxford History of South Africa* (1969, 1971). The publication of this substantial work, which included blacks, prompted a series of critical responses from scholars influenced by Marxist-inspired British social history and French structuralist anthropology. Critiques of the *OHSA* focused on its authors' failure to analyse African societies in a dynamic fashion. Several recent publications have summarized the arguments of the revisionist or 'radical' school which emerged during the 1970s (Bozzoli and Delius, 1990; Smith, 1988).

Over the past twenty years many studies have analysed urban social conditions for blacks in South Africa. Much of this work has been produced at the University of the Witwatersrand or presented at the History Workshop Conferences organized there since the late 1970s (Bonner *et al.*, 1989; Bozzoli, 1979, 1983, 1987). While this literature has expanded knowledge of urban conditions of black South Africans, most of the work has concentrated on the formation of class consciousness and working class culture among urban blacks. Until recently these studies have ignored or only briefly mentioned other forms of consciousness and identity, such as gender and ethnicity.

Charles van Onselen's (1982a, 1982b) pioneering essays on the social and economic history of the Rand between 1886 and 1914 inspired the outpouring of urban studies in the 1980s. Van Onselen was influenced by the work of E. P. Thompson on British working-class history and Eugene Genovese on the culture of slaves in America. Characterized as a 'history from below', van Onselen's research stressed the powerful role played by capitalist development and the state in the shaping of modern Rand society which he called 'the world the mineowners made'. Significantly, he demonstrates how various groups of people responded to the processes of proletarianization, and the opportunities of the market created by the establishment of a large gold mining industry on the Rand in the 1890s and early twentieth century. However, the power of state and capital re-marginalized many new urban residents who had attempted to avoid proletarianization. Belinda Bozzoli (1979) suggested that the history of townships was the unwritten history of the South African working class.

By 1982–83, the focus was shifting to a more nuanced approach which discussed the power of capitalist transformation in shaping blacks' lives. The appearance of van Onselen's essays, a collection edited by Shula Marks and Richard Rathbone (1982) and the second volume of History Workshop papers (Bozzoli, 1983) clearly marks this transition. Rather than depicting blacks merely as members of the 'dominated classes', this new work explored the ways in which class consciousness was generated in cultural, as well as in political, terms. Following E. P. Thompson, Marks and Rathbone (1982: 8) state that consciousness is 'the way in which . . . experiences are handled in cultural terms: embodied in traditions, value systems, ideas and institutional forms', which did not automatically appear from a person's position within 'productive relations'. In sport this can be seen in the exclusion of many South Africans on the basis of race or gender and not just on material conditions.

By the mid-1980s scholars focused on forms of identity generated 'from below'. In her introduction to the third volume of History Workshop papers, Bozzoli (1987: 2) states that there is 'no substitute for the "view from below" in developing our understanding of the interaction and evolution of class and non-class factors in South African common consciousness'. Despite this focus on history from below, and a move towards social and cultural history, few historians of South Africa have examined the role of sport, with early studies being very preliminary in nature (Couzens, 1983; Peires, 1981).

Developing out of studies which start 'from below' has been a widespread, though diverse, use of the concept of 'community'. In South Africa it has been used to mean racial communities, local, regional and 'national' communities and, under apartheid, 'tribal' communities. Bozzoli argues that earlier analyses which discussed large economically-defined classes, 'the working class' or 'the petty bourgeoisie', were problematic. She states that 'ordinary people live in small-groupings, both in urban and rural settings'. In these contexts, they more often identify themselves as members of specific local groups and not necessarily as part of broad national classes. She concludes that 'community' is 'both sufficiently general and sufficiently vague, to cover all situations in which this may be the case' (Bozzoli, 1987: 5).

The Alexandra Township property owner and political leader, E. P. Mart Zulu, provides a clear example of the ambiguity of 'community'. He owned property, was a leader of Zulu organizations, liquor-seller, businessman, and organizer of a workers' party. Thus, he was a member of the Alexandra 'community', the local business 'community', the property-owning 'community', the Zulu 'community', and even the workers' 'community'. Yet, on closer analysis, Mart Zulu often worked against the development of inclusive identities in Alexandra. He did not want tenants to have any rights in local politics and protests, for example. He was on the same side of many issues as another property owner and businessman, R. G. Baloyi, yet, their similar views diverged on the question of the 1940 bus boycott (Nauright, 1992). From these brief examples, it is clear that personal economic and political interests are obscured by reference to individuals as members of one or another 'community'. Serious divisions within Alexandra in the 1940s and 1950s led a group of local scholars to conclude that 'Alexandra never was a community' (*Izwi lase Township*, 1983).[4] Thus from local levels upward, identities in South Africa have been fraught with numerous contradictions shaped by class, race, ethnicity, gender, residential location and other factors. From the myriad of identities that exist, it has been difficult to generate mass cross-class or cross-racial alliances.

Historians of urban social conditions on the twentieth-century Rand relied heavily on early urban studies, and the valuable work of Eddie Koch (1983) on the marabi culture of the slumyards in Johannesburg for the 1920s and 1930s. Until recently, however, historians have not analysed other areas of the Rand where experiences were quite different. Steve Lebelo (1990) and Dave Goodhew (1989) expanded our knowledge of the social formations in Sophiatown, a freehold township inside the Johannesburg municipality. Lebelo argues that, from its origins, Sophiatown displayed a distinctly middle-class culture and contrasted sharply with the working-class and lumpen-proletarian culture of the slumyards. Similarly, Alexandra's initial residents' identity centred around property ownership as opposed to blacks who lived in slumyards. Property owners adopted notions of 'respectability' to differentiate themselves from 'undesirables', or non-propertied urban blacks with no permanent and concrete ties to town.

Work by Phil Bonner (1988, 1990a, 1990b, 1991) on Basotho migrants to the Witwatersrand has begun uncovering various ways in which people organized themselves as they faced a new urban environment, and, additionally the official responses to black urbanization. Bonner (1988) and Sapire (1989) both show how East Rand municipalities responded to processes of African urbanization. These towns were located near mining properties which meant that many people moved into, and out of, urban black settlements. As a result, East Rand municipalities sought to establish greater control over African settlements within their boundaries and created tightly controlled locations in the late 1920s and 1930s. Bonner argues that the problem centred on 'unattached' women who formed temporary relationships with 'unattached' male mineworkers. This engendered disorderly urbanization producing unstable families and uncontrolled children. As a result of such influxes, white officials sought to try and 'control' or order urban African behaviour through sponsoring some sporting activities in the 1930s and 1940s. Increasingly, however, the state turned to repressive measures in their attempts to create order out of what they viewed as the chaos of African urbanization. Thus, social history studies have concentrated on the relationship between control mechanisms of the state, and cultures of resistance among urban blacks and migrant mineworkers. The study of sport among black South Africans has emerged from this broader social history literature.

SPORTS STUDIES AND SOUTH AFRICA

The study of sport has begun to receive much academic attention internationally in the past thirty years. Numerous works of history and sociology have appeared that seek to situate sport within a social and cultural context. Despite this interest there have been few academic socio-historical studies that focus on a national level outside the USA (Cashman, 1995; Holt, 1982, 1989; Metcalfe, 1987), and even fewer studies that situate sport within the context of national identity politics and culture (Sugden and Bairner, 1993; Jarvie and Walker, 1994). A few books have placed particular sports within a nationalist cultural context (Beckles and Stoddart, 1994; Gruneau and Whitson, 1993; Mandle and Mandle, 1988; Black and Nauright, forthcoming). A number of studies have concentrated on sport in the colonial and imperial context, and discussed the process of cultural transfer and resistance (Guttmann, 1994; Mangan, 1986, 1988, 1992; Nauright and Chandler, 1996). While we are beginning to get a fuller picture of sport and society in North America, Britain and Australasia, in South Africa sports studies is in its infancy.

A few preliminary examinations of black and non-racial sport were undertaken in the late 1970s and 1980s (Couzens, 1982; Odendaal, 1977; Peires, 1981). Much of this pioneering work merely scratched the surface of black sporting development, and were offered as part of the broader project of recovering the social history of the disadvantaged communities in South Africa. There is a large and long-established popular literature on white sport in South Africa, especially for the dominant white male team sports of cricket and rugby, so radical social historians tended to ignore white sport. A largely Afrikaans body of sports history, particularly from the University of Stellenbosch, also appeared, but this was very descriptive in nature and offered little in the way of social analysis. Due to apartheid and the movements to boycott racist sport, a substantial international literature developed that critiqued the South African sporting system (Archer and Bouillon, 1982; Brickhill, 1976; Kidd, 1988; Lapchick, 1975; Newnham, 1975, 1978; Ramsamy, 1982; Thompson, 1964, 1973; Woods, 1981). While much of this work was polemical in nature and sought to persuade readers to support sporting boycotts, these studies are invaluable historical documents, as well as sources of information about sport and society in South Africa.

In the late 1980s and 1990s the situation began to change as more so-called mainstream historians and other academics based in South Africa, such as Albert Grundlingh, Christopher Merrett, Robert Morrell and André Odendaal, began to examine sport in greater detail (Grundlingh, 1996; Grundlingh, Odendaal and Spies, 1995; Jeffrey, 1990; Merrett, 1995, 1996; Morrell, 1996; Odendaal, 1988, 1995).

The literature largely continued from the social history studies of the early 1980s and has attempted to place sport alongside other important social and cultural activities. Morrell and Grundlingh in particular have situated the social construction of masculinities at the centre of their work on rugby. Morrell examines how rugby and other sporting activities were used to shore up beliefs of superiority among a small settler population in colonial Natal; while Grundlingh has examined the links between rugby, Afrikaner national-ism and masculinity that drew on British imperial sporting practices in rugby but recast them as Afrikaner. Odendaal has written on the history of black cricket and rugby, and on the way that cricket and tennis were used by African elites to distinguish themselves from the mass of 'tribal' and non-mission educated Africans. Jeffrey examines the role of patrons in soccer in Top Location and Sharpeville, and provides one of the few community studies of sport in South Africa to date. Cecile Badenhorst's PhD thesis is an excellent study of the provision of sporting facilities and the place of sport in the urban black communities of Johannesburg in the period from 1920 to the 1950s. She analyses the links between state officials, capitalist interests, black leaders and sports administrators in looking at the emergence of black sporting activity in Johannesburg and on the gold mines. Christopher Merrett is the first scholar in the post-apartheid era to access Department of Sport and Recreation files from the 1960s and 1970s which has added to our understanding of sport and the apartheid state (Merrett, 1996). He has also written an initial history (1996) of the Comrades Marathon, one of the world's most famous marathons run each year between Pietermaritzburg and Durban.

Several scholars outside South Africa have also contributed to the emerging academic literature on sport and society. Alan Cobley (1994) undertook a similar study to the work done by Badenhorst that emerged out of his earlier (1990) book on the black petty-bourgeoisie in Johannesburg. Douglas Booth has analysed the development of the apartheid sporting system within the context of segregation and apartheid, and analysed the shifts in South African sporting policy in the 1980s and 1990s. Nauright (1997) has contributed to analysis at the local level through his work on Coloured rugby in Cape Town, and has analysed feelings of national identification and racist nostalgia in the white crowd behaviour at the Ellis Park rugby test in 1992 between the Springboks and the New Zealand All Blacks (Nauright, 1996a). Nauright and Black (1994, 1996) have examined the specific impact of rugby sanctions, and attempted to analyse the relative success of sporting sanctions in the international moves to try and force change upon apartheid rulers in the 1970s and 1980s. Douglas Booth (1990, 1992, 1995) has also exploded myths surrounding desegregation and 'unity' in sport during the negotiation for new sporting structures.

While this emerging literature is to be welcomed many gaps remain. Virtually nothing has been written on women's sport – white, black or non-racial – in South Africa even though netball's power structures and ties to Afrikaner nationalism closely resembled those of rugby. Very little has been written on black soccer, rugby and cricket, or other sports in which blacks have participated, and the early historical record is often sketchy as records were not always kept and authorities were not interested in many of the intricacies of black sporting organization. This book draws on the extant literature, popular accounts, press reports and some interviews conducted by the author during the 1990s, in an attempt to demonstrate the role of history in the current situation of sport in South Africa, and the various identities that have emerged around sport and sporting practices during the past 120 years.

GENDER, SOCIETIES AND SPORT

South African society has not been segregated only by race, but also by gender both in the workplace and in public leisure activities. Many bars, for example, were for white men only. Black women were not expected to carry passes allowing them to be in urban areas, as white officials left the policing of black women to black men in a patriarchal alliance that saw them face a triple oppression as blacks, women and workers in poor-paying occupations. White women were advantaged by race and often by class, but disadvantaged relative to white men.

Although some women have played sport in South Africa and participated as political leaders, most have not participated in sport or reached high status occupations. Until very recently, white women were not allowed to work in many occupations once they were married, and most black women were either working and raising families in the rural or urban areas, or employed as domestic labourers working in white households. Both European and African societies are patriarchal, though many white women have been advantaged in having cheap domestic labour which freed up leisure time.

Very little has been written on the history and sociology of women's sport in South Africa as it has not been seen as important as men's sport. Despite this lack of overall interest by male journalists and by academics studying sport, sportswomen such as Zola Budd, Elena Meyer and Frith van der Merwe in athletics, and Joan Harrison, Karen Muir, Ann Fairlie, Mariaan Kriel and Penny Heyns in swimming, have captured the imagination of many in South Africa. Netball star Irene van Dyck was hailed by the British media as the sex symbol that international netball needs (Haigh, 1994). Unfortunately, the focus was not as much on her ability as a goal scorer, but on her supposed sexual attractiveness. All of these women are white. Cheryl Roberts (1992) has tried to raise awareness of sport among black women, and promote sport as a legitimate activity for black women. Few black women have had the encouragement or opportunities to make it to elite level in sports, though many black women do play netball. Additionally, many Coloured women in the Western Cape also play softball. There is a clear need to both better understand the history and social conditions that have prevented South African women from fuller participation in sport, and to develop programmes and create facilities and infrastructure that will address the participation and health needs of South African women and assist them to become top class athletes. The history of women's sport in South Africa is crying out for researchers, particularly in sports such as netball which had a large following among white women and became popular in many townships.

SPORT, MEMORY AND PERFORMING WHITE
SOUTH AFRICAN CULTURE AND IDENTITY

Racist and sexist behaviour, national identity, indeed all forms of identity and behaviour, are learned. Paul Connerton in *How Societies Remember* (1989) sets out the process whereby collective memory and cultural identity is generated and perpetuated in society. He centres his analysis on bodily practices as performed in activities such as ceremonial occasions, parades and other forms of collective public activity. Certainly military parades, commemorations of the Great Trek and the Battle of Blood River were important in generating identities among white South Africans. Additionally, bodily performance in public activities of everyday life also demonstrate particular behaviours. In referring to court life at Versailles in eighteenth-century France, Connerton states that:

> Ceremonies, proprieties and techniques of the body exist along a spectrum of possibilities extending from the more or less formal to the more or less informal. All in varying ways entail cognitive memory. Thus ceremonies of the body, such as are exemplified in court etiquette at Versailles, remind performers of a system of honour and hereditary transmission as the organising principle of social classification. (Connerton, 1989: 87)

In South Africa such performances took place on an everyday scale and the racial order was reinforced repeatedly through bodily actions. Thus blacks in the performing of deference towards whites, and white expectations of such deference, helped perpetuate a racially divided social order. Blacks could manipulate this system, and often did for their own benefit, by playing to white expectations of black behaviour. Additionally, many blacks resisted accommodating expectations of absolute deference.

Sport in South Africa was a central part of bodily performance in the learning of identification and social place. Sport was segregated nearly completely for most of South Africa's history, meaning that whites played with and watched each other, but not with blacks. Thus particular sporting activities and heroes were known to whites, but they knew very little about black sport. Since whites dominated power structures in the society, black South Africans were more aware of white sporting results and heroes. In addition, white and black men learned much about being men through sport. White women, freed from most domestic labour chores by black women and men, played many sports, though these activities were gendered – women did not play rugby union, for example. Peter Hain, British MP and leader of the Stop the Seventy Tour campaign, suggests that sport is an area where whites could seek self-fulfilment in a society that was not really free under apartheid (Bose, 1994: 11). Christopher Merrett confirms the closed nature of South African society in his study of censorship (Merrett, 1995). The media was highly centralized and the state owned radio and later television broadcasting for most of the apartheid period. State officials were so concerned about the possible influence of television, and international culture, that they did not allow television broadcasting until 1975.

SPORT AND NATION-BUILDING IN THE NEW SOUTH AFRICA

Sport in South Africa has been integrated, at least on paper and in terms of administrative structure. As the final chapters discuss, however, apartheid has a deep legacy that still impacts substantially on society. Even though the ANC and President Mandela have used sport as a means of reaching out to whites, old attitudes and divisions are never far from the surface. Evidence of this is seen in the crowd response at the 1992 rugby test match between South Africa and New Zealand, and in the reactions to a series of rugby defeats by New Zealand in 1996, discussed in Chapters 7 and 8. Meanwhile, former white-dominated sports have been actively supported by Mandela and Sports Minister Steve Tshwete, in attempts to use sport in forging a national identity for the new 'Rainbow Nation' of South Africa.

There are many critics of the move back into international sporting structures who argue that insufficient attention is being paid to development issues and mass participation. South Africa is firmly re-entrenched in the global sports order and is actively seeking to host major sports events as part of a strategy to induce the return of more foreign investment and tourists. South Africa hosted the 1995 Rugby World Cup and the 1996 Africa Nations Cup for soccer, Cape Town bid to host the 2004 Olympic Games, and by 1997 plans were well underway for a bid for the 2006 Soccer World Cup. South Africa is indeed in a unique position as the only African country that has anywhere near the necessary infrastructure to host major sporting events, most of which have never been held in Africa. Other major international events are also scheduled for South Africa in the next few years. The broad international discourses of sport, and international success being good for the nation as a whole, have appeared virtually unchallenged in the new South Africa and in the priorities of sports policy. Whether sport can generate a pan-South African identity out of the fragmented identities generated by decades of segregation and apartheid remains to be seen. The burden of the past is indeed strong in South Africa.

The rest of this book explores the historical development of sports, particularly the team sports of rugby, soccer and cricket, that have been used to promote wider identities, and examines the interaction between sport and developments in wider South African societies of the past and present in the shaping of exclusive and inclusive identities. Other sports are discussed only briefly, but this is not to suggest that histories and contemporary studies of many other sports and those where individuals are the primary competitors are not important. We need many more studies of women in sport, boxing, athletics, swimming, hockey, netball and ethnically-based activities such as stick-fighting and *jukeskei*. Only then will we have a fuller understanding of the role of all forms of sport in the formation of collective and divisive identities in South Africa.

NOTES

1. For a more detailed coverage of modern South African history, see Beinart (1994).
2. Although there are many more provinces in the New South Africa, much sporting organization is based around the four original provinces of the Cape, Natal, Orange Free State and Transvaal or regions within these provinces such as Northern Transvaal and Eastern and Western Province in the Cape. Usually major unions have been focused around the major cities of Johannesburg, Cape Town, Durban, Pretoria, Bloemfontein, Port Elizabeth and Kimberley with smaller cities hosting sub-unions.
3. Indeed white women were given the vote initially to dilute the Coloured and African vote in the Cape.
4. *Izwi lase Township*, 1983. The occasional newspaper appeared between 1982 and 1985 and was established by a group of school students and members of a youth group in Alexandra, called the Ditshwantsho tsa Rona. The contributors mostly held union jobs and wrote in their spare time; see Luli Callinicos, 'The "People's Past": Towards Transforming the Present', in Bozzoli (1987: 50). I would like to thank Luli Callinicos for allowing me to photocopy her originals of *Izwi lase Township*.

2

IMPERIAL GAMES: THE EMERGENCE OF WHITE-DOMINATED SPORT

South Africa's return to international sport in the 1990s has been warmly welcomed by many of its former competitors, most especially the white-dominated countries of the former British Empire with whom the old white South African sporting teams had close relations. In order to understand just why such reactions have occurred, we need to place the development of South African sports within the broader imperial and global context. Significantly, South Africa adopted many of the sports played by British elites, that also dominated white settler societies such as Australia and New Zealand. By the 1920s regular tours in cricket and rugby took place between these four countries of the Empire establishing a pattern of close sporting relations within a small network of white-dominated societies.

This chapter explores the development of cricket and rugby in the late nineteenth and early twentieth centuries as they became entrenched as white cultural activities. Additionally, the rise of segregation in sports is also discussed as blacks were excluded from playing with whites. In South Africa, sport was central in the development of a geography of exclusion and division, it became a central factor in the emergence of divergent sporting cultures among spatially divided groups. This chapter concentrates on the development of imperial sports among whites, and the next will focus on those sports in the black communities.

Modern sport emerged in Britain in the middle decades of the nineteenth century, which coincided with its undisputed dominance as a world power. The British navy controlled the seas, its shipping took trade all over the globe. As a result, British sports soon spread to areas of British influence with cricket, horse-racing and varieties of football soon appearing in South America, Africa, India and Australasia. South Africa quickly developed British sporting forms after settlers began arriving in the 1820s. By the 1860s, South African settlers were playing most British sports and soon became linked to a wider imperial sporting community.

Before the building of the Suez Canal in the 1880s, Cape Town was on the main shipping routes to Asia and Australasia, placing it in a central position to receive British cultural developments and contacts from those returning to Britain from India or Australia. English-speaking white schools in South Africa took up British games and used them to instil values of British elite culture. These games took on a greater significance in a colonial context where whites were a small minority of the population. Educationalists and elites equated civilization with Britishness and whiteness. Although the 'virtues' of British civilization and cultural behaviour were promoted on mission stations to a small percentage of the African population, its culture represented cultural, moral and even genetic or 'natural' superiority to settlers and officials who believed these qualities set them apart from the local population. Indeed, for many years British settlers all over the Empire referred to Britain as 'home' rather than the places where they lived. Deference in all matters cultural, including those in sport, was to Britain and British institutions and authorities. By the early 1900s, however, sport was the one cultural activity where colonial men gained a measure of equality, and even dominance, discussed in both the British and colonial media (Nauright, 1991, 1992, 1996b). In particular cricket and rugby union became the team sports that most closely tied white imperial societies together and which captured the imagination in colonial settler societies.

Cricket has long been a significant part of the imperial context in South African history, and the game was imported by military personnel, administrators and settlers from Britain. In particular, coastal towns 'received assistance from the members of the Military garrison' (Swaffer, 1914: 29). Grant Jarvie emphasises that, 'sport must not be understood abstractly or simply in the context of ideas about racial prejudice, but rather in the context of the ensemble of social relations characterizing the South African social formation' (Jarvie, 1991: 182). Cricket in South Africa represented British imperialist classist ideology and increasingly racist exclusivism.

White cricket became entrenched in segregated schools and clubs (often based on old boys' groups) whose purpose was to demonstrate solidarity, superiority and apartness. Elitism and racism were the norm except for rare mixing on imperial holidays. The South African Cricket Association (SACA), established in 1890 to 'foster and develop cricket throughout South Africa' (Parker, 1897: 47), had no need to include racial barriers in its constitution as social custom already achieved that. Significantly, one of the clauses in its constitution specified its managerial role in relation to tours to and from England. SACA originally included a union for Portuguese East Africa while ignoring the aspirations of South Africa's black cricketers. The 1886–7 inter-colonial tournament included a white team from British Bechuanaland (now

Botswana). The Currie Cup, instituted as the prize for inter-provincial white cricket in 1888, was presented by Donald Currie, diamond and gold magnate, of Castle Shipping Line, which provided the sea link between South Africa and England (Duffus, 1980). Rhodesia was admitted to the Currie Cup competition for one match in the 1904–5 season and again from 1930 (Duffus, 1969). Thus, the inclusion of white teams from colonies outside those that formed the Union of South Africa in 1910 was far more important than including teams from black communities inside South Africa. Racial solidarity was more crucial in this context than national-based solidarities.

From 1864 an important (and for a while the premier) fixture in South African cricket was the match between Mother Country and Colonial Born. Implicit in this contest was a deference to 'home' origins and the significance of cultural ties to England. Though not unique to South Africa, as such matches were common in Australia, New Zealand and elsewhere in the Empire, links to British culture were even more important in a setting where whites were surrounded by a large local population linguistically constructed as 'uncivilized', different and ultimately inferior. Morrell (1996) shows how the small white population in Natal used rugby union to culturally demarkate themselves from the overwhelming black majority. The ability to appropriate and dispense English culture as the measure of social acceptability gave English-speaking whites, and those they chose to include, a real sense of cultural and moral power and superiority. As the twentieth century progressed, specific sports became synonymous with particular racial groups, even though nearly all sports were played within the various social and cultural communities in South Africa. As a result, sporting practice and associated popular culture surrounding sport became distinct social signifiers within the country. Such signifiers have been difficult to remove even in the post-apartheid era.

Cricket was *the* imperial game, the epitome of British culture, morality, manners and racism, which served to alienate Afrikaners as well as most blacks. In 1854, a match at the Cape involved 'Hottentots' versus 'Boers' (won by the former) (Archer and Bouillon, 1982), but towards the end of the century, and in particular after the Anglo-Boer War, cricket found little favour among the Afrikaner community and its imperial characteristics limited its reconciliatory potential. Before the war, a number of Afrikaners represented South Africa: Arthur Ochse and Nicolaas Hendrik Theunissen in the first test of 1888; Jacobus Francois du Toit and Charles Gustav Fichardt in the 1891–2 series; and Fichardt again in 1895–6. The fast bowler Johannes Jacobus Kotze, a 'Boer . . . who preferred cricket to war' (Martin-Jenkins, 1980: 265) went on tour with South Africa to England in 1901 while the war was still being fought, although his five tests were played later.

While it is unwise to assign ethnicity on the basis of surnames, it appears that after 1907 no Afrikaner played in a test for South Africa until Jacobus Petrus Duminy in 1927–8. Cricket, as the epitome of Empire, was unlikely to attract those who considered themselves enemies of *die Engelse*. In addition, the British had won the war only after placing Afrikaner women and children in concentration camps, so as to force Afrikaner men out of the bush and into signing a peace treaty. Afrikaners viewed the concentration camps as a British attempt to wipe them out, which fed into emerging explications of Afrikaner nationalism and the Afrikaners as a 'besieged people'.

The apparent Afrikaner reluctance to take up cricket continued for several decades. Just before the Second World War it was reported that 'The Boer element in South Africa is not vastly taken up with the game, although some of the papers do print reports of it in Africaans[sic]' (Pollock, 1941: 121). Cricket thus became a symbol of divisions among the whites of South Africa, as well as separateness and exclusiveness of English-speaking whites from the rest of the population, until 1948 after which it increasingly functioned as a totem of white national unity. For these reasons, cricket never achieved the same status as rugby during the apartheid years when Afrikaner nationalists ran the country. The relative insignificance of cricket to some Afrikaners is evidenced in a story about Prime Minister John Vorster. He was told that '*die Engelse* had lost three wickets for 42 runs in the test between South Africa and England. Upon being given the information, Vorster replied "*Hulle Engelse of ons Engelse?*"' ('Their English or our English?') (Woods, 1981: 46).

Since the 1960s Afrikaners have been more prominent in cricket. This is partly due to a weakening of anti-cricket ideology among Afrikaners, identification with a wider, albeit white-dominated South Africa before the 1980s, and the appearance of more Afrikaner students at elite schools such as Grey's College in Bloemfontein. In the new South Africa, Afrikaners, such as team captain Hansie Cronje and players such as Fanie de Villiers and Alan Donald, have played an important role in the national team.

There is some evidence, however, of a belief in the reconciliatory potential of cricket between the whites of South Africa emanating from early in the twentieth century. A match involving Afrikaners illustrated the imperial use of cricket. In 1901, Afrikaner war prisoners interned at Diyatalawa, Ceylon (Sri Lanka) played against the Colombo Colts. The *Ceylon Independent* described the match as 'a sporting event . . . no other significance need be attached to it . . . The men are on parole; they have given their word that they will not enter into the discussion of any controversial subjects.' The captain of the prisoners of war was P. H. de Villiers of the Western Province Cricket Club in Cape Town and at least two others had played club cricket. Contrary to the newspaper report, the match was significant in at least two ways. First, the Governor attended, the prisoners were given lunch at the Galle Face Hotel and after the match Commandant van Zyl called for three cheers for His Excellency, which were 'heartily given, with great waving of hats and a display of the utmost cordiality'. Second, when a 'native' crowd, described as over-excited, invaded the pitch, the police made 'free application' of canes to control them (Luckin, 1915: 803–6).

The match was thus characterized by white sporting solidarity,[1] deference to Imperial authority and harsh treatment of locals. Although played thousands of miles away, this match captures some of the essence of South African cricket at the dawn of the twentieth century. The notion of 'over-excited natives' who had to be controlled pervaded white international social thought at the turn of the century. Thus, the playing of cricket juxtaposed with the caning of 'natives' reinforced central notions of white superiority. Within a social Darwinist hierarchy, cricket was believed to be the most moral of games and one that demonstrated the inherent superiority of the English over other 'races'. As Will Whittam proudly wrote in 1884, 'No German, Frenchman, or Fijee can ever master cricket, sir, Because they haven't got the pluck to stand before the wicket, sir' (quoted in Nauright, 1992). Cricket developed into a complex system of bodily presence and deportment that defined civilized behaviour itself. Imbued with moral characteristics and an air of superiority, the game was thought to be masterable by only those who had become 'civilized'. In South Africa, the spatial dimensions of cricket also reinforced exclusive discourses surrounding the game. Access to playing facilities was limited as segregation restricted blacks from playing on the same fields as whites. By the early 1900s, cricket represented sporting exclusivity, even among urban educated blacks who played the game.

CRICKET AND IMPERIAL SPORTING LINKS

The role of Anglo-South African capital was crucial to the survival of early cricket and other sporting tours. Donald Currie funded the first touring team in 1888–9 put together by Major Warton, an official at the Cape (Altham and Swanton, 1948; Parker, 1897). The 1895 team to England (frequently referred to as the 'Africans' in *Wisden*) was described condescendingly as 'common-place' and attracted gate receipts of only £500, compared with £3500 worth of expenses. Someone evidently felt the need to maintain the link since 'a collapse was only avoided by the advance of money by South African friends in England'. Maybe they were the 'several gentlemen connected with South Africa' invited to the opening match versus Lord Sheffield's XI (*Wisden*, 1895: 333, 336). It is significant that the 1901 touring side left for England before the end of the South African War (Altham, 1962). Cricket against South Africa failed to rouse the English public, however, and 'The whole expenses of the trip were defrayed by Mr Logan [of Matjiesfontein], with whom the whole idea of the enterprise originated.' (*Wisden*, 1902: 467.) Patronage was important in the development of international sporting tours in the white settler societies of the British Empire. Many early tours were financed by entrepreneurs keen to exploit emerging spectator interest in the colonies and the exotic nature of sporting tastes of British crowds, though often organizers overestimated the market (Cashman, 1992; Ryan, 1993).

The political and imperial leanings of visiting cricketers were clear. C. B. Fry maintains that the 1896 England touring team was sent to Johannesburg at the time of the Jameson Raid 'as an antidote to the inflamed melancholy of that distant city' (Fry, 1986: 109); a motive supported by Lord Hawke who said he was 'telegraphed . . . to go to Johannesburg to play there to turn people's minds from the raid' (Hawke, 1924: 151).[2] The Raid, led by Leander Starr Jameson, protege of Cecil Rhodes, was an abortive attempt to take control of the South African Republic. Team members Lord Hawke, Sir Timothy O'Brien and Charles Wright, dined and played cards with the British captives in Johannesburg Prison. Nevertheless, a match was played against a predominately Afrikaner team in Pretoria, although entertainment by, and a polo match with, the 7th Hussars in Pietermaritzburg was more typical of the tour. The touring team promoted both cricket and Empire.

The touring teams of the 1890s may accurately be described as 'Imperial Wanderers' including as they did the Australians J. J. Ferris and W. Murdoch (1891–2), S. M. J. Woods (1895–6) and Albert Trott (1898–9) (Cashman, 1992; Tozer, 1992). The links went both ways and it was said of the 1894 touring team to England that 'it cannot fail to have a beneficial effect as forming one more link between the Old Country and ourselves . . . one that especially influences the youth of both lands', adding that the tour 'will accomplish as much good as would the visit of a Minister or the efforts of an Agent-General' (*Cape Illustrated Magazine*, 1894: 370). Lord Hawke's touring team of 1899 played two matches at Bulawayo in March (versus 18 of Bulawayo and 15 of Rhodesia) at a time when it was merely 'a town in the making' (Hawke, 1924: 160). Additionally, the 1906 English team led by Pelham Warner followed a match against the Transvaal in Johannesburg with 'an excursion to pretty Potchefstroom to greet the local Britishers before the serious business of the first test' (Dobson, 1988: 10). Cricket closely followed the flag and was significant in the development of British imperial cultural identity across the emerging 'nations' of the Empire (Stoddart and Sandiford, forthcoming).

The insecurity of colonial society was counteracted by invoking the imperial connection and elevating Britain as the source of civilization. Cricket was held up as perhaps the most significant training ground for life and service to the British Empire. At the turn of the century, the tone of writing on cricket was deferential in the extreme: Lord Hawke's team to South Africa in 1895–6 was described as 'the men from the Homeland' (Dorey, 1912: 187); while 'cricketing teams from all parts of the Empire look to Lord's as the home, and to MCC as the head of the game' (Henderson, 1906: 1). Lord Harris, who believed that the MCC was the most venerated institution of the Empire, commenting on the same tour described it as 'a strand in the elastic which unites the colonies and the Mother Country' (Henderson, 1906: 5). South Africa's cricketers and spectators were routinely referred to as 'colonial' and by implication as of a lesser standard than those of the 'Mother Country' (Luckin, 1915: 521). For example, H. H. Castens' team to England in 1894 was described as 'of the calibre of a second-class county' even though it managed to beat the MCC at Lords in one day by 11 runs (Dorey, 1912: 184).

In Johannesburg in January 1906, South Africa beat England for the first time, which Pelham Warner attributed to 'that grit and courage which we are so proud of saying are inherent in the British race' (Warner, 1906: 68). Two of the South African side were born in England, but the rest were native to South Africa. South Africa went on to win the series by four tests to one and, coupled with the victories of the 1906–7 Springbok rugby team in the British Isles, assisted in the development of a sense of white South Africa colonial maturity. Despite this South African success, England sent sides infrequently (10 tours in 50 years) and of less than full strength to South Africa until 1938. Significantly the 1938 tour was the first sent out by England after South Africa defeated England at Lord's in the second test of its tour of 1935. That victory marked the first win by South Africa in a test match in England and was viewed as a coming of age of South African cricket, not unlike interpretations of initial wins in England by other colonial teams.

The generally deferential attitude to English cricket, and English cricket's patronizing attitude about the 'colonials', was not at all in conflict with a South African will to beat England: such events reinforced South Africa's, or at least white and 'civilized' South Africa's, worth to the Empire. Richard Cashman has shown that a similar process occurred in Australian cricket in the 1870s and 1880s as British qualities of Anglo-Australian cricketers were celebrated, and early Australian victories over England were used to stress the ability of the Anglo-Saxon race to thrive in a hostile environment (Cashman, 1988). Despite the unequal nature of the relationship between English authorities at the MCC and South Africa, both, along with Australia, were founder members of the Imperial Cricket Council in 1909, the organizational body for international cricket, later renamed the International Cricket Council.

British military influence in South African cricket was pronounced and the military presence helped to ease psychological fears of inferiority and of being surrounded by potentially hostile forces. Included in South Africa's first test team that played at Port Elizabeth in 1888 was Major R. Stewart. A number of cricketing British soldiers settled in South Africa after the 1899–1902 war, such as Dave Nourse and Frank Mitchell. The military influence on the game is illustrated by the ranks named on score cards: Brigadier-General Reginald Montagu Poore is a good example of this connection. An officer in the 7th Hussars who served in India and South Africa, a noted shot and polo and tennis player, he played cricket for Bombay Presidency from 1893 to 1895 (while ADC to Lord Harris, Governor of Bombay) and for Natal and South Africa (three tests) in 1895 and 1896. Poore then went on to play English county cricket for Hampshire, scoring seven centuries and over 1300 runs in 1899. In two weeks during June 1899 he scored three consecutive centuries, played on the winning team at the inter-regimental polo tournament, and won a fencing title at the Royal Naval and Military Tournament. He later returned to South Africa as an imperial sporting hero and example (Stoddart, 1988).[3]

A particular form of insecurity developed in Natal, often still referred to as 'the last outpost of the British Empire'. The whites of Natal viewed themselves as a beleaguered homogeneous group (Morrell, 1996), the consequence of which was the gross stereotyping of others. 'White attitudes towards Africans at the turn of the century were a curious blend of paternalism, fear and contempt'. White and black were seen as opposites in which the latter occupied a place as minors and were made to understand that 'the presence and predominance of the white race will be preserved at all hazards' (Marks, 1970: 11, 13). While attitudes towards Africans implied that they were 'non-persons', the threat of urbanized, free immigrants of Indian origin (as opposed to indentured Indians) gave rise to virulent racism. Their main transgression was that of effective commercial competition and their presence was countered by racist laws concerning immigration (the 'Natal formula'), the franchise and licensing. Indians were legally declared 'uncivilized' and described in the Natal legislature in 1880 as 'the scum of Madras and Calcutta'. Other racist epithets such as 'Asiatic curse' were common and Indians were sometimes pushed off pavements. Their competitiveness 'aroused the petty bourgeois establishment that held sway in Natal's towns and cities' as they failed to 'wait patiently, hat in hand, outside the shrine of Victorian Anglo-Saxonism' (Huttenback, 1976: 197–8).

South African white society consistently displayed frontier behaviour, insisting upon 'religious, moral, and cultural barriers between itself and its neighbours' (de Kiewiet, 1941: 211). Sports in general, and cricket and rugby in particular, were important means used to create social unity among English-speaking whites and to maintain social distance from the rest. In the words of J. A. Mangan, cricket contributed a 'cultural bond of white imperial fraternity' of instrumental use to the dominant male elite (Mangan, 1992: 6).

In the context of cricket, the opinion of the arch-Imperialist Pelham Warner, who had a quasi-religious approach to the game, was highly valued: 'Mr Warner says the position of South Africa in the cricket world is largely due to the munificence and sagacity of Mr Abe Bailey' (*South African Cricketers Annual*, 1905–6: 120). Warner wrote that 'For South African cricket [Bailey] did much, as he put his hand deeply into his pocket to further its interests and development, as did the great Rhodes . . .' (Warner, 1951: 135). Sir Abe Bailey was interested in South African cricket from the early 1890s, underwrote the South African cricket tours of England in 1904 and 1906, funded the 1902 Australian tour and provided Transvaal with a guarantee for the MCC match of 1905 (*South African Cricketers Annual*, 1906–7: 174). Bailey was an imperialist Rand magnate (with real estate, farming and mining interests throughout southern Africa) and politician who had captained Transvaal in the Currie Cup, belonged to the Reform Committee in 1896 at the time of the Jameson Raid, served as an intelligence officer in the Anglo-Boer War, and raised an irregular corps in that conflict 'continuing his support of imperial interests in South Africa' (*Dictionary of South African Biography*, vol. II: 19). He identified strongly with the philosophy of Cecil Rhodes, whose constituency at Barkly West he took over from 1902–5. A racist who opposed the rights of Indian immigrants in Natal and the Transvaal (by 1922 he was arguing for their expulsion), he worked for the union of the South African colonies, financing *The State* (a journal started by Philip Kerr, one of the 'Milner kindergarten', who supported the post-South African War pro-imperialist policies of Lord Milner), and advocated and promoted Imperial preference. A contemporary writer observed that 'There was no racialism in his composition . . .' (Neame, 1929: 167). By this it was meant that Bailey valued highly good relations between South Africans of British origins and Afrikaners – the idea of not being racist with regard to Indians and Africans was not even considered and explains their absence from the world of South African cricket.

Leveson-Gower maintains that cricket was so important to Bailey that he was moved to greater nervousness over a tight Test match than matters of high finance (Leveson-Gower, 1953: 160). His writings on cricket epitomize imperial prose:

> Sport has played a great part in creating a balance between the two great white races of this Country and . . . the Sportsmen of the Empire have responded in a most gallant manner to the call of their King and Country . . . The part

Imperial cricket has played in the past is known to all. It has added to the union of hearts, it has strengthened the bonds of Empire, it has brought closer together our immense family, and to-day the cricketers of our vast Empire who played with us in the time of peace, are fighting with us in a greater game for liberty. (Foreword to Luckin, 1915)

'Cypher' (H. E. Holmes), writing at the same time about Natal cricket, also used the imperial image when he wrote 'nothing less than a German occupation of the Province will kill the spirit of cricket which prevails' (Cypher, 1915: 81). Cricket as a moral metaphor and imperial symbol was ideally suited to the social anxieties and political allegiances of English-speaking whites of the era. South Africa maintained old imperial exclusivities longer than the MCC itself by only playing against 'white' countries of England, Australia and New Zealand until the post-apartheid era of the 1990s.

Cricket tours by the MCC were intimately connected with the imperial social scene. On the 1905–6 tour, Pelham Warner stayed with Godfrey Lagden, the Basutoland administrator and Lord Cobham, ADC to the Governor-General, Lord Selborne (Warner, 1951: 71). When the MCC met Natal at Pietermaritzburg in January 1910 they found room in the side for R. Ponsonby, Secretary to ex-Governor Sir Matthew Nathan. The 1909–10 tourists were also entertained by Lord Methuen at Government House, Pietermaritzburg and after their win in the third test at Cape Town he sent an encouraging telegram. At the end of the tour in March 1910, Leander Starr Jameson, an imperial visionary who shared Rhodes' dream of British territory stretching from Cape to Cairo and who had been an agent for the British South Africa Company, and Abe Bailey invited the team to Rhodesia, an offer accepted by the amateurs.

This social serenity appears to have been mildly inconvenienced during the 1913–14 tour which was 'marred by the labour troubles in Johannesburg, and owing to an unfortunate misunderstanding, there was a little un-pleasantness in Bloemfontein' (*Wisden*, 1915: 477). Of the match between MCC and a Transvaal XI at Vogelsfontein on 14–15 January 1914 *Wisden* reported, 'The Labour troubles were at their height and the match excited very little interest' (*Wisden*, 1915: 491). Local concerns had clearly eclipsed the imperial connection, if only briefly. The English players made their political loyalties plain by volunteering as special constables (Tennyson, 1950: 73). Such behaviour should not come as any surprise given the overtly English and loyalist associations between cricket and Britain and the Empire.

The suggestion in 1909 of an Imperial Cricket Conference was initiated by Bailey. Two meetings of the British Colonial Cricket Conference were held in London on 15 and 20 July at which the term 'Imperial' was adopted. Bailey represented South Africa at the second meeting along with G. W. Hillyard and H. D. G. Leverson-Gower. People with closer ties to the MCC than Newlands routinely represented South Africa at the ICC: Leverson-Gower at the meeting on 16 July 1912 (with the South African G. Allsop); Leverson-Gower (again) and Pelham Warner at the June 1921 meeting. The power of South African gold was instrumental in setting up the 1912 Triangular Tournament, 'which was brought about through Sir Abe Bailey's efforts' (Taylor, 1925: 125). Unfortunately for Bailey the South African side was no stronger than the average English county and the weather was abysmal. Nevertheless, this was the perfect imperial tournament though resisted by the Australians who saw it as a threat to the primacy of their relationship with England. The founding of the ICC tied South Africa firmly into the international fixture list, at the time consisting of Australia, England and South Africa, so much so that with the outbreak of the First World War South Africa asked that the 'Imperial programme' be advanced by one year to allow Australia to tour in 1915–16. This was turned down by the Australians pending the MCC's wishes. The Australian Imperial Forces team visited South Africa in 1919–20 and the mining magnate S. P. Joel sponsored the England second team tour to South Africa, 1924–5.

In 1929, at a British Empire League dinner in London for visiting South African cricketers, Eric Louw emphasized the role of sport in bringing together South African whites and asserting their identity in the eyes of the British (Paton, 1964: 159).[4] This also extended to whites to the north of the Limpopo River in what was then Rhodesia. In 1935, D. S. Tomlinson was the first Rhodesian to represent South Africa and included on the same tour was R. J. Crisp of Western Province, who had grown up in Rhodesia (Duffus, 1969: 938). The image was created of a small cricketing nation struggling hard to keep up standards, 'It is not surprising that in a country so vast and with so scattered a white population as exists . . . there should have been innumerable difficulties to overcome in the organisation and harnessing of the cricket potentialities that existed' (Webber, 1927: 21).

Clearly only white potential counted in cricket. The inclusion of Rhodesian players in South African sporting teams is indicative of the general attitude of identity among whites in South Africa, with the white race first and foremost, and of a pan-white African and Imperial identity shared between settler groups in different areas. During the 1920s 'White society became more acutely conscious than before of its numerical inferiority, against which neither natural increase nor immigration from Europe showed any promise of prevailing.' Ties with the mother country were strengthened by 'A belief in an innate and invincible white superiority . . . [which] became a faith, and racial and social segregation a creed.' (de Kiewiet, 1941: 222, 226.) At this point, South African whites took British racial attitudes further in promoting full segregation down to the detail of which jobs each race could hold.

In line with the colonial attitudes of the time, blacks were treated like children, if their presence was acknowledged at all. The Newlands scoreboard was operated by a team of Coloured men. During the match between MCC and Natal at Durban in 1938 'a small army of bare-footed non-Europeans periodically sall[ied] forth, armed with brooms, to sweep away the water from the wicket covers . . .' (Pollock, 1941: 116); while on the last day of the Timeless Test in Durban in 1938 'At 3.15pm an Indian came out with a tray of cool drinks . . .' (Pollock, 1941: 152). Louis Duffus, writing in 1947, aptly summed up the attitudes of the 1930s. He opens his book with a day-dream about a cricket match on the Reef: 'Out in the centre of the oval Sixpence, the ground boy, is methodically rolling up the mat. As he wheels away the pitch he chants a tune of his kraal-land, a low-toned drawling song that his proud ancestors were wont to sing as night fell over the rolling hills of Zululand.' In another passage, about schools' cricket, he describes 'The native, Jim Fish . . . pulling up the last strip of matting' (Duffus, 1947: 5–6, 11).

The examples above are revealing. The only proper place for a black man on a cricket field used by whites was as a labourer and his real identity was camouflaged by a nickname intelligible to, and imposed by, whites. In any case, Sixpence, it is implied, really belongs hundreds of miles away, not in a white urban area. The use of the signifiers 'native', 'boy', 'bare-footed non-Europeans', plus links to primeval singing or dancing based in the rural areas, continually reminded whites of the difference between themselves and the black 'others' in the country. Eventually, such signifiers helped draw whites closer together as a social collectivity that was different from, and, as they viewed it, culturally and morally superior to, blacks. The supposed 'excit-ability' of black South Africans and their constructed inability to 'control' themselves and their bodies was also used by whites to keep blacks in isolated sections of grounds or away altogether. Such racial ideologies made sense to white South Africans who were always a minority. Unlike other settler societies, whites never came to dominate the local population by weight of numbers. Thus, racial ideologies in South Africa came to be more rigid and in practical policy terms lasted longer than elsewhere. Fear of miscegenation (interbreeding) and of cultural swamping led whites to close ranks around their everyday experiences, ensuring that blacks were to be excluded except where necessary to perform labouring tasks.

The overwhelming reliance on race as social signifier served to submerge the real and distinct class differences within each grouping. Members of the mission-educated black middle class were far more likely to support 'respectable' British cultural values and play cricket than were the members of the Afrikaner working class who began to arrive in the cities in large numbers after 1907. Racial separation and perceived distinctiveness was so powerful that, even in the early 1990s, many whites believed that blacks had only taken to the 'white' sports of cricket and rugby in the previous ten to twenty years (Odendaal, 1995).

While initially in the later nineteenth century, black cricket emulated the values and cultural practices of white cricket, Coloured, Indian and African cricket culture developed its own forms in the twentieth century, sometimes different from the dominant white culture surrounding the game. Defensive batting was not supported and quality of stroke play and shot making was paramount. Most matches lasted one day or less as that was the limit of available time free from work. The quality of the pitches also made playing 'safe' a potentially dangerous proposition. Many teams were based on areas within communities, particularly in Cape Town, Port Elizabeth, the eastern Cape, Durban and Kimberley, or by ex-school old boys or on occupation, so they were firmly rooted in local community cultures. Matches in Cape Town for example took on a communal atmosphere and food and drink was shared among members of the crowd. While patronized by the black middle classes, cricket took place within communities dominated in numbers by the urban working class and thus expressed the values of that culture – a far cry from the concerns of many white cricket supporters for whom cricket embodied pastoral images of rural England and peaceful isolation from the tensions of life outside the grounds and from the confines of urban space. Indeed the style of black cricket emerged out of the social conditions in which blacks had to learn the game.

While black cricket struggled for finances and facilities, white cricket at all levels benefited from generous donations of capitalists and governing bodies. In 1939, Lord Nuffield, at a function to welcome the visiting England team, announced a donation of £10,000 to further white schoolboy cricket. After the inaugural 1940 tournament, an opinion was ventured that 'tournaments of this nature will make the boys of South Africa just one big family, regardless of considerations of race or birth' (*South African Cricket Annual*, 1951–2: 208). The 'one big family' referred, of course, to whites. The Governor-General was the President of SACA until South Africa left the Commonwealth in 1961; and the cricket literature of the time was redolent of imperial linkage. SACA's annual report of 1955 noted the death of Lady Warner, widow of Sir Pelham; but when C. B. Llewellyn, South Africa's only black international cricketer, died in June 1964, it was five years before South Africa's white cricketing annual recorded it, though with no obituary. Given the overt imperial links in cricket, it is not surprising that Afrikaner nationalists denigrated it as the 'Englishman's game' and took to promoting rugby as a sport worthy of Afrikaner nationalist support (this is discussed later in the chapter). Cricket more than any other sporting or cultural activity remained in this position for much of South Africa's modern history.

Between 1888 and 1970, South Africa participated in 45 test match series consisting of 172 test matches; but the only opponents were the white-dominated countries of England, Australia (from 1902–3) and New Zealand (from 1931–2). Until 1958, England, Australia and South Africa had two votes each on the ICC ensuring the power of the white-dominated nations. The survival of South African whites in international competition in the 1960s was underpinned by 'a pattern of social, political and business relationships' (Thompson, 1964: 67) that owed a great deal to lingering imperial bonds. In the words of Derek Birley, 'South Africa had always occupied a special place in the affections of the cricket establishment' (Birley, 1979: 154). An editorial in *The Times* welcomed the 1960 South African tourists to England, describing them as 'old friends' (quoted in Lapchick, 1973: 84–5). Such characterization survived the period of sporting boycotts and apartheid and reappeared in advertisements for the 1993–4 series between South Africa and Australia, the first series between the two countries for 23 years. Although South Africa had been instrumental in the setting up of the ICC and its representative, Foster Bowley, argued in July 1961 for continued test status, South Africa was required to leave the ICC on departing from the Common-wealth, after which all matches played with the remaining members were technically unofficial. The South African Sports Association (SASA), formed in 1958 to promote non-racial sport, and elements in the government of India pushed for total exclusion, but the ICC solution was a system which permitted the continuation of the status quo while giving an impression of grappling with changed geo-political circumstances. The Australian cricket authorities strongly supported South Africa and made it clear that they would regard all their matches as official. A report in the South African press assessed the situation astutely: 'all countries showed sympathy with the MCC view that nothing should be done which would be detrimental to the interests of South African cricket' (*Rand Daily Mail*, 18 July 1962). The imperial old boys network was alive and well in the 1960s, and as we shall see, it remained alive in the 1990s.

The myopia of the 1960s in establishment cricket circles is illustrated by Geoffrey Chettle, editor of the *South African Cricket Annual*, who explained in an editorial of 1963 that South Africa's future in international cricket depended upon positive, attacking cricket and good performances in forthcoming encounters with the Australians and New Zealanders (*South African Cricket Annual*, 1963: 5). Jackie McGlew, writing at much the same time, emphasized similar concerns adding his worry about the nature of pitches (McGlew, 1965). The view persisted that traditional bonds could be maintained if performances were good enough. Thus Chettle was able to write in 1964, 'After being discarded as a member of the [ICC] and relegated to the position of sharing a tour with another country, the Springboks returned from their fourth visit to Australia and New Zealand having restored the country's prestige as a major cricketing power' (*South African Cricket Annual*, 1964: 5). He added that the core of the South African test side had been set for the next ten years and after the 1965 tour of England he stated, 'This is the dawn of a new era' (*South African Cricket Annual*, 1965: 5). The black cricketers of South Africa remained invisible. Thus, it appeared that only major international boycotts could halt the progress of the South African cricket team. Many experts agree that the South African test side of the late 1960s was one of the better sides assembled and would have been very successful internationally. By the early 1970s, however, South Africa was isolated from international cricketing competition and the establishment had to resort to 'rebel' tours financed by major companies and supported by government subsidies and tax breaks. Right through to the end of the apartheid period, cricket remained identified with the English-speaking white community, though Afrikaners increasingly played at top levels and Coloured and African cricketers also began to succeed when given the opportunity, usually overseas, before 1990.

Through the imperial connection and identifications with British imperial cultural practices, English-speaking whites always had an internationalist aspect to their national identity as South Africans within a larger British 'family' of nations. Afrikaners always suspected that English-speaking whites were somehow less South African than themselves and labelled them as less patriotic. As Nixon (1994) puts it, English-speaking whites were assailed by Afrikaner nationalists for their flawed patriotism – they were not 'true' South Africans but 'a section of a nation overseas', and a conduit for foreign capital and cultural interests. Cricket was labelled as one of these 'foreign' activities, though ironically rugby, with nearly an equal imperial pedigree, was not.

SOUTH AFRICAN RUGBY AND THE IMPERIAL CONNECTION

As with cricket, British officers and settlers also brought rugby to South Africa in the nineteenth century. The acknowledged founder of rugby in South Africa is Canon George Oglivie who became headmaster of Diocesan College, or Bishop's, in Cape Town in 1861 where he remained until 1885. A version of football began at Bishop's from this time and the first recorded match took place on 23 August 1862. The *Cape Argus* on 21 August 1862 promoted the match:

FOOT-BALL

We are happy to find this fine old English school-game has been introduced amongst us. On Saturday next sides consisting of fifteen officers of the army and a like number of gentlemen in the civil service will open the Ball with a game on the race-course at Green Point.

Of course this example will be speedily followed, and we shall have foot-ball treading closely on the likes of cricket and other imported manly games.

Included in this first match was future Cape Prime Minister John X. Merriman and other local notables. The imperial connection was evident at the outset as the Governor of the Cape Colony, Governor Wodehouse, attended this initial match (Joyce, 1981). Bishop's and South African College also began to play against each other at this time. The version of football initially played resembled the game played at Winchester School in England, and many Winchester Old Boys played important roles in starting rugby in South Africa. William Henry Milton, a former England rugby union international, arrived in Cape Town in 1878 and he persuaded Capetonian men that they were playing an outmoded game. His recommendation that rugby rules be taken up was followed, though Oglivie thought rugby was too violent a game. Rugby spread rapidly, however, and soon embodied all the elements of manliness promoted in the British game.

In 1879, the first two rugby union clubs, Hamilton and Villagers, were founded in Cape Town. In 1886 the first Coloured rugby clubs appeared, also in Cape Town. On 31 May 1890, the first match was held at Newlands in Cape Town. As the official history of the Newlands ground puts it:

Special trains were arranged from Stellenbosch and Southern suburbs, and the Wynberg Military Camp band was in attendance. The Governor, Sir Henry Loch, and his entourage were accommodated in cane chairs.

A crowd of about 2 400 turned up, which was considered excellent....
(Western Province Rugby Football Union, 1990:1)

As this passage shows, rugby, as with cricket, was initially tied closely to concepts of British civilization, culture and imperial power. Similar to England, white rugby began as a private school and Old Boy club-based clique. In this period, British attitudes towards Afrikaners were not much removed from those of black Africans. As late as 1903, John Buchan commented on Afrikaners and sport in harsh, and quite unfair, terms:

It is worth while considering the Boer in sport, for it is there he is seen at his worst. Without tradition of fair play, soured and harassed by want and disaster, his sport became a matter of commerce, and he held no device unworthy . . . [The Afrikaners] are not a sporting race – they are not even a race of very skilful hunters (quoted in Archer and Bouillon, 1982: 18).

The South African Rugby Board (SARB) was founded in 1889, 21 years prior to the formation of the Union of South Africa, and international tours by British teams became regular occurrences in the 1890s. British teams toured South Africa in 1891, 1896 and 1903 with the Anglo-Boer War of 1899–1902 briefly preventing tours. The British teams were initially successful, winning all their matches in 1891 and only losing one test match to the South African team in 1896. Imperial links were stressed during these tours. The 1891 British Isles team, consisting of twenty English and Scottish players, were greeted by a large group of officials and supporters led a procession to the Royal Hotel where the team received flowers and ferns. The British team was treated to many smoking concerts, dinners, picnics and a formal ball at Government House. The Cape Town newspapers discussed the tour in detail and worked to generate great public interest. In typical colonial reportage of matches against British teams, the *Cape Argus* reported that the tour would be a trial for South African rugby (Greyvenstein, 1995: 11). During the 1891 tour, Sir Donald Currie, founder of the Castle Shipping Line donated a trophy for an internal South African competition. The Currie Cup as it was to be called was first presented to the team who gave the British tourists the best game. Griqualand West was presented with the trophy which was then used in subsequent years as the trophy for the South African provincial champions.[5]

The links between Empire and rugby in the 1890s can be best illustrated by the Irish Banquet held in Cape Town on 5 September 1896 for the British Isles touring rugby team. At the Banquet were leading members of the Cape Government and local and sporting officials, as well as most of the players for the British and South African teams. Toasts were proposed to the Queen, the Governor and the Cape Ministry, the latter of which, Sir James Sivewright, leading minister in the government, responded. The *Cape Argus* reported Sivewright's reply to the latter toast as follows:

They had had an awful year in South Africa. There had been a great deal to forgive and forget, and the sooner the better, but they were not going to forget the representative cricket and football teams that had visited South Africa (applause), and the visits would be enshrined in their memories. . . . The British race seemed to make football their prerogative and the parents of the game had sent out a team to teach the children, and Mr Hammond [British captain] would testify that they had learned their lesson well since the visit of the first team (cheers). The bull-dog characteristic of the race was called upon in the football field, and it did a great deal to make their men, not the game itself so much as the qualities which it encouraged (cheers). Such visits as the present one bound them to the Old Country with stronger bonds than ever (*Cape Argus*, 7 September 1896: 6).

This passage demonstrates how sport could be used to divert attention from political strife (the tour took place at a time of increasing tension between the British and Afrikaner communities, culminating in the infamous Jameson Raid on 29 December), but more significantly just how important rugby and cricket tours were in cementing ties to England and the bonds of Empire and Imperial culture. While the tone is deferential to England, it is clear the local success was viewed as evidence of reaching a certain stage of maturity. Fittingly, South Africa won the fourth and final test on 5 September at Newlands, 5-0 for their first victory over a British team. It was in this match that the South Africans first wore the green jerseys that were to become such a familiar sight in international rugby.

By 1903 the tide had shifted and South Africa began to dominate rugby encounters with British teams. South Africa defeated the British tourists of 1903 in the final test after the first two were drawn, thus winning its first international series. South Africa was not to be beaten in a rugby series until 1956 in New Zealand. South Africa's overwhelming success in international rugby can really be dated, however, from its tour of the British Isles in 1906. Although the 1903 team defeated the British tourists, it was success in the 'mother country' that secured sporting reputations for colonial societies. South Africa's rugby successes in the British Isles in 1906 pre-dated their first official cricket test match win by 29 years, thus assisting the development of rugby as the most significant 'national' sport.[6] South Africa has always been more successful at international rugby than in cricket, though cricket results in official matches in the 1960s and 1990s began to approach those of rugby.

THE SPRINGBOKS AND WHITE SOUTH AFRICAN IDENTITY

The 1906–7 Springbok rugby tour was significant in helping to unite white South Africans, coming only four years after the Anglo-Boer War. The War fostered a deep animosity for the British on the part of Afrikaners as we have seen. For the tour, however, both British Isles-descended players and Afrikaners were picked for the team, with Paul Roos, an Afrikaner, as captain and 'Paddy' Carolin as vice-captain. By this time, South African rugby had advanced dramatically and the Springboks were superior in organization and physical ability in comparison with their British opponents.

The 1906 tour followed closely on the success of the first All Black tour of Britain in 1905. The New Zealanders won all their matches except for a controversial test against Wales and were hailed as 'all conquering colonials' in the British press (Nauright, 1991, 1992, 1996a). The South Africans were not quite as successful as the All Blacks, but they handily defeated Wales 11–0 in front of 50,000 spectators in Swansea. The British media who had constructed the All Blacks as superior, did the same for the South Africans. After South Africa defeated Midland Counties 29–0, the *Daily Chronicle* stated that 'The Colonials have met the cream of the Midlands, and have made them look like thin skim milk' (Nauright, 1996a: 133). The South Africans played an innovative style of rugby. They experimented with various formations and set plays and were the first national team to utilize the 3–4–1 scrum formation that had appeared in South Africa by 1906. It seems most plausible that the 3–4–1 scrum developed as a response to a 1905 rule change that did not allow forwards to put the ball back into the scrum with their feet. The South Africans also felt that the new formation would help them on wet grounds and thus used it in Britain in 1906–7. The Springboks also communicated in Afrikaans so that their signals could not be interpreted by opposing players.

Upon the conclusion of the tour, assessments in the English newspapers confirmed the overall dominance of the South Africans. The *Daily News* reported that there 'are many points of superiority left to the Old Country, but not as regards football'. The *Daily Express* went further in stating that at the time 'the English national genius is dormant, while the enterprising spirit of the Colonial never flags'. On a more hopeful note, the *Morning Post* echoed the emerging sentiments of many observers, 'The South Africans have demonstrated that the colonies are capable of rejuvenating the methods of the Motherland, and have shown that the race from which they spring is equal to ours in courage, chivalry and sportsmanship' (Laubscher and Nieman, 1990: 212).

The 1906 South Africans also invented the nickname 'Springboks' for themselves early on the tour so that the British press would not invent one for them (Laubscher and Nieman, 1990). The Springboks followed their 1906 successes with a tour in 1912–13 during which they defeated Scotland, Ireland, Wales, France and England. The victory over England was the first loss inflicted on them at Twickenham, which opened in 1909. The Springboks went from strength to strength by not losing a home test match series they played before 1974, and winning or drawing all of their series of tests both home and away from 1903, until their 1956 loss in New Zealand. After the First World War, the number of Afrikaners playing rugby rose dramatically and in the 1930s rugby began to shift from a broader imperial focus to a South

African nationalist focus, particularly as the Afrikaner Broederbond and the National Party targeted rugby as a central site for the expression of Afrikaner nationalism.

Already by the 1890s, representative South African sides were mixed between English-speaking whites and Afrikaners. Initially, most Afrikaners were from Stellenbosch and Cape Town, but increasingly in the 1900s, Afrikaner players also came from the Transvaal and Orange Free State. The University of Stellenbosch, as Grundlingh (1996) shows, became the most significant training ground for top Afrikaner players. In the 1890s, there was little to suggest that an Afrikaner ethos of rugby had emerged to challenge British and Imperial values. Such challenges were located later as Afrikaner nationalism developed in the 1920s and 1930s as a potent force in white South African society.

OTHER SPORTS AND IMPERIAL MASCULINITY IN SOUTH AFRICA

As whites settled in South Africa, they brought with them pastimes and sports from Europe. By the 1820s, hunting, horse racing and cricket were regular occurrences as the social trappings of elite English sport appeared on the South African scene. Hunts, horse races and cricket matches were social occasions where white officials and leading citizens could mingle and display their cultural superiority over the majority of residents. These occasions were similar to many held throughout the British Empire in the nineteenth and first half of the twentieth centuries as Imperial culture sought to bedazzle locals with its power and superiority. In particular these sports and social occasions were also about demonstrating the cultural superiority of white men, especially government officials, military officers and leading local landowners and entrepreneurs. Through sporting prowess and financial support, leading white men could demonstrate their supposed dominance.

Numerous national governing bodies for sport appeared in the 1890s and early 1900s, and by 1910 most major sports were organized on a national basis. The Football Association of South Africa, the South African Cyclists' Union and the South African Amateur Athletic Association formed, in 1892, all white-only organizations. Swimming's national association appeared in 1899. Golf and tennis also began to appear in the late nineteenth century and while these sports were also played by white women, they served to reinforce white power and difference as they also remained socially segregated. Tennis began in South Africa during the 1870s. In 1884, E. L. Williams became the first South African to appear in a Wimbledon final in the men's doubles, partnering an English player. Port Elizabeth was the centre of early tennis activity and hosted the first national championships in 1891. National associations were organized in tennis in 1903 and golf in 1909. Hockey was first played in 1899 introduced by British troops during the Anglo-Boer War. The first women's hockey club appeared in 1901 with the Western Province Union being established in 1907. In golf, whites played on segregated courses where blacks caddied for the white players, thus explicitly reinforcing the wider South African social order in a very visible and easily interpreted way. A succession of internationally successful golfers has assisted in the development and cultural significance of golf in the white communities of South Africa, from Bobby Locke to Gary Player and others on to Ernie Els, winner of the 1994 and 1997 United States Open Golf Championships.

A prominent, though vastly under-researched sport full of imperial cultural connotations is lawn bowls. In South Africa, New Zealand and Australia, the sport developed as a cultural haven for older whites who sought cultural security in the social activities in and around the sport. South Africa's first lawn bowls club appeared in Port Elizabeth in 1882 with the first interclub matches beginning in 1884. By World War II there were 13,000 registered lawn bowlers (9800 men and 3200 women) in nearly 400 clubs. By 1947 players numbered 24,000, playing in 365 men's clubs and 200 women's clubs. Imperial contact at elite level was important, with South Africa competing in the Empire Games and in tests against white colonial societies. South Africa won world championships in 1972, in Australia, and in 1976, when it hosted the tournament.

One of South Africa's earliest local sporting heroes was Laurens Smitz Meintjes who became world cycling champion in 1893. Although he was officially a representative of his Wanderers' Amateur Cycling Club in Johannesburg, foreign newspapers referred to him as a South African representative during his trip to England and the USA in 1893. Meintjes was the first major South African sportsman sent overseas to compete and his success led to calls for sporting tours to Britain in other sports (van der Merwe, 1991). Jan Hofmeyr, a member of the Cape Legislative Assembly chaired a dinner in honour of Meintjes in Cape Town in 1893. Hofmeyr clearly stated the role of sport in white South African society at the time:

> Sport has almost invariably been the pioneer of diplomacy in cementing the relationships and good understanding between Great Britain and her Colonies. . . the sporting associations of this country, which for the most part represent combinations of sportsmen throughout the various States, have set an example which politicians are all too slow to follow in the aim for a United South Africa (quoted in van der Merwe, 1991: 195).

As was the case in the late 1980s and early 1990s, sporting organizations in the 1880s and 1890s led the way in forming national associations prior to the political union of 1910. Clearly sport was one of, if not the most important areas where national feelings were generated, at least within the white communities of the Cape and Natal colonies and the former Boer Republics in the Transvaal and Orange Free State. Though, prior to the 1920s, national identification was situated firmly within the British imperial tradition and the connections through imperial sporting and other links.

South Africa was one of the early participants in the Olympic Games and in the Empire and Commonwealth Games up until the 1960s when nationalist politics and international protest forced the country out of these competitions. South Africa first competed officially in the 1908 Games in London, the year in which the South Africa Olympic Association was formed (later the name changed to the South African Olympic and Empire Games Association). Between 1908 and 1960, white South Africans won 72 Olympic medals (17 gold, 28 silver and 27 bronze) and from 1930 through 1958, they won 190 medals (72 gold, 60 silver and 58 bronze) in the British Empire and Commonwealth Games (Joyce, 1981). White South Africans took to the full range of British sports and, in this context, white South African sport developed in a similar fashion to British sport and to sport in other settler societies such as Australia and New Zealand.

CONCLUSION

Although the development of modern sport in South Africa took on many of the characteristics present in Britain and other English-speaking settler societies, South Africa became most rigid in its enforcement of racial segregation which became one of the central organizing principles in sport. While segregation existed in Australia, it was not enforced in totality or evenly across all sports. In New Zealand, Maoris played regularly in provincial and national rugby teams, except when the All Blacks toured South Africa before 1970 (Nauright, 1993). Similar to the United States, blacks in South Africa were excluded from most sporting competitions in which whites participated by 1900. The Imperial sporting model was a racist one. In the West Indies, no black player captained their cricket team on tour until 1960, and for years before that the captain was often the only white player in the team. Thus sport became one of the central cultural practices whereby white supremacy and difference were performed and learned over time, and in segregated spaces both in South Africa and many other areas in the British Empire. White South African sports closely allied themselves with similar sporting organizations in Britain and in the white settler colonies of Australia and New Zealand. Thus, South African sport was initially infused with imperial ideologies of the power of the white and British race, of masculinity expressed through sporting prowess and of class distinctions learned through cultural performances such as sport.

NOTES

1. Ironically, the Boers were forced to play against a number of Singhalese in the Colombo side.
2. The team was held up by an armed group of Transvaal men at Vereeniging who were given two cricket bats as a peace offering.
3. Though held up as an example of an ideal imperial sportsman, Poore's team solidarity was somewhat elastic: after playing for Natal he tried to transfer to Lord Hawke's side only to have permission refused by the army (Hawke, p. 152). Poore was born in 1866 and died in 1938. He played county cricket for Hampshire from 1898 until 1906 and in 1899 scored 1309 runs at an average of 115.58.
4. Eric Louw later became the National Party's Minister of External Affairs, 1955–63.
5. As a point of historical accuracy, some suggest that the Cup was given to Griqualand West who then generously donated it to the SARB. Currie's instructions were, however, that the trophy was to be for an internal competition (Greyvenstein, 1995: 12).
6. Though a South African team did defeat an MCC side at Lord's in 1894 by eleven runs. This was the first cricket team from South Africa to venture to England.

3

RESPECTABILITY, URBAN CULTURE AND THE DEVELOPMENT OF MODERN SPORT IN SOUTH AFRICA'S BLACK COMMUNITIES

Despite the evidence of black sporting clubs and associations existing for decades, the predominant white South African attitude about black sport in general centres on beliefs that blacks have not played 'Western' style sport for nearly as long as whites, or that blacks have their own sporting culture centred on soccer and boxing that is very different from that of whites. In 1994, Springbok rugby hero Uli Schmidt stated that rugby was not in the culture of blacks and was not natural for them to play; rather they should play soccer (*Cape Times*, 26 October 1994). In a recent chapter on black rugby, Odendaal reports how Hannes Marais, convenor of the South African selection panel in 1995, suggested in 1971 that 'The Coloured populations [sic] does not seem very interested in sport. They do not play much rugby and cricket'. Additionally, Dawid de Villiers, former Springbok captain, National Party minister and a minister in the post-apartheid government of national unity, said in 1980, 'Don't forget that the Blacks have really known western sports [only] for the last ten years . . . they have not reached the same standard [as whites]' (Odendaal, 1995: 24–5). Even in the academic literature, statements about blacks not having the opportunity to play 'white' sports have appeared, thus assisting in the perpetuation of the myth of low sporting participation among Africans. Stoddart, in an otherwise excellent article on imperial sport, argues that given the 'concern with reconciling Boer and Briton, black and coloured communities had few if any opportunities to play rugby union' (Stoddart, 1988: 662).

Contrast those statements with the following from Coloured men who have played and watched sport in Cape Town since the 1930s. Gassan Emeran, a former school principal and cricketer stated that in District Six and the Bo-Kaap, the two main Coloured areas in Cape Town up to 1970, 'whenever you meet people it was just rugby, there was nothing else it was just, rugby, rugby, rugby. That was their life – rugby.' When the cricket season came along they followed cricket, but 'they talked of nothing else but rugby, that is why they are very knowledgable.' Furthermore, 'rugby was the game that everybody played. Even some girls played rugby with the boys in their younger years' (Emeran, 1995). 'Meneer' Effendi, a long-time rugby administrator also relates the significance of rugby in the Coloured community of Cape Town, '. . . each club had a huge following . . . we played our matches at the Green Point Track on the Saturday and on the Sunday – you had to witness a Sunday match to be able to get that feeling to see the families come with their picnic baskets and whatever, it is a day' (Effendi, 1994). As Odendaal puts it, 'Contrary to general knowledge, black South Africans have a long, indeed remarkable, rugby and sporting history' (Odendaal, 1995: 25).

It is perhaps not surprising that many whites believe that blacks have not had similar experiences of sports. Most whites still only come into contact with blacks as workers and few whites venture into black townships. As a result, most whites have little direct cultural links with blacks and had not played sport with or against them before the 1990s. A geography of the mind pervades South African society, allowing whites to safely tuck most blacks away into the out-of-sight townships, and either forget about what they might be doing in their leisure time, or assume that they are drinking and committing crime as the media and their educational system taught them to think in the apartheid era.

This chapter and Chapter 5 on soccer follow recent pioneering work on urban black sport (Magubane, 1963; Peires, 1981; Couzens, 1983; Jeffrey, 1992; Badenhorst, 1992b; Odendaal, 1995). The focus is the development of a rugby culture among Coloured men in Cape Town and the rise of urban sporting cultures centred on cricket, rugby and, especially, soccer in Johannesburg and Durban, and how urban black cultures progressed over time in the large South African cities. This is not a comprehensive survey as much research remains to be done on black sport, however, the richness of material from Cape Town, as well as work on Johannesburg, Vereeniging and Durban (Magubane, 1963; Jeffrey, 1992; Badenhorst, 1992b), suggests possible directions for future research. Additionally, this chapter highlights the emerging role of sport in urban black popular cultures up to about 1960.

Social divisions affecting sport and other activities did not emerge based solely on government dictated racial lines. In Cape Town, two distinct rugby unions emerged amongst Coloureds: one that was predominantly Muslim and one that banned Muslims until the 1960s. Among the Indian community, especially in Durban, divisions between Muslim, Tamil and Hindu meant that cultural divisions remained within that group. Of course, gender differences were also crucial and urban black sport became closely linked with notions of urban black masculinity.

As modern forms of sports and urban culture began to develop among whites in the latter half of the nineteenth century, blacks also became exposed to British cultural forms that included sport through the role of missionaries and the establishment of African elite cultural organizations. If we are to adequately understand the position of many ANC and leading black sporting officials in the new South Africa, then we need a solid grasp of the historical development of black sport.

COLOURED RUGBY, MASCULINITY AND
COMMUNITY IDENTITY IN CAPE TOWN

Rugby and cricket were the first sports to be organized among blacks in urban areas, with soccer and boxing following later. What we know of Coloured rugby in Cape Town dates from the formation of the first rugby clubs in 1886. Two rugby Unions emerged in the Cape Town area that administered two distinct competitions, the Western Province Coloured Rugby Union (WPCRU) founded in 1886 and the City and Suburban Rugby Union (CSRU) founded in 1898. Rugby dominated the Coloured sport scene in Cape Town from the 1880s through the 1960s, it was an integral part of local culture and masculinity was displayed through physical performance. Some rugby clubs gained reputations from their use of intimidating tactics, while other provinces feared Western Province because of its physicality and psychological ability to frighten opponents before matches even started. Perhaps there was more to muscular Islam than to muscular Christianity (Nauright, 1996c, 1997). The primary reason for the WPCRU retaining a reputation for tough and robust play is that the base of its clubs remained in the working-class areas of District Six and the Bo-Kaap, while the centre of CSRU activity increasingly moved to suburban Cape Town in the 1950s and 1960s. District Six and the Bo-Kaap were tightly-knit communities where people lived in close proximity and where survival for working-class males often meant developing a sense of toughness centred on physical abilities. School teachers recognized the need for such toughness, and both Muslim and Christian teachers stressed the significance of rugby as a game that created physical and mental toughness and group solidarity.

District Six became South Africa's first working-class area. When the slaves were freed in 1838, more than 5000 needed homes. The Muslims, mostly of Malaysian, Indonesian and Sri Lankan origin settled in what was later to become the Bo-Kaap or the 'Malay Quarter'. Others moved to the opposite edge of Cape Town beyond Roeland Street in the area that became District Six. Overcrowding affected the District by the time the Cape Town City Council 'named' it in 1867 as the sixth district of the Cape Town municipality. In 1900, during the Anglo-Boer War, a concerted building programme began in District Six, providing the physical structure for the community. The official population figures for District Six stood at 22,440 in 1936, 28,377 in 1946, but by the early 1950s the population passed 40,000 (Pinnock, 1984). Don Pinnock describes District Six aptly, as it was known for the 'ingenuity, novelty and enterprise of its residents, engaged in this mode of small-scale production and services. By day it hummed with trade, barter and manufacture, and by night it offered the "various pleasures of conviviality or forgetfulness"'. Pinnock then shows how the extended family acted as networks of social control and enabled poor families to survive in the District (Pinnock, 1984: 21–23).

The two main areas of Coloured settlement in Cape Town developed their own distinct, albeit related communities. Muslim and non-Muslim culture did not mix readily, yet the communities had common cultural practices in music and especially in sport. Rugby became the dominant winter sport by the early 1900s, though soccer grew to prominence from the 1920s. Male school-teachers promoted rugby in particular and viewed it as an ideal means of teaching discipline and for generating social cohesion (Emeran, 1994). Such promotion of rugby union is not dissimilar to other areas where the game was actively encouraged in schools, though it would be wrong to assume that, because whites played rugby in their schools, Coloureds merely copied white sporting structures and cultural values attached to sport. Rugby emerged as a manly and character-forming game among Cape Town's elite Coloured schools, developing from the influence of British missionaries plus the need to deal with the harsh realities of everyday life in the cramped working-class areas of District Six and the Bo-Kaap. There was a strong influence of 'respectability' notions that were important for the urban African elite, however, in Cape Town this was also infused with concepts of respectable behaviour and self-discipline that stemmed from Muslim culture and the teachings of the Koran.

The first known rugby clubs among Coloureds were formed in 1886. Five important clubs were founded in that year. Roslyns, Good Hopes, Violets and Arabian College came together to found the WPCRU. A fifth club, Wanderers, became the prime mover behind a second union formed in 1898, the CSRU. Several clubs that formed in the late 1880s and 1890s did not join the WPCRU, but joined with Wanderers to form the CSRU, a union that excluded Muslims until the 1960s.[1] The founding clubs of the CSRU were California (1888); Perseverance (1889); Thistles (1891); Woodstock Rangers (1892); and Retreat (1898). Primrose joined in 1901, Progress in 1906 and Universal in 1931 to form the core of CSRU clubs to the 1960s. The WPCRU was well connected with the national South African Coloured Rugby Football Board

(SACRFB), founded in 1897 and based in Kimberley, and very successful in Rhodes Cup competitions, but it nearly collapsed in the early 1930s, with only Roslyns and Violets surviving from the original clubs. Several clubs emerged in the 1930s, however, to revitalize the union. These clubs included Young Stars (1928); Orange Blossoms (1931); Caledonian Roses (1934); and Buffaloes (1936). Other clubs in the competition by 1940 were Hamediahs, Evergreens, Watsonias, Young Ideas and Leeuwendale. The WPCRU clubs were all based in the Bo-Kaap and District Six, with CSRU clubs located in District Six, Woodstock and later in suburban Cape Town.

District Six was a vibrant area of cultural activities, with sports playing an important part in local culture. Of the sports played, rugby was the most prominent in the District as well as in the Bo-Kaap. Gassan Emeran states that culture, politics and even life itself revolved around rugby and for the Islamic majority of District Six and the Bo-Kaap, rugby was the 'second religion' (Emeran, 1995). Effendi argues that the 'non-white community as such was a very sport loving community' and that rugby 'brought the whole community together' (Effendi, 1994). In addition to organized rugby, many matches took place on Sundays which were not covered by the media. Some Sunday teams decided to play more formally which led to the entry of additional clubs into WPCRU competitions in the 1930s and 1940s. These Sunday matches allowed far greater numbers of men from District Six and the Bo-Kaap to participate in a physical team sport where masculine attributes could be displayed on a less organized level.

While participation was an important element in rugby's cultural significance among Coloureds in Cape Town, spectating was even more broadly inclusive as it included women and children. All the informants I interviewed discuss the community element of the game, though this was clearly a community in which men dominated. Men controlled most public spaces, and rugby clubs met on street corners or in houses of administrators for pre- and post-match meetings and for social functions during the week. Many activities were homosocial, though clubs raised money through dances that involved women in club activities. The working-class areas of Cape Town increasingly came under the influence of gangsters and protection rackets in the 1940s and 1950s and some of these linked themselves closely with rugby clubs. In particular, the dominant gang of the 1950s, the Globe Gang, strongly supported Roslyns, the most powerful and oldest club in the WPCRU competition.

Rugby clubs initially met on street corners in District Six and the Bo-Kaap. Clubs from both unions congregated at different corners for team meetings, to announce team selections, and to discuss and analyse previous perform-ances. Roslyns, for example, met in front of the Globe Furnishing Company,

side-by-side with the Globe Gang who also met there (Effendi, 1994).
Pinnock describes how the Globe Gang came into being in the 1940s. As
greater numbers of people moved into the District from other areas, the
incidence of petty-theft by young males increased. In response to this threat,
the sons of shopkeepers began to meet outside the Globe Furnishing Company
in Hanover Street opposite the Star Bioscope. They began by smashing a 'tax-
racket' at the cinema where patrons were forced to pay a penny to youths
before entering. Leaders of the Globe Gang were bricklayers, hawkers and
painters. The core of the gang formed around the Ishmail family, one of whom
was a City Councillor. Pinnock points out that as more people moved into the
District, 'the Globe was an organisation that sought to assert and maintain the
control of the more wealthy families and the hawkers' (Pinnock, 1984: 26).
According to one Globe member:

> The Globe hated the skollie[2] element in town, like the people who robbed the
> crowds on [celebrations] or when there were those marches in town with the
> Torch Commando or Cissy Gool's singsong [demonstration] outside
> Parliament buildings. Mikey and the boys would really bomb out the skollie
> element when they robbed the people then. They tore them to ribbons. (Quoted
> in Pinnock, 1984: 26)

The Globe Gang had a close relationship with the police who counted on
the gang to help control the District. The Globe soon became a protection
racket with all in their area having to pay allegiance. Pinnock explains that by
1950 'the Globe was controlling extortion, blackmail, illicit buying of every
kind, smuggling, shebeens, gambling, and political movements in the District'
(Pinnock, 1984: 28). Slowly, prison elements took control of the gang
throughout the 1950s and more direct acts of intimidation, theft and murder
became a regular part of Globe activities. Globe influence also affected rugby
as the gang was a strong supporter of the Roslyns club.

While Roslyns' specific ties to the Globe Gang are not entirely clear, the
club and its fans had a reputation for intimidating referees and opposing
players. Former Montrose players state that when they played for Young Stars
they had trouble finding referees for matches against Roslyns, as 'the referees
were frightened because Roslyns must win, if Roslyns doesn't win, it's a fight
because they got their stones and their chains ready and their big swords ready
that means they're going to attack. . . .' (Benjamin *et al.*, 1994). In one game
between Stars and Roslyns, Rajab Benjamin, a founder of the Montrose club
in the WPCRU, scored near the end of the match and Stars only had to kick
the conversion for a win. Benjamin says he knew the chains would come out
when he made the kick since the Roslyns fans knew they would lose. 'When
we passed the Globe corner and they had their table decorated because they

were winning the trophy back this year. . .' (Benjamin *et al*., 1994). Some fans had pangas and chains and Benjamin readied for a quick escape after the match by moving to the opposite area of the field from the Globe Gang. Montrose players argued that it was mainly Roslyns and their fans who behaved this way, asserting that they had to win partly because they had all the delegates in the Union (Benjamin *et al*., 1994). Despite such incidents, Roslyns supplied many important and widely respected administrators, such as 'Meneer' Adams and 'Meneer' Effendi, both school teachers and long-serving Roslyns and WPCRU administrators. Adams also played at the top level longer than almost any other rugby player in South Africa, beginning with Roslyn in 1932 and playing into the 1950s with most of his career also spent in the Western Province team. Effendi did not play as long at the top but instead was known for his boxing skills (Effendi and Adams, 1994).

Richard Rive recounts the story of one gang, the Jungle Boys, and their links with rugby in his autobiographical novel of life in District Six, *Buckingham Palace, District Six*. Three gang leaders formed the front-row of the Young Anemones Rugby Football Club's first team. Rive states that they 'practised in Trafalgar Park and played hard and dirty. They turned up regularly with their team to fulfil fixtures but these seldom materialised because most of the teams they were scheduled to play would rather forfeit the match than meet the Jungle Boys head on' (Rive, 1986: 24–5). Rough, intimidating play was a feature of District Six and Bo-Kaap rugby, at least among some clubs. Roslyns had a reputation for toughness among WPCRU clubs, but the WPCRU also had a general reputation for playing hard, intimidating rugby. Given the social conditions in District Six and to a lesser degree in the Bo-Kaap, this tough style of play should not be surprising, though many leading rugby players tended to be from better-off families.

Rajab Benjamin relates that violent play was part of the tactics of rugby, but that any roughness or violence stayed on the field of play and did not continue outside the ground after a match. He explains how he stopped Eastern Province one year in the Rhodes Cup when Western Province were being overrun by an Eastern Province winger:

> I said to our captain, you must make a change man . . . we gonna lose. So he ask me what can we do? So I say the only thing you can do is change me from my position. . . . I was a loose forward and I went to go and play in his position. The first time he come past, the second time he's gone off the field, so there are no more tries coming from their side. . . . It shows you the tactics you must use – you must use your brains (Benjamin *et al*., 1994).

Here it appears that using one's brains meant figuring out a way to stop the opposition in any way necessary to achieve the desired result. Again, this mentality flowed from the rough conditions faced in working-class areas of Cape Town, but is indicative of the tough masculinity taught in schools and promoted in the Muslim community in particular. In this context, the use of 'trickery' was an important part of playing the game. 'Trickery' involved a range of intimidatory tactics, some of which were viewed in white rugby circles as unacceptable. The differences in acceptable on-field behaviour has led to a number of problems since the rugby's unity in 1992, particularly in the Western Cape where the provincial tribunal has been faced with different perceptions of acceptable violence among players.

Evidence from the *Cape Standard* and the *Cape Sun* from the 1930s and 1940s suggests that violent play on the field occurred regularly. Despite this, the CSRU records show that the Union took a hard line with those found guilty of rough play with suspensions ranging from a couple of matches to two years. The WPCRU also suspended players for exceedingly rough play, but the documents do not exist to establish whether there was a consistent policy of punishment. What is clear, is that a culture of rough play was an accepted part of the game, though there were defined limits to the levels of violence tolerated.

Matches between the two unions drew large crowds whether played at the WPCRU home ground at Green Point Track or the CSRU grounds. City rarely defeated Province, though often there was little difference in ability between top players in the two unions. Gassan Emeran suggests that Province was more successful because they could intimidate City, with Province players starting months in advance. Players from both unions worked together and met each other outside the rugby arena so the intimidation was purely linked to rugby, unlike the periodic violence that accompanied some club rugby (Emeran, 1995). Although divisions existed, rugby enabled men who played and watched it to generate a sense of respect for each other that extended beyond any religious differences. Often this respect was based on violent physicality as displayed on the rugby field, though union officials frowned upon violence beyond accepted parameters and punished offenders, thus maintaining an aura of 'respectability' around the game.

Women were not allowed to play rugby generally, though as Emeran mentioned, some girls played rugby with boys when they were young. By puberty, women were cut out of the game and encouraged to play netball and hockey (Emeran, 1995), though sports participation was much higher among non-Muslim women.[3] Occasionally a woman's game formed part of the festivities at the annual Charity Rag matches in Cape Town, though it was not taken seriously by men. Despite this exclusion from playing, many women attended rugby matches and were strong supporters of the game. Matches involving leading teams, inter-provincial play and Rag matches[4] united the community, with men, women and children attending these matches together. As with rugby in other places, women provided domestic support. They also spent much time knitting scarves for players and supporters, and made the special uniforms and scarves for Caledonian Roses and Stars for the Rag matches each year. The general attitude of Muslim men towards female participation in sport is evidenced in an interview with an Islamic woman who attended Trafalgar High School in District Six in the 1940s. She stated:

> I enjoyed PE because I could have a break from the classroom. I was not very good. But my other problem was that as a female coming from an Islamic background my father was not too pleased about me wearing a short skirt for classes. He allowed it [only] for school hours. This meant I could not play sport after school. (Quoted in Jones, 1995: 5)

Other than the famous 'Coon Carnival' that takes place at New Year each year, the Charity Rag match between Young Stars and Caledonian Roses became the focal point of annual community cultural celebration. Charity Rag began in 1936 as the two clubs adopted the annual fixture, based on the model from the match played each year between the Universities of Cape Town and Stellenbosch. Notable features of the day were the four rugby matches played between the four teams from each club, colourful scarves knitted by women supporters of the clubs, songs composed for the occasion and the massive crowds at the Green Point Track to watch the matches. Ten thousand or more people from the Bo-Kaap and District Six used to walk down for the matches, and processions from the District through the Bo-Kaap and down to the Track featured prominently.

Rag matches, along with other elements of 'Coloured' culture in Cape Town, are evidence of a distinctive culture that drew upon some aspects of white culture but recast them into forms that fit the working-class culture of District Six and the Bo-Kaap. As with the Carnival, Rag provided a sense of cultural release, an event for community focus and solidarity, and one where the wider system of oppression could be forgotten for at least a short period of time. Rag and Carnival were celebrations of the community's vibrant culture and its resilience in the face of wider social, economic and political domination by whites.

Beyond Cape Town, black sport began to develop rapidly in the 1890s and early 1900s. Originally black sport was centred among an elite keen to promote itself as 'civilized' and 'respectable', but by the 1930s and 1940s, sport in general and soccer in particular developed in the townships of major cities such as Johannesburg, Durban and Pretoria. Soccer generated mass community followings similar to that for rugby in District Six and the Bo-

Kaap areas of Cape Town, as Chapter 5 discusses. The early appearance among Africans of imperial sporting culture took place among an elite educated in mission schools and colleges established by missionaries, such as Fort Hare. Rapid urbanization brought on by the mineral revolution brought educated men together in substantial numbers, first in Kimberley and then in Johannesburg, the two key centres in the emergence of modern sporting forms among Africans.

The central component of sport for elite Africans and Coloureds was its role as a part of 'civilized' British culture, which was important in establishing 'respectability'. Thus, sport was used as a means of social exclusivity for the educated African urban elite. This group has been frequently called an African petty-bourgeoisie in attempts to better explain their position within the wider South African economy and society, however, the term is misleading when we place culture at the centre of our analysis. Through the acceptance of Christianity, British social and moral values, and a limited franchise for blacks, this group became an African elite that has remained at the forefront of African political organizations and struggle for the past century. While more Africans from outside this group began to rise to positions of leadership in the ANC and PAC during the late 1940s and 1950s (Lodge, 1983), there remains a strong presence within the ANC of Africans who can trace their lineage back to the mission stations of the nineteenth century, and who have held professional or clerical occupational positions.

Mary Benson, in her biography of Mandela, describes him as being 'Groomed from childhood for respectability, status and sheltered living...' (Benson, 1986: 23). Indeed the movers behind the formation of the ANC as the South African Natives National Congress in 1912 were four lawyers. The leader, Pixley ka Izaka Seme, studied at Columbia and Oxford Universities, and spent time at the Inns of Court in London, before calling for a national organization to break down divisions between various black groups in southern Africa, and to create a broader black nationalism within South Africa. The ANC was revitalized in the late 1930s after a period of inactivity through the leadership of Dr Alfred B. Xuma, and a social anthropology, native law and administration lecturer from Fort Hare, Z. K. Matthews, among others. Although the ANC developed into a mass movement in the 1950s, its leadership has been dominated by members of the elite educated class among blacks in South Africa. Many of the ANC's leaders, and leaders of other nationalist movements in southern Africa, were educated at Fort Hare College in the eastern Cape town of Alice. Fort Hare was founded in 1916 and quickly became a centre of learning for aspirant African elites. It was at Fort Hare that the future ANC leaders Nelson Mandela and Oliver Tambo became close friends during their time there in 1939 and 1940.

While it is clear that this group of formally educated Africans suffered under the systems of segregation and apartheid, it is important to remember their social and historical background in understanding their relationship to sports, and the role of sports in building character and in the gendered context of making men out of boys. Sports Minister Steve Tshwete, for example, has often been quoted as stating that soccer is a game for sissies in comparison with the real man's game of rugby. Tshwete and/or Mandela have been present at nearly all of South Africa's post-apartheid sporting triumphs, thus linking themselves with South African international sporting success. So where did the focus on sport within the black elite come from and how did it develop over time?

THE MISSION EXPERIENCE

White missionaries used cricket at mission stations such as Healdtown, Lovedale and Zonnebloem, in their attempts to inculcate 'respectability' to an emerging black middle class. Cricket became a crucial cultural activity that helped to define a 'civilized' man as the black middle class sought to achieve wider acceptance through tests of civilization rather than of race. The first recorded cricket match involving blacks dates from an 1854 match in Cape Town between 'the Hottentots and the Boers' (Bowen, 1970: 277). Organized sport, including cricket, tennis, croquet, soccer and rugby, was particularly well developed in the Eastern Cape. In 1862, John Shedden Dobie reported that Africans on a farm near Queenstown were playing cricket with the farm owner (Archer and Bouillon, 1982; Odendaal, 1977). The first African cricket club was founded in Port Elizabeth in 1869; and by 1887 *Imvo Zabantsundu* (the King William's Town African newspaper) had a sports edition that reported news of cricket and other emerging sports in the black elite community (Odendaal, 1988). The Eastern Cape showed high levels of black political organization, and an important part of that mobilization was the visibility of political leaders through their involvement in sports clubs. The links between politics and sport among black political leaders continued into the 1970s and 1980s, as leaders from groups such as the Black Consciousness Movement and the United Democratic Front (UDF) used soccer matches to make speeches to large crowds where they could also escape police detection (Lewis, 1992/3).

Throughout many areas of Africa sporting clubs provided the initial location for interaction between different groups of African elites within a colony, as educated Africans gravitated to administrative, professional and educational posts in colonial capitals and large regional towns. John Iliffe in his history of Tanganyika demonstrates that the earliest forms of African urban political organisation emerged from soccer clubs in Dar-es-Salaam in the 1930s (Iliffe, 1979). This pattern occurred throughout sub-Saharan Africa as soccer and other sporting clubs were uniformly encouraged and were also legal urban African organizations (Martin, 1991; Ranger, 1987; Stuart, 1996). Ossie Stuart points out that soccer teams often became the focus of protests and strikes in colonial Zimbabwe (then known as Southern Rhodesia) in the 1950s and 1960s. He goes further to state that soccer 'became an embodiment of the political aspirations of the African people' (Stuart, 1995: 34). Yet despite its role in galvanizing local elites and urbanizing masses in protest against colonial rule, sport in Africa after independence has proved to be a conservative institution closely linked to new post-colonial power structures, not unlike modern sport globally.

By the early 1900s, many African mission-educated elite males played cricket, some played rugby, and soccer also began to develop. This process similarly occurred among Coloureds and Indians. Few Indian South Africans played rugby, though they have played cricket and have been just as passionate about soccer as Africans. Sports were also promoted by missionaries and mine owners as ways to 'moralize leisure time' (Couzens, 1982), or control and direct the leisure activities of migrant workers in order to prevent the emergence of serious social unrest. While missionaries and white officials played key roles in the establishment of British sporting practices among Africans, the sports themselves were quickly organized and run by Africans in local, provincial and national associations.

Chapter 5 will explain the role of soccer and other sports in urban black culture, but first we need to understand the historical process whereby Africans began to play British sports, and adopt some of the meanings and values attached to those sports while incorporating some cultural practices from indigenous culture. Cobley (1994) argues that there was a clear divide in black sports between 'elite' and 'mass' sporting forms. For the 'elite' the mission experience was crucial. Cobley states that 'graduates of mission institutions in towns formed themselves into teams and practised the skills they had learned at school as much from a desire to emphasize their social advantages, class position and consciousness, as for the joy of the games itself' (Cobley, 1994: 213).

From about the 1830s, a number of mission stations began to appear throughout present-day South Africa where Africans began to be educated to European moral and social standards. Brian Willan, in his biographical study of Sol Plaatje, describes the process whereby one group of Africans, the

Barolong, came to be on mission stations and how some like Plaatje's family came to be educated into a system of values that were European-focused. When missionaries first encountered the Barolong they met with resistance from chiefs. Chiefs in many cases used the presence of missionaries to try and protect themselves and their people from dispossession, but they did not really want a permanent missionary presence that could ultimately undermine their authority. Many early converts were refugees following the disruptions of the *mfecane* while others were social outcasts from their own societies. A number of Barolong people went to Thaba Nchu in the present day Orange Free State during the 1830s and came under the influence of missionaries (Willan, 1984).

The most successful area of missionary endeavour, however, was in the eastern Cape region in the areas near East London, Queenstown and King William's Town. Willan (1982) points out that the concepts of 'civilization' and British imperial power went hand-in-hand. Mission-educated Africans held on to the notion of 'civilization' as the criteria for acceptance into wider Cape colonial society rather than race or colour. The Cape Colony had a non-racial franchise, though with such strict provisions that only a handful of Africans could qualify for the vote. As mission-educated Africans moved to the cities, they clung to the concepts of 'civilization', Christianity and British culture as the determinants of social position and worth. In 1865 there were 2827 students in mission schools which rose to 15,568 in 700 schools by 1885. British sports and recreational activities were important at these schools as African 'traditional' culture was deemed 'incompatible with Christian purity of life' (Odendaal, 1995: 33).

URBAN BLACK ELITES, RESPECTABILITY AND SPORTS

As Africans became more Christianized and moved to the cities for employment opportunities, they had to settle in racially defined areas and construct new patterns of social existence. Those from the better-off peasant and sharecropping areas of the Transvaal and the Orange Free State often moved to the freehold townships of Sophiatown and Alexandra near Johannesburg between 1912 and the 1930s. Many of these people migrated to the cities as a means to accumulate resources for marriage, or to buy property and houses in the rural areas. In addition, it became prestigious to have a job in Johannesburg, and those who did not were increasingly looked down upon by their cohorts from the rural areas (Bozzoli, 1991: 89–92). Once migrants married they often settled in Sophiatown or Alexandra which had more 'respectable' reputations than inner city slums in Johannesburg.

A number of scholars have asserted that township residents were divided into a form of 'classes' based on property ownership and tenancy, though recent research suggests a more complicated picture of township social relationships (Bozzoli, 1989). Links to rural areas through friends and relatives, often called 'homeboy' and 'homegirl' networks, attracted migrants to specific areas of certain townships. In some cases rooms were occupied or rented from friends and relatives already established in town. Township residents had to adjust to the presence of many ethnicities which led to a redefinition of pre-existing ethnic boundaries. Bozzoli (1989) suggests that a transformed ethnicity was a key category of social understanding in townships. Broader definitions of self as Tswana rather than Bafokeng, for example, led to the conception of others as members of broad ethno-linguistic categories of Xhosa, Zulu, Basotho or Coloured.

Research on social and early political organization in Johannesburg and Kimberley demonstrates that the impact of mission education was strong in the establishment of an urban black elite (Odendaal, 1984; Willan, 1982, 1984). Attracted to skilled positions such as clerks in the rapidly expanding towns of Kimberley and Johannesburg in the late nineteenth and early twentieth centuries, these educated Africans adopted an 'ideology of respectability' (Nauright, 1992). This was based on English high culture and served to set themselves apart from African migrant workers, and from the poorer whites who also flocked to the cities in the wake of the mineral revolution, drought, and reorganization of land-use and farming patterns in the countryside.

By the early 1900s, the African educated elite had mobilized itself into political organizations which the South African Native Affairs Commission noted 'were taking an active and intelligent interest in political affairs' (Odendaal, 1984: 62). This group developed newspapers to promote greater communication about social, political, economic and cultural events that affected their interests. Odendaal (1984) shows that many early political organizations focused on local issues and had short lifespans, however, they were 'symptomatic of an ever-increasing African interest in political affairs and organization at grassroots level' (Odendaal, 1984: 62). In addition to these local political organizations, many teachers associations, social clubs, financial self-help groups and sporting clubs also appeared in this period. In Kimberley, Africans formed the South African Improvement Society in 1895. The society promoted the use of the English language (Willan, 1982) and its very name suggested the notion of moving to some 'higher' state of being, of becoming something 'civilized' or 'respectable'. At one of its early meetings, the society heard a lecture entitled 'Civilization and its Advantages to African Races' (Willan, 1984: 247). In Cape society, the use of the English language was central in the 'civilizing' process, as was the adoption of British attitudes and cultural activities including cricket and rugby. Stoddart discusses the way that British culture was transferred to colonial elites through 'informal authority systems' such as the English language which became 'not simply a conveyer of information between otherwise differing cultural groups, it was a medium for the exchange of moral codes and social attitudes. Attaining command of the "proper" English language, accent as well as vocabulary and syntax, became the goal of innumerable colonial peoples' (Stoddart, 1988: 650–1).

Brian Willan encapsulates the attitudes of the African elite in Kimberley in recounting an incident from 21 August 1896, when a celebration was held for two men who had won places at Wilberforce University in the USA. One of the men, H. C. Msikinya, had his social accomplishments listed including his role as President of the Come Again Lawn Tennis Club, Secretary to the Eccentrics Cricket Club, member of the Rovers Rugby Football Club and member of the South African Improvement Society (Willan, 1984). Significantly, three of the four societies mentioned were sporting and included the noted imperial and 'cultured' sports of tennis, cricket and rugby. J. T. Jabavu, editor of the newspaper *Imvo Zabantsundu*, a churchman and educationalist involved in cricket and tennis, supported a Cape Bill of 1891 designed to outlaw 'tribal amusements' (Altham, 1962). Imperial sports, therefore, were significant in attempts of the African elite to establish their 'civilized' credentials both in terms of their own community and in relations with whites. Everyone who wanted to be anyone in the black establishment in Kimberley sought to be office holders in the Duke of Wellington or Eccentrics Cricket Clubs, whether they actually played or not (Willan, 1982). Willan describes how Sol Plaatje became Joint Secretary of the Eccentrics Cricket Club even though he had not been taught cricket on the German mission station where he grew up. Willan states that it was in the company of cricket club office holders where Plaatje internalized and subsequently retained the qualities and values embodied in cricket. In 1930 Plaatje dedicated one of his translations of Shakespeare to his friend Arthur Motlala, stating that Motlala was 'a loyal friend, a splendid cricketer, and an able Penman' (Willan, 1982: 252). The role of sport in the lives of elite blacks is evidenced in Mweli Skota's *African Yearly Register* published in 1932. Many of the African personalities included by Skota listed sport among their principal leisure activities. Additionally, Skota obviously selected some of the personalities because of their sporting prowess. Of those who mentioned sport, the most popular sports were cricket (44.5 per cent), tennis (30 per cent) and football (22.4 per cent) (Archer and Bouillon, 1982).

By the mid-1880s there were several well-established African cricket clubs in the Eastern Cape playing in regular competitions. The first African newspaper, *Imvo Zabantsundu*, founded in 1884, helped establish the importance of these competitions through regular reporting of matches. By 1887 the newspaper had a 'sporting editor' and many advertisements targeted cricket and cricket clubs (Odendaal, 1988). Not only did African teams play against each other, but some inter-racial matches also began to take place in the 1880s. In 1885, a black team beat the local whites at King William's Town, and in the same year blacks from Port Elizabeth defeated the whites of Cradock.

Matches between whites and blacks were a feature of imperial public holidays, in particular, in the late nineteenth century. Black cricket clubs frequently had imperial-sounding names and in Kimberley the highlight of the annual social calendar in the mid-1890s was a Christmas Day cricket match. This emulated the social role of cricket in the white community; in the nineteenth century matches at the Western Province Cricket Club (WPCC) at Newlands in Cape Town were accompanied by military bands and the presence of the Governor and his staff (Altham, 1962).

Team names often emulated those used by white clubs in Britain or South Africa. A simplistic analysis of the use of imperial names by black teams would suggest a form of cultural mimicking of whites. The real reason, however, was more complex and part of an elaborate process of proving respectability. The ideology of respectability was crucial in the aspirations of middle class blacks. Colonial and later South African governments would only converse with those men whom they believed behaved in a 'European' manner, even if they simultaneously denigrated them in discussions with other whites.

The paternalistic and long-term assimilationist cultural approach, character-istic of Cape liberalism in the nineteenth century, gave way, however, to concerns about the competitiveness of blacks manifested in segregationist policies. By the early twentieth century, social institutions were adapted to play a role not only of social control but also for purposes of exclusivity. White officials increasingly thought that the proper place for blacks was in the working class. Blacks were progressively consigned to inferior social, political and economic positions by exclusion from the vote, land ownership and commercial opportunity. In this climate, it is hardly surprising to see the small amount of cross-racial sport rapidly eliminated by the early 1900s. Despite being excluded from sporting competitions with whites on the basis of race, however, urban African elites organized their own competitions in cricket, rugby, soccer, boxing and other sports and these competitions grew and flourished despite frequent opposition from municipal officials and the police (Badenhorst, 1992a).

Black experiences of English culture became increasingly fraught with contradictions as the push for rigid segregation increased. King William's Town's black cricketers were 'rewarded' for their 1885 victory over Cradock's whites by being banned from the pavilion (Odendaal, 1988). Segregation became the norm by the late 1890s, although white facilities were made available to Coloureds. An example of this was the Malay tournament played at Newlands, home of the white Western Province cricket and rugby associations, in Cape Town during the 1889–90 season, involving teams from Cape Town, Johannesburg, Port Elizabeth and Claremont (a Cape Town suburb) (Bowen, 1970). Additionally, some Coloured rugby matches were held at Newlands as late as 1919 for a fee comprising 25 per cent of the gate (Dobson, 1989).

In 1892, W. W. Read's England cricketers played a Malay XVIII at Newlands, but the amateurs withdrew rather than play against blacks. An alternative interpretation, that the match was played for 'the benefit of the professionals' (West and Lucker, 1965: 21), amounted to the same disdain for black cricketers. Two years later, Krom Hendricks, a Coloured fast bowler thought to be among the fastest in the world of his era (Odendaal, 1977), who had taken 4–50 in 25 overs in the Newlands match, was named in the fifteen from which a tour party to England was to be chosen. His selection was, however, declared 'impolitic' (Bassano, 1979: 17) and after pressure he was omitted. Thus, it was not South Africa who invented notions of racial exclusivity in sport and other social activities, but rather the English who refused to mix with 'racial inferiors'. The whole construction of imperial discourse may have something to do with these English attitudes. Already white settlers were constructed as 'colonials' as opposed to Englishmen from the 'mother' country. An air of cultural and social superiority continued among the English elite in their attitudes to white colonial men well into the 1900s. White colonial references to England as the 'mother' country and as 'home' reinforced conceptions of Britain and British culture as superior to derivative white colonial cultures, which were then constructed as superior to black cultures.

In colonies outside the Cape, segregationist thought and policies took a harsher tone much earlier. As early as 1856 Natal passed legislation for the establishment of segregated African locations, and laws passed in 1874 and 1902 established control over African workers (Merrett, 1994a). Natal, often called 'the last outpost of the British Empire' was the area of South Africa where whites were the most outnumbered and where British segregationist attitudes were most advanced. Even in the Cape, a segregationist policy began to replace liberal attitudes in the 1890s.

Black cricket went into gradual decline by the early 1900s and mixed matches became the exception, although there are records of Coloured players in Cape Town hired to take part in practice sessions with white teams, and of white farmers (ex-British soldiers) playing the Barolong of Thaba Nchu in the Orange Free State (Odendaal, 1977). A British army officer who included his servant in a team, however, was told that this defied local custom (Archer and Bouillon, 1982). The Barnato cricket tournament began in 1904 as a segregated, national black competition, its trophy having been presented by Sir David Harris, director of the De Beers company, politician and soldier, to the Griqualand West Coloured Cricket Board in 1897. Thus, imperial capitalist interests endorsed cricket segregation. As blacks were excluded from white provincial and national sporting organizations, they had to form their own competitions and sporting bodies. Many national governing bodies appeared by the late 1890s soon after white organizations became established along racial lines.

KIMBERLEY: CRADLE OF NATIONAL BLACK SPORT

In 1860, it would have been unlikely that a spot in the middle of nowhere, not even really claimed by any existing colony, would become the centre for black national sporting organization in South Africa. The discovery of diamonds in Kimberley in 1867, however, insured that there would be a large influx of people of all backgrounds to the diamond fields. Kimberley was at the forefront of South Africa's version of the industrial revolution, and though outstripped by Johannesburg after gold was discovered on the Witwatersrand in 1886, Kimberley was the first boom city in the country. Whites, Coloureds and Africans all flocked there to make money from diamonds or the necessary supporting industries. As Bill Worger puts it:

> Diamonds encouraged British imperialism to move tack into the interior to secure the newfound wealth for the Crown, established a huge urban community in the middle of the subcontinent, brought tens of thousands of blacks and whites into daily contact in the industrial workplace, and attracted millions of pounds of capital from foreign investors (Worger, 1987: xi).

After initial uncertainty and the scrambling for claims, the diamond claims at Kimberley were concentrated in a few hands by the late 1870s and more stable and larger-scale production ensued. After a speculating crisis in the early 1880s, Kimberley began to appear as a more settled town rather than merely a temporary mineral boom location.

Many blacks from the Eastern Cape and Orange Free State missions and Cape Town moved to Kimberley seeking the best jobs on offer for blacks such as interpreters, clerks and teachers. This group included early black nationalist leaders such as Sol Plaatje and Isiah Bud Mbelle. Members of this emerging black middle class began to set up sporting associations, church-based organizations and mutual aid groups (Willan, 1982; Odendaal, 1995). Odendaal points out that perhaps the first non-racial sports organization in South Africa began in Kimberley. Founded in 1894, the Griqualand West Colonial Rugby Football Union (GWCRFU) consisted of Coloured, 'Malay' and African clubs. The use of 'colonial' rather than the common racial or religious designation, Odendaal argues, suggests that the founders consciously wanted to include all black groups in the organization. Isiah Bud Mbelle, educated at Healdtown and the first African to qualify for the Cape civil service, was the founding secretary of the GWCRFU. Mbelle reportedly earned the highest wage of any African government employee at £25 per month (Willan, 1982; Odendaal, 1995), and was instrumental in the establishment of a national rugby board for blacks. The white SARB had been founded in 1889 and provincial teams played for the Currie Cup. Mbelle, captain of the Native Rovers Rugby Football Club, wanted to establish a similar organizational structure and provincial competition for blacks. He called a meeting for 19 August 1897 in Kimberley. Though only local men attended, the SACRFB was launched with Robert Grendon as the first President. He had been educated at Zonnebloem College in Cape Town and was employed as a teacher. The SACRFB leaders secured a Cup from Cecil Rhodes and the first Rhodes Cup competition was held in 1898. Due to financial difficulties and the great travelling distances involved, the Rhodes Cup was only held 27 times between 1898 and 1969, when it was replaced with the SA Cup. In both rugby and cricket in Kimberley, African teams played with Coloured teams in unified competitions in the 1890s. The Duke of Wellington and Eccentrics Cricket Clubs played alongside six Indian, 'Malay' and Coloured teams in the Griqualand West Coloured Cricketers Union (1892–5) and then in the Griqualand West Colonial Union.

Sol Plaatje married Mbelle's sister, though they were from different ethnic groups, evidencing the broader social and cultural connections and links being made among Western educated Africans. Willan argues that Kimberley, as the Cape Colony's leading marriage market, 'contributed more than anywhere else to the process of creating a national African petty bourgeoisie out of a diverse set of regionally and ethnically defined local groupings' (Willan, 1982: 252). Importantly, English became the language of communication among the African elite, and both African and Coloured clubs used English as the language of their meetings and in their minute books, even when officials spoke Xhosa, Tswana or Afrikaans as their first language. The mere fact of communicating in English was an outward sign of 'civilized' behaviour, as English was viewed as the language of culture and symbolized 'respectability' and difference from the mass population of blacks.

In addition to the presence of educated blacks at Kimberley, the location of African elite education at a handful of institutions meant that a national elite network formed rapidly in the late nineteenth and early twentieth centuries. Fort Hare, in particular, was a centre of African learning, and was also important in fostering a national black elite sporting culture out of the sporting interests of its students. According to the college's official historian, one of the first acts of new Fort Hare students, led by Hamilton M. J. Masiza, was to lay out cricket and football pitches (Kerr, 1968; Archer and Bouillon, 1982).

Although the founding ideologies around early rugby and cricket associations were those of 'respectability' and similarity to white sporting culture and organizations, in reality, black sports had to constantly struggle for financial resources and decent grounds on which to play. As a result, black sports were often dependent on the assistance of whites. Most organizations had prominent white men as patrons and many leaders of black sporting bodies were selected on the basis of their ability to secure funds from white benefactors (Peires, 1981; Odendaal, 1995). A handful of white sportsmen also assisted their black counterparts. Famous Springbok rugby player Bennie Osler, who worked for the United Tobacco Company, secured small amounts of financial and in-kind support for Cape Town Coloured sporting groups (Effendi and Adams, 1994), though these amounts were very minimal. As the urban black middle class grew and a few within the group began to prosper, some support for sporting teams and organizations developed within local communities. In Transvaal and Natal townships, in particular, research has shown that owning or being patron for local soccer teams was one of the most important ways that relatively well-off black men could publicly demonstrate their position in society (Magubane, 1962; Jeffrey, 1992). Denied most other outlets by segregation and apartheid, the support of sporting teams was a crucial way that patronage could be displayed.

SPORT AND SOCIAL AND MORAL ORDER IN THE URBAN ENVIRONMENT

In Natal, the Native Beer Act of 1908 enabled municipalities to fund African welfare programmes and recreational facilities through revenue generated from a municipal monopoly over the sale of African beer in municipal beerhalls. Thus, as Merrett states, 'the bizarre idea that African welfare and recreational facilities should be financed from the profits derivative of potential inebriation was established at an early stage' (Merrett, 1994: 98). After 1910, a number of national segregationist laws followed the lead of

Natal and attempted to create a legislative framework for the social, economic and spatial control of blacks (Davenport, 1969). Although blacks were forced into segregated locations in the late nineteenth and early twentieth centuries, or housed in migrant labour compounds in the mines, the spectre of thousands of blacks huddled near areas of white settlement caused continual concern for white officials. From Natal's black rape scare of the 1870s (Etherington, 1992) to the 'black peril' election of 1929, and removal and slum clearance debates of the 1930s and 1940s (Nauright, 1992; Sapire, 1989) and beyond, control over the lives of urban blacks was a priority for whites who felt threatened merely by the presence of any group of blacks who were not performing necessary labour tasks.

Badenhorst demonstrates just how strong white concerns over black leisure time activities became in the period from the 1920s to the 1950s. She points out how white liberals, missionaries and the Johannesburg City Council (JCC), through its Non-European Affairs Department (NEAD), instituted a series of programmes 'to create "healthy uplifting" recreation as an antidote to political militancy and popular protest. The organization of urban African sport was seen as a major vehicle for urban social control' (Badenhorst, 1992b: 32). She argues that there was a deliberate pattern of sporting expansion among blacks from the early twentieth century whereby white liberals and missionaries promoted and assisted black sporting organizations, though blacks did not merely adopt all of the sporting culture and organization that whites urged, but rather resisted them when necessary. While it is true that whites were prominent in the 'moralizing of leisure time' as Couzens (1982) argues, it is also clear that black men in particular actively worked to shape their own sporting experiences. This was part of their attempts not only to emulate European and 'civilized' culture, but also to uplift themselves from the mass of working-class blacks so that they could legitimately portray themselves as 'civilized' and worthy of equality of opportunity that supposedly went along with the cultural appellation 'civilized'. In order to understand the current strategies towards sport in the new South Africa, it is important to remember just how strong the concept of 'civilized' culture was for educated urban Africans, although material realities meant that this concept was fraught with contradictions.

BLACK URBAN SETTLEMENT AND SOCIAL DEVELOPMENT

Archdeacon Francis Hill of the Anglican Church reported to the Native Economic Commission in 1931 that significant numbers of tenants who had come to Johannesburg townships had left white farms in the late 1920s, because farmers would no longer let them keep cattle and demanded more labour from tenants. Some left farms and came to town, but had to sell their cattle because they could not find inexpensive grazing land close to areas of black settlement (Nauright, 1992).

In freehold townships such as Sophiatown and Alexandra, divisions existed between those who owned property (known as stands), and those who rented from these standowners. Only 4 per cent of the Sophiatown population owned stands in the 1930s and only a quarter of these could afford not to have tenants on their property. Steve Lebelo argues that Sophiatown property owners faced a dilemma: they needed tenants to maintain their income, property and way of life; but the presence of large numbers of tenants came to threaten their position and status (Lebelo, 1990). A 1950 survey showed that only 102 families out of a total population of 66,000 in Sophiatown and Martindale could afford to buy homes if they were relocated. Alan Cobley suggests that, although property owners were not much better off than tenants, aspirations surrounding freehold rights had a psychological significance that often led to a special pleading for protection. He argues further that poor living conditions faced by all classes of urban Africans helped develop common cultural references in urban African communities that ensured the potential for cross-class mass action (Cobley, 1990). Phil Bonner posits that those who invested in property were indicating their permanent tie to the urban area where they had to raise all of their costs of reproduction. The necessity for women to work in this context and the constant struggle for survival and accumulation, Bonner argues, drove this property-owning group towards the rest of Africans living in urban areas (Bonner, 1982).

Despite these suggestions of material closeness, an African elite in towns aspired to respectability through education at the best available schools for Africans, attending church at the 'more respectable denominations – Anglican, Methodist, Presbyterian and African Methodist Episcopal – through 'proper' behaviour and cultivation of some 'Western' values. This behaviour earned them the appellation 'scuse-me-please' from other township dwellers. Bozzoli points out that 'often ties between standholders and tenants were complexly mediated by kinship relations in ways that made it difficult to identify hard-and-fast classes . . . often the decision not to buy a stand was less a matter of lacking the financial strength to do so, than lacking the desire to remain permanently in the city' (Bozzoli, 1991: 124). Those who chose to remain permanently in the city adopted more European social and sporting practices, while those with greater links to the countryside remained closer to African local culture and recreational forms.

The members of the urban black elite were caught between liberal-Christian values of self-improvement and advancement, and their emerging anger at being confined to an inferior position along with other blacks who did not share their cultural and ideological values. Only 15,214 (37.6 per cent) of the estimated 40,000 school-age children in Johannesburg in 1939 had access to schools, which led to a rise in juvenile delinquency and crime. Additionally, many new migrants were single men (and later women) who came to the city searching for economic means of survival. Townships became overcrowded during the late 1930s and 1940s and crime rose dramatically. In 1941–2 there were 38 murders in Alexandra Township whereas a decade earlier there had only been one or two a year (Nauright, 1992).

Elite blacks into the 1940s continued to believe that behaving 'respectably' was the key to their advancement. But European notions of respectability were not simply adopted *in toto* by urban African elites. For example, white notions of respectability were combined with missionary, Victorian-influenced ideals of female domesticity that were hostile to women's involvement in the production and sale of beer and other alcoholic drinks. Yet the potential for profit here was much greater than for other activities and most families had to have income from both men and women. Thus, an outward appearance of Christian and Western influenced culture, and respectable behaviour, merged with the harsh economic realities of urban life.

White missionaries continually promoted notions of respectability in their attempts to 'uplift' and Christianize Africans. The centre of organizing efforts in Johannesburg was the Bantu Men's Social Centre (BMSC) which first opened in 1924. Much has been written on the role of the BMSC in urban African elite culture of the 1920s to 1940s period (Badenhorst, 1992b; Cobley, 1990, 1994; Couzens, 1982). The BMSC was crucial in the development of African sporting organization as it was one of the few venues within the municipality of Johannesburg where African sporting competitions could be held outside of mining properties. While the BMSC was instrumental in the development of African male sporting activities, women were not encouraged into sports on nearly the same levels. African schoolgirls were taught netball, basketball, hockey and athletics, but tennis was the most important sport for urban African elite women. As the *Bantu World's* Women's section declared in 1934, 'With all of us it is work, work, work. And when there is time for a rest we are only too glad of the chance for tennis, dancing or visiting our friends' (quoted in Cobley, 1994: 213). Magubane (1963) also identified tennis as the sport of men in the 'excuse me' class who emulated British upper-class culture, whereas real men, those who are 'fit and strong', play soccer (Magubane, 1963: 12).

WHITES AND URBAN BLACK MEN

Many anthropological studies of the 1920s and 1930s examined the detrimental effects on black culture caused by cultural contact between whites and blacks. In almost all cases, it was thought that black culture suffered. In particular, blacks who moved to urban areas and became 'de-tribalized' were viewed as existing in a cultural vacuum, neither white and urban, but no longer rural and African. Thus, missionaries and social reformers thought that the construction of proper leisure time cultural activities was of the utmost urgency in urban areas. Badenhorst points out that 'tribalized' and 'detribalized' became the prime categories for labelling Africans during the 1920s and 1930s. These terms evolved from earlier terms of 'primitive' and 'civilized' that categorized thinking in the nineteenth century (Badenhorst, 1992b).

Several initiatives linking white liberals and African urban elites developed during the 1920s. The Joint Council movement which began in 1921 was modelled on Booker T. Washington's beliefs in moderate reform of race relations in the United States. While whites maintained effective control of these councils, they were a point of contact between racial elites. The Joint Council movement failed by the late 1920s, but several white liberals, in particular John David Rheinallt-Jones, were instrumental in forming the South African Institute of Race Relations (SAIRR) in 1929. The SAIRR studied and reported on the social and economic conditions of Africans, particularly in the towns. It also worked to pressure municipalities, and provincial and national governments, for social and economic reforms that would assist urban blacks and improve their lives. The SAIRR was not involved in the organization of sporting activities, but many of its members were and so influenced the SAIRR to pressure the Johannesburg municipality, in particular, to provide better recreational facilities for Africans (Badenhorst, 1992b).

The Joint Council movement, the SAIRR, and other liberal initiatives, were closely involved with the dominant strains of action by members of the educated black elite in the inter-war period. Protest centred on issues of health, sanitation, housing and provision of recreational facilities, while not initially concentrating on issues of segregation *per se*. Many members of the black elite followed the conservative approach used by Booker T. Washington and his followers in the United States, focusing on individual and group improvement, and immersed themselves in British imperial and 'civilized' culture. Most newspapers aimed at the black market had social pages where the activities of elite blacks were reported. Events such as marriages, engagements, visitations by relatives and friends from other places, and social gatherings dominated the social pages and emulated social reporting in the English-language press aimed at the white market. Thus, for most of the first half of the twentieth century, there was very little noticeable difference in the cultural behaviour and activities of educated blacks and educated whites. The basis of cultural activity and acceptability was that of British imperial culture, and the concepts of 'civilized' behaviour that flowed out from the cultural belief system of the Victorian English middle class. Indeed, the men who frequented the BMSC were thought of as elitist. Ray Phillips revealed that the BMSC was seen by the masses 'as a "high hat" club of White Man's "Good Boys"' (Phillips, 1930: 303).

Added to the activities of white liberals and educated blacks were those of white missionaries. The American Board Mission (ABM) became especially concerned with urban living conditions in the 1920s and 1930s and was involved in the development of recreational and health facilities for Africans in the Johannesburg area. While the role of the ABM was significant in the organization of black sport in Johannesburg and Durban, it would be wrong to reduce the emergence of sporting organizations to the ABM. Indeed, urbanized Africans were instrumental in the establishment and administration of sport, though the assistance of missionaries and white liberals was vital in extracting meagre funding and zoning for sporting facilities from municipalities. Despite the creation of black sporting organizations, and a few facilities for the playing of matches, black sport remained segregated and conditions for the playing of sport remained poorly funded.

A key area of ABM and liberal interest lay in what Couzens calls the 'moralizing leisure time' of urban blacks. In particular, Phillips and other ABM missionaries worked with mine owners to establish organized recreational practices in the mines. Following from the ideals of the rational recreation movement of the nineteenth century, attempts were made to organize and control leisure activities of urban blacks in general, and among mineworkers in particular. Two elements of leisure time activities predominated in ABM and mine efforts at filling non-work hours of migrant mineworkers – movies and organized soccer.

As with the English rational recreation movement, efforts to generate organized leisure activities for the mass of urban Africans had very limited success. At the end of World War II there were 32 boys clubs and 22 girls clubs on the Rand with a total of only 2892 members (Archer and Bouillon, 1982) out of the tens of thousands of youth on the Rand by that time. These clubs, along with the BMSC, helped to create a group of Africans who adopted most of the rudiments of British culture that separated them off from the majority of urban Africans. While this group successfully moved into leadership positions in local politics and the nationalist struggle, they were initially viewed with an element of mistrust as being merely black white men or the cultural and political dupes of whites. A younger generation emerged in the late 1940s, who challenged older conservative politics and moved towards the concept of non-racialism as a unifying principle for political protest against white domination and apartheid policies. In sport, non-racialism dominated nearly all forms of non-establishment sport by the 1960s, as nationalist and non-racial protest challenged white-dominated society and culture on all fronts.

Many political battles in sport had to be fought before non-racialism could be achieved because black sports officials often jealously guarded their own administrative positions. From the early 1900s to the 1960s, sport remained almost totally segregated because each of the four main population groups played only other clubs and organizations from within the same group. Early non-racial organization among elite blacks collapsed under the weight of segregation by the middle of the twentieth century. International sporting tours were increasingly organized on a racial basis with white teams playing whites, teams from India playing Indians, and tours of Africans between various British African colonies. The separateness of black cricket in the 1920s and 1930s, for example, was illustrated by the first known overseas tour by a team from the Indian community to India in 1922 (Bowen, 1970: 329). In the inter-war period, cricket survived precariously as an activity for middle-class blacks with social aspirations, and on special occasions whites played black teams; for instance, at the opening of the Bantu Sports Club in 1932 when 15,000 turned out to watch. In the Eastern Cape, a small amount of mixed cricket survived in matches between Rhodes University and the University of Fort Hare (Archer and Bouillon, 1982). There is also a record of a Malay XI playing a white XI, including Dave Nourse and Xenophon Balaskas (presumably in the 1920s); while tourists such as Clarrie Grimmett came into contact with, and commented favourably upon, aspects of black cricket (Odendaal, 1977). But unified black cricket ceased, due to 'divergent opinions among the cricket administrators' (S. J. Reddy, 'South African Non-European Cricket' in Swanton and Woodcock, 1980) and under the heavy pressures of segregationist policy.

In 1926 the South African Independent Coloured Cricket Board broke away from the South African Coloured Cricket Board (SACCB), and by the time the South African Bantu Cricket Board had departed (in 1932) and the South African Indian Cricket Union had deserted (in 1940) the SACCB was effectively the Malay Board. The SACCB ran a strong competition in Cape Town that produced a number of players of high quality. A. J. 'Dol' Freeman, for example, regularly scored centuries in cricket on poor matted wickets, and was rated as the best black rugby player of the inter-war period. One of his nicknames was the 'Black Bennie Osler' in reference to the great white Springbok rugby player on whose game Freeman's was modelled. Many in the Coloured community, and those few whites who had seen him play, believe he could have played for the Springboks in either rugby or cricket. Salie Abed, a wicketkeeper, also played in Cape Town, and most agree that he would have easily been selected for the South African team if he had been classified white. Later, Basil d'Oliveira, who played for England, came out of this competition (Adams *et al.*, 1994).

In some parts of South Africa (Transvaal and the Cape Province) inter-race bodies kept alive links between the different groups and, in the Transvaal, some whites were included. These inter-race bodies remained a distinct minority, however, as segregation divided the sporting population and each group largely identified with its own sporting heroes. Ultimately, though, white national teams received some support from blacks, particularly in the case of rugby in Cape Town. So many Muslims attended rugby matches played by Western Province and the Springboks that one of the stands at Newlands was called the Malay Stand. As early as the 1930s, however, many blacks cheered for teams visiting South Africa and against white national teams (Hendricks, 1994) and this became a factor in government policy arguing against letting any players of colour tour as members of international teams visiting South Africa (Nauright, 1993).

Examples of exclusion based on racial background highlight the frustration felt by many black sportspeople in the old South Africa who wanted equal recognition and opportunity but, as they became more successful, whites eliminated those opportunities. This was particularly hard for sportspeople in cricket, rugby, netball, tennis and golf, since it was mostly well-educated blacks who played these sports which were viewed as elements of 'civilized' culture. As a result, blacks were left with white standards as the norm for national teams, and top players were frequently compared with white stars to see if they 'would have made the grade' (Effendi, 1994). Due to better facilities, media coverage, opportunities to play and international competition, white elite sports remained the standard into the post-apartheid era. Much internal protest against apartheid in sport centred on the quite un-radical notion of selection based on 'merit', rather than on fundamental structural changes to the system. Attitudes hardened in the 1970s and 1980s, as we shall see, but the fundamental principle of merit selection survived into the post-apartheid period, and has helped to entrench the old sporting structures in the new South Africa.

CONCLUSION

Despite divisions caused by spatial segregation and cultural separation, sport became an integral part of all urban communities in South Africa by the middle of the twentieth century, though by this time it was firmly rooted in the traditions of modern British sport. Many mission-educated black sportspeople adopted elements of British elite sporting culture in an attempt to establish a civilized pedigree or 'respectability'. Black sporting cultures did not merely copy white sporting culture, however, as sporting competitions increasingly became significant parts of local community culture, and sport spread throughout the black urban population. As we shall see, in most townships soccer became the dominant sport by the 1940s, and the present-day National Soccer League generates massive followings among black spectators. Additionally, rugby remained popular in the Coloured communities of the Western Cape and among Africans in the Eastern Cape. Cricket is played in many black areas, and baseball and softball have a substantial following in the Western Cape.

Due to segregation and difficulties caused by lack of facilities and resources, much sporting identity among Coloureds, Africans and Indians remained focused on local sporting heroes and competitions. Increasingly throughout the twentieth century, however, national and inter-provincial competitions gained in importance. Black South Africans were almost completely barred from any international competitions before the 1980s unless, like Basil d'Oliveira, they moved overseas. Thus, identification with a national South African team, in any sport, was fraught with difficulties for many black sportspeople, because they were not allowed to represent the country in which they lived. As a result, many blacks supported overseas sporting teams against the white South African ones, thereby making any form of truly national identity in sport a virtual impossibility. In addition, wider black identities through sport were not easily developed, as those who became too Europeanized, the 'excuse-me's', were denigrated by the majority of blacks who rejected a mere acceptance of European culture and behaviour.

While some black sportspeople aligned themselves with white structures, the vast majority joined the non-racial sports movement, or competed in events run by blacks. South Africa thus had multiple sporting systems and organizations that were shaped by either support for the status quo or opposition to segregationist structures in sport and society. A long and often dirty campaign was fought during the apartheid era to isolate white South African sport from its international allies and to create a new sporting system that would select participants on the basis of merit and not skin colour.

NOTES

1. The first records of Muslims playing officially in the CSRU I have found date from 1961. Minute Books of the Perseverance Rugby Football Club, 1961. Thanks to Mark Wilson for providing me with access to the club records.
2. 'Skollies' referred to street youths who committed petty crimes. It is thought to be derived from a Dutch word meaning 'scavenger'.
3. Softball also attracted a number of Coloured women players by the 1950s and remains popular among Coloured women.
4. Charity Rag, a key cultural event in the Coloured communities of the Bo-Kaap and District Six, began in 1936. Two clubs, the Young Stars and the Caledonian Roses, from the Bo-Kaap and District Six respectively, organized a charity match in aid of the hospital fund launched by the mayor of Cape Town. This match became an annual event and its organization reveals much about the cultural life of Coloureds in Cape Town, being played every year except in 1959. Rag is the subject of a paper in progress by the author entitled 'Charity, Community and "Coloured" Rugby in Cape Town'.

4

'WHITE TRIBE DREAMING': RUGBY, POLITICS AND WHITE IDENTITIES IN 'WHITE' SOUTH AFRICA 1948–90

It was the way that we could show the world that we were good at something
. . . Rugby was the one area where the Afrikaner could live and show
superiority . . . We were young men fighting for what we loved which was
rugby . . .

Morné du Plessis, former Springbok captain and manager in *Voortrekker Ruck.*

On Saturdays the referee told them which interpretation held sway on the rugby
field; dominees told them on Sundays which interpretation of the Bible to
believe; on Mondays their bosses brought them the latest interpretations of the
secret Broederbond masterplan.

Hans Pienaar, former rugby player, *Sidelines* (Spring 1996: 10).

The face of modern South Africa was shaped during the apartheid period from
1948 to 1990. During that time Afrikaners, who formed about 8 or 9 per cent
of the total population, took political control of the country and created
alternative cultural institutions and ideologies that challenged British imperial
cultural hegemony. Black South Africans, over 85 per cent of the population,
continued to be excluded from access to power in the mainstream of South
African society, and they were told that their political future lay in a series of
'homelands' or areas where the National Party government deemed various
African 'tribes' to have originated. In reality, the homelands were never viable
and they became rural dumping grounds for surplus labour and wives and
children of migrant labourers. As part of their strategy of dividing the entire
country into precise areas for each race, the NP government forcibly resettled
an estimated 3,522,900 people between 1960 and 1982. Under the Group Areas
Act, a number of urban areas settled by blacks were razed and re-developed as

whites-only suburbs. As many as 834,400 people had their lives disrupted in this way (Unterhalter, 1987). The removal of entire communities, such as District Six in Cape Town and Sophiatown in Johannesburg, significantly disrupted sports and many other social activities in those communities, as we shall see. In this chapter, however, we examine the rise of Afrikaner nationalism, particularly as it involves the sport of rugby union which Afrikaners imbued with new messages that were closely linked to the success of Afrikanerdom and white South Africa. Archer and Bouillon quite aptly sub-titled their discussion of Afrikanerdom and rugby 'The chosen sport of a chosen people' (Archer and Bouillon, 1982).

WHY RUGBY?

Rugby union became the dominant sport in South Africa (and New Zealand) in the latter part of the nineteenth century for a number of reasons. Rugby by that time was being encoded as the most masculine of games, and one that best demonstrated the relative vigour of a nation (Nauright, 1996b). In South Africa, rugby was established in the private schools and in clubs by English-speaking whites who sought to replicate British cultural activities that enabled them to signify themselves as different from, and superior to, the rest of the population in southern Africa. Afrikaners, however, soon took up rugby, thus making it a sport played by most white males. In the early 1980s, over 5 per cent of the white population were rugby club members, 37,000 adults and 180,000 school players (Archer and Bouillon, 1982). Therefore, at least 10 per cent of white males were involved in organized rugby. Others played more informally. In Natal, rugby was constructed as an elite social activity to link a small English-speaking minority together. Natalian settlers believed that rugby was too violent a game for Africans (Morrell, 1996), a view that gained currency across South Africa in the early twentieth century. While Coloureds also played rugby, and Africans on mission stations and in townships in the eastern and western Cape participated in their own competitions, these groups were not allowed to participate in a wider rugby-playing culture. Thus, whites identified rugby as their game, particularly as the national Springbok team went from success to success during most of the twentieth century. Cricket remained the sport of the English-elite, with few Afrikaners taking it up in the period before apartheid. Soccer became identified as a black sport, though some whites had always played. In rugby, however, South Africa was the most successful country on the international stage, thus the game became closely intertwined with the success of white South Africa as a whole.

South Africa is no different from other nations in that sport has played a crucial role in the development and maintenance of national identity. Within

South Africa, however, specific sports have assisted in the emergence of particular, often fragmented national identities, or what might better be called community identities, within a larger 'nation' whose definition and composition has been contested by many groups over the past 150 years. Afrikaner nationalists in particular used rugby to bolster their own cultural identity. Rugby, however, also provided for a more inclusive white identity, centred on the Springbok national rugby team and on provincial level teams who compete each year in the Currie Cup competition. Rugby has also been a strong source of Coloured identity, especially in the Western Cape, and African identity in the Eastern Cape. Cricket remained largely an English-speaking white game linked to its history as *the* imperial game, as Chapter 2 outlined. Soccer, although played by many whites in the first decades of the twentieth century, became identified with resistance, and with black cultural and national identity. All of these games are played by men. Large numbers of white women played netball and hockey, and the netball power structures closely resembled those of rugby during the apartheid period.

South African international sporting success, as with other colonial societies, was initially a way to prove that the white race could prosper in distant settings. From the 1920s and 1930s, however, sporting success by the white-only national teams became a source of proving internal power and, during the apartheid period, as a source of strength internationally as countries began to pressure white South Africa to reform or dismantle its system of apartheid. Through pronouncements by politicians and rugby officials and a largely uncritical media, rugby came to symbolize the power of white South Africa over other societies. For some, the ability to defeat societies that had instituted forms of racial integration by the 1960s, such as British Isles teams, France and New Zealand, helped reaffirm white South African racial policies and moral superiority.

UNIFYING THE AFRIKANER *VOLK*

After the Second World War there was an increasing difference between the views of English-speaking whites and Afrikaners on the future course of South African society, and the constitution of the South African nation. While most English-speaking whites believed in segregation and the superiority of white culture, they did not go as far as Afrikaner nationalism in its emerging formulation of a series of distinct 'nations' within South Africa. During the 1930s and 1940s, Afrikaner intellectuals and businessmen worked hard to establish Afrikanerized institutions and an identity among Afrikaners that would see them identify themselves, first and foremost, as members of the Afrikaner *Volk* and not as workers, women or merely South Africans (Moodie,

1975; O'Meara, 1983). The Afrikaner nationalist movement, led by the secret organization the Afrikaner Broederbond and the cultural body the *Federasie van Afrikanse Kulturvereeninginge*, sought to wrest political, economic and cultural power from English-speaking whites and elevate the position of Afrikaners. The first *Ekonomiese Volkskongres* (Economic People's Congress), held in 1939, launched the rallying slogan of *volkseenheid* (unity of the *Volk* or people) which sought to unite all Afrikaners as members of an organic *Volk*. By 1948 the cry of *volkseenheid* was successful in obtaining enough Afrikaner unity to gain election for the NP and bring in its policies of apartheid. The Dutch Reformed Church (NGK), the Broederbond and its related cultural organizations, the National Party, and a compliant Afrikaans-language media, all combined to influence and coordinate all aspects of Afrikaner cultural and political life. With the attendant Christian national education programme instituted under apartheid, Afrikaner identity and culture was closely managed throughout life. The Sauer Commission of 1948 summed up the NP position linking a particular Christian interpretation with justification for apartheid ideology:

> The party [NP] subscribes to the view that God determined that there will be a variety of races and people whose survival and natural growth must be respected as part of the external and divine plan. In South Africa God in his all-wise rule has placed the white race and the non-white race groups with deep racial and other differences. Every race and race group possesses its own character, talents, calling and distinction. (Quoted in Muller, 1987: 148)

This quote evidences the crucial point about identity in the apartheid era. South African identity historically has been predicated on divisions rather than unity. Although the focus on white South African identity remained strong, particularly as Afrikaner nationalists needed English-speaking whites to help skew their numbers in justifying white domination, division rather than unity marked the development of broader identities in South Africa at least into the early 1990s.

Despite apparent coordination and centralized influence, Afrikaner leaders were not entirely unified. In particular, differences existed between the Cape NP and the Transvaal NP. By 1948, the Cape NP was led by wealthy farmers and financial capital interests located in Samlam and Rembrandt, the largest Afrikaner-controlled economic companies. In the Transvaal, the Broederbond was all powerful, and ideological constructions of the *Volk* more crucial. By the late 1950s, Cape financial capital was strong enough to be independent from agricultural interests and slowly aligned itself more closely with English speaker-controlled interests in mining, secondary industry and finance. This group of Afrikaner capitalists began to press for reforms that apartheid hardliners resisted. The period from the late 1960s to 1990 was marked by a struggle for dominance in Afrikaner political circles, with splits from the NP in 1969 and 1982 and a massive information scandal called 'Muldergate' in 1978. While state interests competed over the pace of reform, versus interests wanting to maintain apartheid, on a cultural front attempts were made to generate a unified white identity once the Afrikaner nationalist objective of creating a Republic was realized in 1961.

During the late 1940s and 1950s the Broederbond sought to shore up Afrikaner support through taking control of all cultural institutions and public discourse. Sport in general, and rugby in particular, was a significant element in the project of Afrikaner advancement. It was more difficult, however, for the nationalist movement to totally take over older forms of national popular culture, such as international sporting teams, but they were, nevertheless, targeted for Afrikanerization. As a result of apartheid ideology, and discourse and political divisions within all groups in South Africa, unity in a wide range of spheres was difficult, but in sport and through national sporting successes, white South Africans had a cultural activity that they shared and which generated a broader identity. While rugby was put into the service of Afrikaner nationalism, it remained widely popular in the English-speaking white community and focused feelings of national identification.

Paul Roos, Danie Craven, Bennie Osler, Boy Louw, Johann Claassen, Dawid de Villiers, Janie Engelbrecht, Frik du Preez, Morné du Plessis, Naas Botha, François Pienaar . . . these names and many others are national heroes for most white South Africans. They are some of the 'nation's' rugby heroes, based on their past performances with the all-conquering Springboks, and have become integral parts of the 'knowing' of white South African society, especially if one is a white South African male. While some whites thought that politicians of whatever party let down the white population in the past, the Springboks very rarely let the 'nation' down before the 1990s. All new Springboks must measure up to the heroes of the past, and Springbok rugby teams are repeatedly compared with those that have gone before. Many have argued that rugby is the second religion of Afrikaners or of white South Africans more generally, and rugby is certainly one of the most important cultural activities among white South Africans. Rugby was the one cultural activity that went furthest in uniting white South Africans and the Springbok became the most potent symbol of white South African national identity.

While rugby became a significant part of white South African identity in the first half of the twentieth century, it developed into a central core of white consciousness and power during the apartheid era. This chapter uses a metaphor from Marq de Villiers' (1988) book on generations of his Afrikaner family, which he entitled *White Tribe Dreaming*, to explore just how rugby and rugby success developed into a part of a white identity that was 'dreaming', or as anthropologist Vincent Crapanzano (1986) put it in his study of a white South African community, many whites appeared to be 'waiting' for the end to apartheid and of white power in Africa without a strong sense of future direction; rather, life was lived even more in the present and past than has been the case elsewhere. To borrow from Connerton (1989) the white South African nation was 'remembered' through its cultural practices, and the continual use and manipulation of the past, to shore up identity in the present. In their dreaming and waiting, most whites drew on their culture, parties and social gatherings as means of escaping or avoiding the inevitable emergence of majority rule.

By the late 1980s, whites increasingly drew on their nostalgic conceptions of the past when the Springboks ruled the world, before the turmoils of post-1976 black protest, the 1975 independence of the former southern African colonies of Portugal (Mozambique and Angola), and the transition to majority rule in Zimbabwe from the white-controlled former Rhodesia. The loss of Rhodesia, coupled with the immigration of former 'Rhodies' into South Africa, left South Africa as the last bastion of white power in Africa, as white English-speaking and Afrikaner settlers fled majority rule from Kenya to Rhodesia to South Africa. If South Africa went over to majority rule, there was nowhere else for whites to go in Africa where they could be in political control. Thus, South Africa became a symbol for the white race, and success or failure of white settlement on the African continent. A beleaguered mentality crept into public consciousness, and the preservation and security of the white nation became a central part of public and private discourse by the 1980s. The places where white South Africans appeared most secure were locked together behind their security gates and walls, and in sporting arenas where the 'crowd' was white. Rugby was an important element of this culture throughout the apartheid period, evidenced in white crowd expressions at rugby matches when South Africa was readmitted to world rugby after several years in isolation.

WHITE SYMBOLS: THE FLAG, *DIE STEM* AND THE SPRINGBOK EMBLEM

In order to make sense of what rugby symbolizes for white South Africans today, we must first examine the historical development of nationalism, national symbols and national identity in South Africa. In addition, we must understand the broader social, political, cultural and sporting context in which international rugby returned to South Africa in 1992. Rugby bodies had unified at the national level, but programmes to generate some form of equity in the sport were still few and far between. The future direction of South

African sport, society and the (re)shaping of identity(ies) was uncertain and demonstrated by the behaviour of the white rugby fans at the first post-apartheid rugby test match at Ellis Park in Johannesburg. The place of rugby in the new South Africa will be discussed in detail in Chapters 7 and 8.

Dunbar Moodie (1975) refers to Afrikaner nationalism as a 'civil religion'. Others have called Afrikaners the 'white tribe of Africa' (Harrison, 1985). Culturally, Afrikaner nationalism centred around symbols of a mythic symbolic culture and identity. Leonard Thompson (1985) examines the development of Afrikaner historical myths, using the term 'political mythology' to discuss the use of history in mobilizing a national, in this case Afrikaner, identity. Afrikaners have used their political mythology to create a sense of identity rooted in recollections of a heroic past, now often used nostalgically in fondly, if quietly, recalling the days of Afrikaner power between 1948 and the more troubled times since the 1976 Soweto student protests.

During the 1930s and 1940s, Afrikaner intellectuals repackaged Afrikaner culture and history through an emphasis on a common past. Afrikaners were thus cast as a 'chosen people' surrounded by hostile forces of English-speaking whites and Africans. Official Afrikaner versions of South African history were taught in schools after 1948 and were only beginning to be dismantled in 1997. Although Afrikaners maintained a political hegemony from 1948 to 1994, they were never able to culturally subdue other South Africans. Indeed, white South African culture retains many connections with, and elements of, a broader Western international culture. Former Springbok rugby captain Wynand Claassen puts it well: 'we're not in our own little world here, we're part of a bigger world' (Claassen, 1992). Once the Afrikaner Nationalist political dream of a Republic was realised in 1961, the government attempted to include English-speaking whites in a more inclusive white South African identity. Despite such moves, many cultural and social differences remained between English-speaking and Afrikaner whites. Whites did, however, share many of the symbols that helped to define their identity in cultural terms.

The old South African flag and national anthem have been important symbols of white identity. In discussing a white South African identity and indeed a white national identity, however, the primary symbol is that of the Springbok emblem. The flag and the anthem were products of Afrikaner nationalism, but the Springbok has been shared by all whites despite Broederbond attempts to take control of rugby. The willingness of most whites to accept the new flag by 1995 and for many to begin learning the new co-national anthem, *Nkosi Sikelele Afrika*, was coupled with the retention of the Springbok, thus allowing white identification with their most important cultural symbol to remain. The Springbok emblem and name were first used in the 1906 South African tour of the British Isles. The team arrived in England with the Springbok badge on their jerseys. They also realized that the English media would create a name for them unless they chose their own. The captain and vice-captain (an Afrikaner and English-speaker respectively) decided on Springboks and the name stuck (Sweet, 1989). Surveys of white South Africans in the early 1990s showed that many were willing to give up the flag and the anthem, but very few would relinquish the Springbok (Gleeson, 1992). While Afrikaners may have taken rugby more seriously, or imbued it with more national and ethnic characteristics than English-speaking whites, both groups were united in their support of the Springboks and in their identification with Springbok success.

In the first half of the twentieth century, rugby was promoted at national level primarily as a means of forging links between Afrikaners and English-speaking whites. Almost continual Springbok success in international rugby, since 1903, meant that rugby also became closely intertwined with white South African national identity. The Springboks continued their international success by not losing a series, home or away, until their 1956 tour of New Zealand. While rugby and Springbok success was used to help unify the white groups in the early 1900s, by the 1940s, Afrikaner nationalists took a keen interest in making rugby distinctly Afrikaner.

That one of the most quintessential of English public school elite sports should be chosen for Afrikanerization has puzzled researchers. Explanations vary widely from linking rugby as a rough and tough game suited to life on the frontier, to those suggesting that the very form of rugby itself is linked to Afrikaner mentality. Archer and Bouillon (1982) suggest that the scrum is representative of the *laager*, the circular wagon formation Afrikaners used when protecting themselves while trekking into the interior of the country. This assertion is surely far-fetched but there is, nevertheless, a strong link that developed between rugby and Afrikaner masculinity and nationalism in the period from the 1920s onwards. Van der Merwe's recent work uncovers the significance of rugby being played in the prisoner-of-war camps during the Anglo-Boer War (van der Merwe, 1997). Prisoners from the interior, he argues, were exposed to the game for the first time and took it with them back to their farms and towns after the war. Grundlingh (1996) locates the early success of the game at Stellenbosch and the Afrikaner college there. Most early Afrikaner players who made it to the national team had played at Stellenbosch, and Afrikaner elites from all over southern Africa attended the College there by the early 1900s. Grundlingh thus accounts for the spread of rugby as these men took the game back to their communities, but he does not precisely tell us of any defining moment in which rugby 'became' Afrikaner or when Afrikaners clearly viewed rugby as their game.

The 1906 Springbok tour, with Afrikaner Paul Roos as captain, played an important role as one of the few arenas of 'mixing' between English and Afrikaner men after the Anglo-Boer War. Successful Afrikaner rugby players demonstrated to the Afrikaner community that they were not inferior to *die Engelse* and could compete with them at their own games. Rugby was also a violent game where Afrikaner men could legally exact a measure of violent revenge for what many felt was the humiliation of the war, and the under-handed way in which the British won it. Rugby, therefore, made symbolic victories over English-speakers possible. Losses by Afrikaner-dominated provincial or national teams to British ones took on a special meaning, and symbolically repeated the humiliation of the Anglo-Boer War, while victories vindicated Afrikanerdom and exacted revenge for military defeat.

Although the Afrikaner-English conflict in rugby played an important role at school, university and club level matches, white South Africans were, nevertheless, unified in their support for the immensely successful Springbok national team. Grundlingh is the first historian to have analysed the links between rugby, Afrikaner masculinity and Afrikaner nationalism. He takes a more plausible line in arguing for the historical role played by the University of Stellenbosch which became the first Afrikaans university in 1918 (before that it existed as Victoria College). Grundlingh argues that Stellenbosch's proximity to Cape Town meant that rugby started there much earlier than in the interior. The first club in Stellenbosch dates from 1880 while the university club officially began in 1919 (Grundlingh, 1996).

The significance of Stellenbosch should not be underestimated for a couple of reasons. First, as Grundlingh suggests, it was the first, and for a while, the only 'institution where young, predominantly Afrikaner men were concentrated in one place for a reasonable period of time and which afforded them sufficient leisure to indulge in' rugby (Grundlingh, 1996: 182). The other prominent reason Stellenbosch has been so important in the history of South African and Afrikaner rugby, is that the two dominant rugby coaches and administrators of the century, A.F. Markötter and Danie Craven, were based at the University and coached the university's first team. In 1991 there were 80 rugby teams (translating to about 1500 players) at the university and 8700 of the 14,500 students played some form of sport, a testament to the role of rugby and sport in general in the Afrikaner community (Roger, 1991).

While Stellenbosch became an Afrikaner rugby stronghold, the game developed among Afrikaners more slowly in the Transvaal. Middle-class English-speaking clubs in Johannesburg took little interest in promoting rugby among working-class Afrikaners, who flocked to the city after the South

African War of 1899–1902. By 1930, only a few Afrikaners had played for the top clubs. In Pretoria, Afrikaners began to take to the game in large numbers from the 1920s, partly through the efforts of Stellenbosch-educated men who moved into government administrative positions, and once the bilingual Transvaal University College was transformed into the Afrikaans-medium University of Pretoria in the 1930s (Grundlingh, 1996). It has been difficult to mark the moment at which rugby became Afrikanerized, though it appears that the convergence of the Afrikaner nationalist movement with the rise of Afrikaner professionals and government servants, and the development of Afrikaans universities in the 1930s, played a key role. Additionally, by the 1930s many Afrikaners had been successful members of the Springbok national team and began to outnumber English-speakers in selections. Thus rugby became one of the first areas where Afrikaners were visibly successful in competition with English-speakers.

Rugby in South Africa became mythologized as rural, though the key influences in its development were in the university town of Stellenbosch and the administrative capital city of Pretoria. Rugby spread quickly throughout the small towns across South Africa and became compulsory for boys in white schools. Like rugby in New Zealand, or baseball in the United States, the rural imagery around rugby remains strong, though the realities of modern sporting competition are that large cities provide the impetus for development of sports for spectators. The main provincial centres of Transvaal (Johannesburg), Northern Transvaal (Pretoria), Orange Free State (Bloemfontein), Natal (Durban), Eastern Province (Port Elizabeth) and Western Province (Cape Town) are all located in the largest city within that region, and these centres are home to the largest rugby arenas in South Africa (see Table 1). New modern facilities have been built at the University of Stellenbosch (Danie Craven Stadium) and at Rustenburg (Olympia Park), while other facilities, such as Ellis Park in Johannesburg and Newlands in Cape Town, have been upgraded in recent years.

In small towns across South Africa, however, the local rugby stadium marks the landscape, along with Dutch Reformed Churches (or Anglican ones in areas of the Eastern Cape and in Natal), as common elements of the small town landscape. These common markers allow white South Africans to share a common link through the similar landscapes present in towns across the country. Larger rugby stadia in the cities are beacons of white power, culture and identity, and now form the venues for the largest gatherings of whites in contemporary South Africa. While public gatherings at monuments and on 'national' holidays could outstrip rugby matches in the 1930s, by the 1960s, international rugby tours provided the motivation for the largest public gatherings of white South Africans.

The rugby ground thus became a symbol of white power, identity and collective consciousness within a society that was increasingly violent and hard to control outside the confines of the rugby stadium. John Bale (1994) and others have begun to analyse the centrality of the sporting landscape to the creation and maintenance of identities, however, there has been little discussion of this in the South African context. Lewis points out that sporting landscapes make up part of people's 'unwitting biography, reflecting our values, our aspirations and even our fears in tangible, visible form' (1979:11). Thus, when white South African sporting stadia are read along with monuments and other forms of architecture as part of the landscape, they provide constant reminders of white South African society, culture, identity and power. Transformation of the landscape has been a large feature in urban South Africa which is constructed as the nation that whites 'built'. Cities themselves have been constructed as 'white' entities and the segregation and apartheid systems ensured that blacks were not allowed full status as urban dwellers. The constant building and rebuilding in the large cities has created a geography of white power over 'nature', over Africa itself. Rugby stadia thus represent white South African power and achievement, while also representing the playing of rugby itself.

Table 1 Major Rugby Venues and Capacities in South Africa

Location/Union	Stadium (opening date)	Capacity
Johannesburg/Transvaal	(New) Ellis Park (1977)	62,000
Durban/Natal	King's Park (1962)	52,287
Pretoria/Northern Transvaal	Loftus Versfeld (1909)	51,762
Cape Town/W Province	Newlands (1890)	51,317
Bloemfontein	Free State (1954)	37,119
Port Elizabeth/E Province	Boet Erasmus (1960)	33,900
Rustenburg/Stellaland	Olympia Park	30,204
Stellenbosch/Boland	Danie Craven (1979)	17,302
East London/Border	Basil Kenyon (1934)	15,476

RUGBY, POLITICS AND AFRIKANER NATIONALISM

During the 1930s and 1940s as Afrikaner nationalism developed and became more powerful, rugby as a bodily practice was viewed more as an arena to demonstrate Afrikaner success and as an excellent practice for instilling moral discipline (Grundlingh, 1996). Thus, Afrikaner nationalists viewed rugby as part of the overall project of instilling bodily control and discipline, coupled with moral and religious righteousness in the public presentation of Afrikaner nationalism. As Archer and Bouillon (1982) state, rugby was 'ideally suited to ideological investment and the Afrikaners, who considered themselves to be a civilizing elite, a pioneer people conquering barbarism, recognized an image of their own ideology in its symbols' (1982: 66). By the 1950s Afrikaners, led by the Broederbond, took over nearly all the key administrative positions, even influencing selection of the Springboks national rugby team and the team's captains (Nauright and Black, 1996; Wilkins and Strydom, 1979; Woods, 1981).[1] Only in Ireland with the links between the Irish Republican Brotherhood and the Gaelic Athletic Association (GAA) in the period from 1884 to the 1920s, and the role of the GAA in Northern Ireland subsequently (Cronin, 1994; Mandle, 1987; Sugden and Bairner, 1993), has there been a comparable long-term link between nationalist politics and sports.

In Afrikaner hands, British attitudes to rugby as a training ground for sportsmanship, fair play and gentlemanly conduct were transformed to the constructed Afrikaner qualities of 'ruggedness, endurance, forcefulness and determination' (Grundlingh, 1996: 187). Support for the Springboks among Afrikaners was at least on the same level as support for the National Party and rugby gave Afrikaners a chance to beat the 'English' at their own game (Grundlingh, 1996). In addition, rugby is a game that promotes group cohesion, and the subordination of the individual to the coach and for the greater good of the team.

This kind of bodily discipline was important to the project of Afrikaner nationalism. Afrikaners were to control any urges that might lead to racial mixing or sexual activity outside marriage, and to display a public air of superiority in bodily relations with blacks. Individual identity was to be subordinated to the larger cause of Afrikaner nationalism in the efforts to achieve parity with English-speaking whites in the economy, and to obtain and maintain political control over the whole of South Africa. A godly, 'chosen people' discourse overlaid such bodily discipline and control giving it moral power. Afrikaners were thus constructed as the divinely chosen rulers of South Africa, because of their bodily restraint, religious piety and group loyalty. Apartheid society was built on the promotion of distinct group identities, and rugby can be seen as a public forum for the promotion of white and Afrikaner 'group' identities. Rugby is also based on the forceful control of the ball and displays of masculine physical power. Along with military parades, international and provincial rugby matches were large public displays of defiant white South African power in the face of perceived hostile internal and external enemies.

From the late 1940s, close links developed between Springbok captains, the ruling NP and the secret Afrikaner Broederbond, formed in 1918 by Afrikaner nationalists and whose members controlled many positions of power in post-Second World War South African society (Wilkins and Strydom, 1979). From the NP's accession to power in the 1948 elections to the 1992 unity agreement between SARB and SARU, nearly all Springbok captains were NP members, or members of both the NP and the Broederbond. Leading Springboks outside the NP and Broederbond, both English-speaking and Afrikaners, such as Basil Kenyon, Stephen Fry, Roy Dryburgh, Tommy Bedford, Morné du Plessis and Wynand Claassen, suffered various degrees of criticism based on politics. In almost all cases, however, they did not last long as captains (Claassen, 1982; Woods, 1981). Claassen points out that, although he was selected as captain of the 1981 Springbok team to tour New Zealand, Broederbond members played key roles as tour officials, and some of the team were also Broeders (Claassen, 1982).

Danie Craven remarked in 1991 on how the 'public' mood was against English-speakers in 1955, when Stephen Fry was chosen as Springbok captain to lead the team against the British Lions. Craven states that the slogan used was 'You don't play an Englishman against an Englishman, you play a Boer against an Englishman' (Clayton and Greyvenstein, 1995: 131). Despite opposition to Fry, 95,000 fans poured into Ellis Park to see the Springboks against the Lions, then a world record attendance for rugby union. In 1956 Craven was voted in as President of the SARB, though Broederbond members occupied most other senior positions in the ensuing years. In 1956, the Broederbond arranged for Dan de Villiers to go on the tour of New Zealand as assistant manager, to keep an eye on Craven who managed the team (Roger, 1991). Despite Broederbond influence in rugby and the SARB, Craven was not challenged by a Broederbond-supported candidate for the position of President. When asked why he thought he had not been challenged for the presidency from 1956 to 1990, Craven stated that it was due to his inter-national contacts, and, perhaps, to a letter sent to SARB from the English Rugby Football Union in the 1960s that said, 'Touch Craven and South Africa is out of the International Board' (Clayton and Greyvenstein, 1995: 135).

Craven argued that the 1965 team that toured New Zealand was a Broederbond team, and that was a reason for their failure to win the test series (Clayton and Greyvenstein, 1995). The manager of the 1965 tour to New Zealand, Kobus Louw, a Broeder, was a Secretary in the Department of Coloured Affairs, and later became a Cabinet minister, as did tour captain, Dawid de Villiers, also a member of the Broederbond (Archer and Bouillon, 1982; Wilkins and Strydom, 1979). Former Springbok captain Avril Malan was the brother of former Defence Minister Magnus Malan. Craven argued that many of the team selections were politically motivated:

> The appointment of the scrum halves Dawie de Villiers and Nelie Smith as captain and vice-captain respectively of the 1965 team was a silly selection. That, and a few other selections of some players proved to me that politics played a part at the cost of the Springboks' success. (Clayton and Greyvenstein, 1995: 143)

Ironically, for many years after 1965 Craven accused opponents of South African racially-based sport of bringing politics into sport. In addition to politics affecting Springbok selection in 1965, Craven was told by a South African diplomat that the government wanted the Springboks to 'ease off their friendly relations with the Maori people' after he pointed out to Craven that the Springboks should not 'indulge in contact in New Zealand with people they would never associate with in their own country' (Partridge, 1991: 92).

From 1965 on in particular, Craven had running battles with the Broederbond and the government about rugby and outside political interference in the game. Meanwhile, the SARB had to deal with mounting international pressure as the NZRFU postponed their scheduled tour to South Africa for 1967, and protesters disrupted Springbok tours of Britain and Australia in 1969–70 and 1971 (Hain, 1971; Harris, 1972; Nauright, 1993). Craven's direct government contacts were with Piet Koornhof and Gerrit Viljoen, Ministers of Sport in the late 1970s and early 1980s, who were also Secretary and President respectively of the Broederbond during much of the same period.

The links between the Broederbond, the government and Springbok rugby during the apartheid era cannot be overemphasized (Nauright and Black, 1994, 1996). In 1949, the year of the first post-war and apartheid period tour by the New Zealand All Blacks, the Broederbond began to take an active interest in shaping South African international rugby. Having suffered the annoyance of seeing a supporter of the opposition United Party, Felix du Plessis (father of future Springbok captain Morné) appointed Springbok captain in that year, and then (worse) English-speaker Basil Kenyon named as his successor for the fourth test against the All Blacks, the Broederbond determined to take closer control over Springbok rugby (Woods, 1981). Although Craven was not a member of the Broederbond, many key positions of leadership in rugby circles, particularly in the provincial unions of the Northern Transvaal, Transvaal and Orange Free State, were controlled by Broeders for thirty or more years. In addition, Johann Claassen, who was a leading Broederbond member during the last two decades of the apartheid era, and a Springbok from 1955 until 1962, was the national coach in the

1970s, manager of the 1981 Springbok tour of New Zealand and the first post-unity tour overseas to France in 1992. And, in 1997, Claassen remained in a leading rugby administrative position as a vice-president of the South African Rugby Football Union (SARFU). In 1980, a leading Natal referee quit rugby over 'internal politics' and the extension of the Broederbond's 'tentacles' through the South African Rugby Referees' Society.[2]

The involvement of leading Broederbond members in the highest levels of rugby administration and in the South African government, meant that rugby relations and international relations were closely connected between the 1940s and 1990s. This connection is explored in the context of rugby boycotts in Chapter 6. Additionally, the significance of rugby as a political tool is closely related to Afrikaner nationalist awareness of its cultural power in white South African cultural identity; rugby was too important an activity to be left to its own devices. In addition to the Broederbond and government links to rugby, the South African Defence Force (SADF) was involved in the promotion of the sport. Magnus Malan, head of the SADF in the 1980s, stated that, 'you can take a rugby player and within half an hour make a soldier of him' (quoted in Grundlingh, 1995: 103). The links between all of these nationalist and white South African institutions meant that the identity promoted by establishment rugby had little appeal to the majority of people in South Africa.

The cultural significance of rugby, overlaid with its political position in apartheid society, meant that rugby became the closest thing to a secular religion in white South African society. Wynand Claassen put it well when he stated that:

> Rugby holds a special fascination in South Africa . . . In every little town, at every little school, a rugby field can be found, and the goalposts alongside a corrugated iron pavilion are as familiar as the church towers in these towns.
>
> All little boys playing rugby have their heroes. Great names running on the field in their green-and-gold jerseys and Springbok emblem.
>
> . . . I am sure most little boys have this ambition, this dream, to become one of those special men who have worn the green-and-gold jersey – to become a Springbok (Claassen, 1992: 4).

The popularity of rugby among white South Africans was evidenced in the 1955 British Lions tour. Although the All Blacks were the biggest rival, the Lions also occupied a special place. On tours of the British Isles, South Africa played each home union in a test. When British teams came to South Africa, however, the four home unions combined to form one, more powerful, team. Chris Greyvenstein records the immense interest in the first test of 1955 at Ellis Park in Johannesburg:

The interest in this test was unbelievable. There was a flourishing black market; people paid the most ridiculous prices for tickets and eventually the biggest crowd ever to see a rugby international – estimates varied between 90,000 and 100,000 – crammed into Ellis Park for the match. The crowd, so huge that there was something frightening about it, saw a match to remember (Greyvenstein, 1995: 115–16).

The links between rugby and Afrikanerdom were well illustrated during the 1974 tour of South Africa by the British Lions. One of the few English-speaking players recounted to Donald Woods that during the series, as the Lions succeeded, team talks were progressively Afrikanerized. The Springbok coach, Johann Claassen, eventually spoke only in Afrikaans and 'the burden of his message no longer had to do with tactics but with the patriotic duty of Afrikaners to strike a sacred blow for the *Volk*' against the old English enemy. (Woods, 1981: 49–50) The depth of the defeat was summed up in the headline of the Afrikaans Sunday newspaper, *Rapport*, following the Springbok defeat in the third test at Port Elizabeth: *Sies, wat 'n kefferpak!* which Woods translates into English as 'Ugh! What a nigger-hammering!' (Woods, 1981: 50). Woods also states that the 1974 Lions tour shook the confidence of white South Africans, who had come to expect victories over the usually smaller and slower men from the British Isles. Furthermore, losing to the British ranked near the top of any Afrikaner humiliation list.

In the wider context of South African society, black protest, which had been largely subdued through the massive clamp-down on the ANC and Pan-African Congress in the early 1960s, resurfaced in a series of strikes begun in Durban in 1973. Although a measure of confidence in rugby was restored in a series win over the All Blacks in 1976, that tour occurred at the time of the Soweto student revolt against Afrikaans-medium education. The 1976 protests launched a massive campaign that ultimately culminated in the ending of apartheid in the early 1990s. As these protests increased, the government placed an even greater importance on maintaining international rugby contacts, as international rugby union was one of the few remaining official sporting contacts left to white South Africans, and rugby success was so significant in shoring up white confidence at home.

As we shall see in Chapter 6, regular international rugby began to disappear in the 1980s, with an official tour to New Zealand in 1981 and one by England to South Africa in 1984 being the only official contact with leading rugby powers. However, South African isolation from major international rugby contact effectively only occurred between late 1986 and mid-1992.

Table 2   International rugby tours of South Africa 1891–1996

Country	Tour years
New Zealand	1928, 1949, 1960, 1970, 1976, 1986†, 1992§, 1996‡
Great Britain/British Lions	1891, 1896, 1903, 1910, 1924, 1955, 1962, 1968, 1974, 1980
Australia	1933, 1953, 1961, 1963, 1969, 1992§, 1996‡
France	1958, 1964§, 1967, 1971, 1975, 1980§, 1993
England	1972, 1984, 1994
Ireland	1961§, 1981
Wales	1964§
South America/Argentina	1980†•, 1982†•, 1984†•, 1994◊
Western Samoa	1995
World XV	1977, 1989

† Rebel or unofficial tours (though the SARB awarded Springbok caps for these matches)
§ Single test tours
‡ Tri-nations annual series, plus full New Zealand tour
• South American team from Argentina, Chile, Uruguay, Paraguay, and 1984 Spain
◊ Official Argentina tour

Source: Adapted from Greyvenstein, 1995

THE WHITE NATION AT WAR: SPRINGBOK–ALL BLACK RUGBY

While rugby was a significant element of white culture and identity in South Africa, and international rugby in general was an important part of that, test series against the New Zealand All Blacks became the most defining moments in white South African sporting culture, perhaps for white identity itself. Springbok rugby great Boy Louw told the team prior to the first rugby test against New Zealand in 1949 that, 'When South Africa plays New Zealand, consider your country at war' (Dobson, 1996: 9). Wynand Claassen, captain of the Springboks during their 1981 tour of New Zealand put the rivalry between the two countries in context:

> A series between the Springboks and the All Blacks became a battle of the giants; the unofficial world championship. In both countries rugby has been regarded as the national sport, played with awesome power and passion, it has become a religion (Claassen, 1992: 4).

Although rugby developed rapidly in all white schools and at the Afrikaans as well as the English-medium universities, it was first and foremost South Africa's success in international rugby that cemented rugby's position in white society. The main rivals of South Africa were the New Zealand All Blacks. The 1905 All Black and 1906–7 and 1912–13 Springbok successes on their tours of the British Isles established the two nations as leading rugby powers prior to the First World war. Unfortunately, perhaps, the two sides could not meet until after the war, which served to heighten the sense of anticipation when the sides finally met for the first time at Carisbrook in Dunedin, New Zealand on 13 August 1921, in front of an overflowing crowd of 25,000 spectators. The All Blacks won by 13 points to 5 but the series was drawn. The return series in South Africa, in 1928, was also drawn, which enhanced the mystique surrounding encounters between the two rugby powers. South Africa won in New Zealand in 1937, and claimed the crown of unofficial world champion. Through to the end of 1996, the Springboks and All Blacks had played 47 tests. Remarkably each side had won 22 tests, with three matches being drawn. South Africa won series in 1937, 1949, 1960, 1970, 1976 and the Rugby World Cup final in 1995, while New Zealand won series in 1956, 1965, 1981, 1994 and 1996 and a one-off test in 1992. From 1996 with the formation of the South Africa-New Zealand-Australia rugby (SANZAR) tri-nations annual series, the All Blacks and Springboks play home and away test matches each year against each other, and with the Australian Wallabies. In addition to official test matches, an unofficial New Zealand rebel team (dubbed the 'Cavaliers') toured South Africa after the planned 1985 tour was cancelled due to a court injunction in New Zealand (this is discussed in Chapter 6). Although the tests were not official, the SARB gave the matches official status at home, and South African rugby histories usually count these matches in official statistics (Dobson, 1989, 1996; Greyvenstein, 1995).

In his popular history of the historic rivalry, Paul Dobson vividly describes a scene from Cape Town in 1949 as the first post-war test between the two rivals was played:

> The whole of Cape Town had been in a fever of excitement in the week leading up to the test. Thousands queued through the night. The gates were shut and people scaled the old galvanised iron fences. When they could not see they got a ladder and climbed up onto the roof of the South Stand then popularly called the Malay Stand. When the police came to dislodge them they fought the police until forced to yield. Newlands was packed. In those simple, austere days after the war, rugby was a passion, a test an experience beyond thrill, a test match with the All Blacks an ecstasy (Dobson, 1996: 67).

Warwick Roger recounted similar scenes at Eden Park in Auckland in his book *Old Heroes* (1991) which nostalgically recalled the 1956 Springbok tour of New Zealand. Before either country had television, Springbok and All

Black players assumed a much larger than life status that further heightened the cultural power of Springbok v. All Black rugby. In 1949, the South African Parliament took the afternoon off so that MPs could go to Newlands to see the first tour match between the All Blacks and Western Province Universities (Dobson, 1996).

SEGREGATION, RUGBY AND WHITE IDENTITY

As the NP implemented apartheid and made the old segregation system more rigid, black protest increased in the 1950s. At the same time, white culture and the white South African 'way of life' emerged as something that had to be defended against a possible black takeover – and increasingly a black takeover was equated with 'communism'. The apartheid government quickly labelled all forms of racial mixing as 'communist' and banned the Communist Party in 1950. Rugby was identified as one of the key elements of white culture, and thus something that was to be defended, a point not missed by marketing strategists either. Perhaps the most famous advertising campaign in South Africa was that for Chevrolet automobiles, which was similar to the American slogan of 'Baseball, hot dogs, apple pie and Chevrolet'. In South Africa, this became, '*Braaivleis*, rugby, sunny skies and Chevrolet'.[3] The political, economic and cultural use of rugby was thus a central part of white South African society during the apartheid era, and rugby's centrality in that society has spilled over into the post-apartheid period.

Before the 1970s, there was no suggestion that Coloureds or Africans would ever be selected for the Springboks and very few whites would have even considered a 'black Springbok' as a likelihood or an option. Afrikaner nationalists repeatedly asserted that whites were superior to blacks, and that whites were cultured while blacks were closer to nature. Such conceptions were even applied to beliefs that soccer, played more widely among blacks, was a more 'natural' game, while rugby was more sophisticated and therefore 'cultured'. In addition, the NP pursued its policies of separate development, and of promoting group identities for Africans who were to be relocated to 'homelands' where they would become citizens. Africans were thus to be denied South African citizenship and reclassified as citizens of 'tribal homelands' such as Kwa Zulu (Zulu), Transkei (Xhosa), Bopthuthatswana (Tswana) and others. Not only would Africans thus be racial 'others' but also 'foreign' others and, as a result, would not then be eligible for Springbok selection anyway. The problem of dealing with Coloured and Indian South Africans was much more difficult: there was no geographic rural space to send them which could even loosely be defined as a 'homeland'. As a result, Coloureds and Indians were ultimately given their own chambers in parliament, though the citizenship issue and its relationship to sport was never completely resolved.

The issue of Coloured South Africans was a particularly difficult one for the government and for whites. Many whites had some African or Coloured blood in their distant past, though they did not want to admit to any such traces as this went against the construction of racial separateness. Additionally, many Coloureds had come to South Africa initially as slaves and were linked to the menial tasks that Africans performed in areas outside the Western Cape. The majority of Coloureds spoke Afrikaans, and along with blood relations, this made definitions of the *Volk* and of Afrikanerdom difficult. In the 1980s, the NP adopted a strategy to win Coloured and middle-class black support. The NP targeted the fears of Coloured voters in their 1994 election campaign (Norval, 1996), and it appears that the NP was at least partially successful as they were able to win control of the new Western Cape province due to large Coloured support.

From 1980, some Coloured schoolboys were allowed to participate in the annual Craven Week national schools rugby tournament. Craven had lobbied the government as early as the 1970s for the inclusion of one or two Coloureds in Springbok teams in order to alleviate foreign pressure on the SARB. Also in 1980, the first Coloured was selected in a Springbok team. The inclusion of a Coloured rugby team in Craven Week threatened to split the NP (*Star*, 7 March 1980). Some Afrikaner schools boycotted the tournament, and the issue was a factor in the most significant split in the NP, as Transvaal NP leader and Cabinet minister Andries Treurnicht, and several MPs resigned from the NP and formed the Conservative Party in protest over P. W. Botha's 'reformist' policies. Their response echoed that of members who left the NP in 1970 over allowing Maori All Blacks to tour South Africa. For some Afrikaner nationalists, any social mixing was too much.

AFRIKANER AND ENGLISH SOUTH AFRICAN MEN: RUGBY AND WHITE IDENTITIES

While the Springbok team and provincial sides galvanized white identity at broader levels, rugby not only played a crucial role in the making of white South African men, but also in sustaining mistrust and hostility between Afrikaners and English-speaking whites. Although the game was promoted as a form of white unity at national level, at regional and school levels the meanings attached to rugby were quite different.

Robert Morrell (1996) demonstrates how the English public school ethos in rugby transferred to colonial Natal and became embellished with notions of white cultural superiority and white masculinity in a hostile and remote colonial setting. In the white schools, rugby promoted a sense of group identity and sublimated individualism. Soccer was identified as a 'coolie game' and rooted out of the schools by 1910. Thus, rugby and soccer were discursively designated as 'white' and 'black' sports that promoted particular cultural values of the groups who played them. Even within the elite Natal school, however, there were differences that showed in and through rugby. Boarding students from the farms more generally played in the early days, and were viewed as tougher than the more 'effeminate' and 'soft' day students from the towns. House matches were established in the 1890s and early 1900s and boarders played day students, often winning by huge margins (Morrell, 1996). Thus, rugby, success and identity became enmeshed in the education of white Natalian boys in the early part of the century.

Similar patterns to that of Natal appeared in other parts of South Africa, though in the Eastern and Western Cape and Griqualand regions many Coloureds and Africans also played rugby. Segregation was less rigid in the Western Cape, though after 1918 inter-racial matches were extremely rare. In the Orange Free State and Transvaal rugby emerged much along the lines of Natal in promoting white group identity and cultural difference, superiority over other groups and a masculinist culture. Segregation in sport remained complete in the northern provinces. In the documentary *Voortrekker Ruck* the position of rugby in the Free State was summarized in the context of masculinity: 'If you're not a rugby player here in the Free State, then you're a sissy and you're out. It's one of the main ingredients of being a man, a man amongst men or whatever'.

Rugby is a violent game, but perhaps fewer games have been more violent than when Afrikaner schools played English-speaking white schools in the segregation and apartheid periods. Many English-speaking white men recount their love for rugby and their playing experiences from school, but Afrikaner teams were different. As with international rugby, school rugby provided a forum where Afrikaners could do better than the 'English'. As Grundlingh (1996) puts it, 'Clashes between Afrikaans and English schools, universities and clubs gave the lie to the cliché that rugby was "only a game"' (Grundlingh, 1996: 188). Sadie Berman, commenting on rugby in the 1930s, states that:

> When Witwatersrand played Pretoria [universities], it wasn't just rugby they were playing, there was an enmity and a bitterness and a hatred of each other. The overtones were quite clear. The major goal was to beat the other university *not* only in the game. I think the competition between two such universities was naturally bitter . . . because it was the child of the hatred of the Afrikaans [sic] for the English-speaking. . . . (quoted in Archer and Bouillon, 1982: 73).

John Horak commented on such matches in the 1960s:

> Rugby is the Afrikaners' game: they got their kick nationally, as a people out of playing it. And they were hard, they pushed it: when you were playing an Afrikaans school, those guys played in a kind of way we English schools didn't. They used to play it hard and they used to play to win, they were dour about it and they were always rough. We never used to play to kill, just to win.
> . . .
> The big match of the year was always Wits versus the Tucs – Tucs being the Afrikaans university at Pretoria. They always used to beat us. (Quoted in Archer and Bouillon, 1982: 73)

While the divisions between Afrikaner and English-speaking teams was pronounced at school, university and sometimes at club levels, whites unified in support of their provincial and national teams. Numerous studies of soccer in Scotland have demonstrated that divided loyalties are commonplace, as local divisions turn into national unity when the Scottish soccer team plays.

White rugby was thus violent, tied to imperial culture for English-speaking whites, national identity for Afrikaners and English-speakers, and cultural superiority and masculinity for all white men. To play rugby was to play a civilized game, one that denoted difference from blacks who were supposedly unable to really master the game. As a result, soccer was denigrated as a working-class and, increasingly, a black game, and also a game that real men did not play. Although this separatism existed in rugby, the ideology of civilized manliness filtered through to the Coloured and Eastern Cape African middle classes, though the cultures that developed around the game were much different.

Despite assertions of superiority and 'culture' by nationalist intellectuals, a hooligan element has always existed among male Afrikaner rugby fans that belies the notion of rugby as a 'cultured' activity. Such behaviour is not uncommon when sports are accorded such levels of significance within a community or society, and it is not surprising in South Africa given the cultural centrality of rugby and its subsequent elevation to the status as a measure of white power and national self-worth. As fanatical supporters of their provinces and the Springboks against visiting rugby teams, some fans have participated in 'hooligan' type behaviour. During the match between Transvaal and the New Zealand All Blacks at Ellis Park in 1949, only a year after the initial political victory of the National Party, fans threw oranges and bottles on to the field in protest over decisions made by the referee that went against the Transvaal. The incident was condemned overseas and by the white and black press in South Africa. The press accounts of the incident, and the subsequent match between the Springboks and All Blacks at Ellis Park, provide a valuable insight into the thinking of whites and blacks at the time. The incident caused the white press to cover up instances of thuggish behaviour so that such problems might stay hidden from mass black view. Any 'un-civilized' or hooligan behaviour remained hidden from broad view in a media controlled by tight restrictions and government censorship.

Hans Pienaar reports on a much more violent incident that took place outside Ellis Park before the Springbok test match against the All Blacks in 1965. It is worth quoting at length:

> It was hot and the liquor flowed; the loudmouths began to strut and bully. The blacks who were walking past us to Ellispark station after the morning shift stared fixedly ahead. When the first naartjie[4] flew, everybody laughed . . . Not for long. The street soon turned into a hell run. Workers walked or ran unexpectedly around the corner, bang into a volley of orange fruit. . . . A few brave ones pressed on . . . and it was not long before a few ringleaders began to give chase to these 'cheeky' intruders. They tackled them like players on the field, or set them up against the walls and pounded and kicked them until the blood turned the juice on the walls into a darker orange. The police pitched up, only to swiftly bundle the victims, who dared not complain, into their green vans, to the screaming delight of the queues. . . (Pienaar, 1996: 13–14).

While this incident reveals much about the attitudes of many rugby fans towards black South Africans, it was not reported in the media and the police did nothing to the attackers. Many blacks learned to stay far away from white rugby crowds during the apartheid era. Despite such outbursts of violence, a myth of white cultured and civilized behaviour had to be maintained both for the control of white culture and for the continued efforts at dominating the black majority.

Since the late 1960s, Afrikaner identity in particular has been subject to significant pressures on the political, religious and cultural fronts (Muller, 1987: 152–73). A political split occurred in the late 1960s, partly over the decision to invite Maoris as part of the All Blacks rugby team (Nauright, 1993; Nauright and Black, 1994). A far deeper political rift developed in the early 1980s when the Conservative Party was formed out of protest against the new constitution, as well as out of the increasing racial mixing in rugby and other spheres allowed by the government. NGK leaders distanced themselves from apartheid by the early 1980s, reversing their position on biblical justifications for apartheid. Johan Muller argues that a clash of discourses emerged within the community of Afrikanerdom that led to 'a complex negotiation of Afrikaner identity' (1987: 154). In this context of cultural and political crisis, rugby relations were also placed under strain as international isolation intensified.

. South African rugby was in a state of deep crisis by 1987. After the 1981 tour of New Zealand, the Springboks' exposure to top level competition consisted of a short series against England in 1984 and a tour of rebel New Zealanders known as the 'Cavaliers' in 1986. In addition, the IRB excluded South Africa from the first Rugby World Cup held in Australia and New Zealand in 1987. Many observers in South Africa, buoyed by success against the Cavaliers, thought that South Africa deserved to be in the final against the All Blacks, the Springboks' historic rivals for world rugby supremacy. The South African press produced numerous stories comparing the All Blacks with a potential South African side, and writers argued that it would only be a true world championship if the winner played the Springboks after the World Cup (see *Cape Times*, 5 June 1987 for an example).

Despite these popular reports, SARB President Craven argued that South Africa was nowhere near the standard needed to compete successfully at the top level of world rugby. His admission amounted to a confession of the success of international rugby boycotts. Springbok rugby captain, Naas Botha, supported Craven's view in 1991 when he stated that South Africa's re-entry into international rugby must be undertaken carefully, 'After all, the Springbok has a strong image and we must not harm it. We do not want to start by losing, but we also must not play against too many ordinary sides' (*Sunday Times*, 30 June 1991). Soon after the 1987 World Cup, Craven and the SARB began to hold discussions with non-racial sports officials and black leaders, both inside and outside South Africa, in the hope of achieving a unity that would allow regular tours to resume. Rugby and other sports led the way in negotiations to remove apartheid from South African society, and when unity was achieved by early 1992 test matches were hastily arranged with the All Blacks and the Australian Wallabies, the 1991 World Cup champions.

CONCLUSION

Attachment to rugby as a central defining cultural symbol for white South Africans, most especially for men, has reinforced long-held notions of dominant white masculine power. That the ANC-led government of national unity firmly supported the 1995 Rugby World Cup held in South Africa, even though the national team contained only one Coloured player among its numbers, suggests that the change in government has done little to challenge the old hegemony surrounding sport in the new South Africa. Indeed, rugby during the 1995 World Cup, and beyond, was promoted as a sport to generate national unity. This seems ironic given the history of rugby's links to Afrikanerdom and white South African identity and power. In the rapidly shifting contours of identity and the moves towards reconciliation in the new

South Africa, anything appears to be possible. Results during 1996, however, suggest that the remnants of rugby's racist past, both on and off the field, may resurface in a nostalgic racism centred on white-dominated cultural events such as international rugby.

The final chapters turn to the situation of, and prospects for, sport in the new South Africa. There is a discussion of the pervasive role of soccer in urban African popular culture and society, the boycotts against apartheid sport and their effect, and the emergence of sport in post-apartheid South Africa.

NOTES

1. Danie Craven, President of the South African Rugby Board from 1956 until unity with black rugby officials was agreed upon in 1992, was not a member of the Broederbond, though they tried to recruit him, and he resisted attempts by the Broederbond to politicize and take over South African rugby. Craven was a known supporter of the United Party.
2. *Sunday Express*, 20 April 1980. The article also reported on the involvement of Broederbond members in the highest levels of South African rugby. Broeders listed included Jannie le Roux, President of the Transvaal Rugby Union; Professor Fritz Eloff, President of the Northern Transvaal Rugby Union; Butch Lochner, convener of the Springbok selectors; rugby officials Piet du Toit, Mannetjies Roux and Willem Delpoort; former Springbok captains Avril Malan, Dawie de Villiers, Hannes Marais and Johann Claassen; Steve Strydom, head of the Orange Free State referees (and later President of the Orange Free State Rugby Union); and Wouter du Toit, head of the Transvaal Referees' Society and formerly of the South African Rugby Referees Society. The Secretary for Sport, Beyers Hoek was also a member of the Broederbond.
3. *Braai* is the Afrikaans term for a barbecue and *vleis* is the Afrikaans word for meat. White South Africans eat the most meat per capita in the world.
4. A small orange-coloured citrus fruit (satsuma).

5

THE DEVELOPMENT OF SOCCER
AND URBAN BLACK CULTURE AND IDENTITY

After a week's work in the world of the white man, the Africans stream onto
the football grounds to watch the feature matches of the week, and there they
cheer the clubs they support. Momentarily their emotional life which is often
subdued and repressed during the week . . . is allowed to break through. From
the day the fixtures are out, the important matches of the weekend are
discussed in the buses, on the pavements during the lunch hour and in the long
bus queues where Africans wait for hours in the morning and afternoon to be
carried to their destinations. The drudgery which their life imposes on them is
temporarily forgotten. . . . This pre-occupation with football matches makes life
worth living despite its frustrations.

                                                    Bernard Magubane (1963: 53).

Though written over thirty years ago, Magubane's assessment of the place of
soccer in urban black communities captures the influence of the game in
South Africa. Although Magubane's approach is functionalist, it nevertheless
resonates with the experience of thousands of urban black men in South Africa
over the past several decades. Soccer is played and watched by more South
Africans than any other sport and given the significance of soccer in urban
black culture, and for some white South Africans, it is surprising that little
academic or popular written work on soccer has appeared in South Africa. It
is also a mystery why so little has been written about soccer when there was
an explosion of literature on black urban social history in South Africa during
the 1970s and 1980s. Indeed, the history of soccer is the great unwritten
history of sport in South Africa. Although the literature is limited, it is possible
to reconstruct elements of the history of soccer and to discuss its meaning in
the popular culture of various communities in South African society. Cricket
and rugby have been promoted as possible unifying sports for the new South
Africa, but it is soccer that resonates most with the great majority of South
Africans. To merely depict rugby as a white man's game and soccer as a black

man's game is a deterministic mistake. For just as there have been great black rugby players and many black rugby supporters, there have also been some great white soccer players from South Africa, such as Gary Bailey who kept goal for Manchester United in the English League for many years in the late 1970s and early 1980s, and 1990s national team captain Neil Tovey and defender Mark Fish among others. Albert Johannsen, who was designated Coloured, played in England from 1959–70 with Leeds United and for two additional years with York City. Several black South Africans currently play in Europe as well. Perhaps the most successful of these players has been Phil Masinga, also of Leeds United, who frequently scored the goal of the month in the English League in the mid-1990s. In the 1970s, South African football legend Jomo Sono played for the New York Cosmos alongside Pele and Franz Beckenbauer, and returned to buy a professional team in South Africa, the Jomo Cosmos. These are just some of the more recent players from South Africa who have played overseas. As early as 1939 it was recorded that 'Boksburg, a place of less than twenty thousand inhabitants has contributed no less than nine players to first-class English and Scottish soccer in the last eighteen years' (Wells, 1949: 373).

Soweto, the conglomeration of townships to the south-west of Johannesburg, has been the centre of South African soccer in terms of support, and for supplying the leading teams and many of the top players. The teams with the largest and most fanatical support have been Kaizer Chiefs (founded in 1970), Orlando Pirates (1937) and Moroka Swallows (1947). These teams are all based in Soweto, as is the Jomo Cosmos. Orlando Pirates are so widely popular that they are also known as the 'People's Team'. Matches between Pirates and Chiefs are popular nationwide, even eclipsing the popularity of national team matches in the immediate post-apartheid era. Another leading team which has had much success in recent years is Sundowns (1962), based in Mamelodi Township in Pretoria. Durban also has a long history of soccer and teams there have played at a high level.

The first white player for Kaizer Chiefs, Lucky Stylianou, who signed in 1979, stated that the passion for soccer in Britain and South America was nothing compared to that passion of the South Africans (Murray, 1994: 254). Repeated commentaries from within South Africa have for decades noted the fanatical support for soccer in black South African communities. Where did this passion come from and what is the significance of soccer in South African urban culture? What other sporting activities have been popular among black South Africans? The remainder of this chapter will address these questions.

AMALAITA AND URBANIZATION

While an increasing number of Africans moved to the cities in the first few decades of the twentieth century, the majority of black workers into the 1940s remained migrant workers who had ties to rural areas in southern Africa. Often, men from the same district would go to work in the same compounds, townships, or work as domestic labourers in the same suburbs. The majority of migrants went to the Witwatersrand or to Durban as there were more employment opportunities in these areas. In the rural areas, these men participated in various forms of dancing, stick-fighting and boxing. *Ngoma,* which were competitive dances, were popular in Natal, along with stick-fighting battles and, in the urban areas, these cultural physical activities took on new forms and meanings.

Congregations of young men in towns were soon generically labelled *amalaita*, a name first used in Durban at the turn of the century. These groups varied in size, function and organization from loose gatherings of young men at weekends to elaborate hierarchical groups that resembled rural social structures. Beinart demonstrates that *amalaita* gangs were highly masculine and anti-authoritarian in nature, but also quite fiercely independent. They rarely became involved in wider political struggles, though *amalaita* groups did participate in the Durban beer hall riots of 1929–30, and in Industrial and Commercial Workers' Union (ICU) activities of the time (Beinart, 1994). Though *amalaita* had its roots in rural culture and was popular among some urban Africans, in the 1950s and 1960s officials tried to use a form of *amalaita* to help in their policies of re-tribalization of blacks. While *amalaita* helped some young men to adjust to life in compounds or in urban areas, soccer rapidly became the dominant sport among young black men in urban areas.

THE DEVELOPMENT OF SOCCER

The first known soccer club was the white club, Pietermaritzburg County, founded by white settlers in 1879 with the first recorded soccer match played in the same town in 1866, only three years after the formation of the English Football Association. The white Natal clubs – Natal Wasps, Durban Alphas and Umgeni Stars – formed the first football association in South Africa in 1882, called the Natal Football Association, with six more clubs joining them the following year. In Cape Town teams from four military regiments formed an association in 1891 (Couzens, 1983; Parker, 1897). The Football Association of South Africa was founded in 1892, with additional provincial associations appearing in Western Province in 1896 and the Transvaal in 1899 (Archer and Bouillon, 1982).

As with other sports developed in Britain and exported throughout the Empire, soccer links were cemented through contact with 'home' in the form of sporting tours. In 1897 the great English amateur club Corinthians played 23 matches in South Africa (Walvin, 1994). Additional tours followed after the Anglo-Boer War, with a South African tour of South America in 1906, and the first professional tour by a British team in 1910. A tour to India by Indian footballers took place in 1921 which helped lead to the formation of the All-India Football Association, one match on that tour taking place in front of 100,000 spectators. An All-India FA team toured South Africa in 1933 (Archer and Bouillon, 1982). These tours did not stir the same imagination in the local press as did rugby tours. By the First World War rugby was clearly the dominant sport among white men, and the successes of the 1906 and 1912 Springbok tours of the British Isles and France confirmed this status through glowing British and local press reports. By 1900, both British and Afrikaner men played rugby, while soccer remained a sport played by working-class white immigrants, Indians, and increasingly by Africans. Soccer was the one sport played by whites that did not develop an elite white following. As late as 1981, a popular history of (white) South Africa did not even mention soccer in the section on 'Sporting Life' (*Reader's Digest*, 1981).

Across South Africa, black soccer associations formed in the first few decades of the twentieth century. In 1898 the Orange Free State Bantu Soccer Club was formed, followed by other clubs in Bloemfontein leading to the establishment of the Orange Free State Bantu Football Association in 1930. In 1931 the Natal Bantu Football Association was formed, with its headquarters in Pietermaritzburg. During the early 1900s many African national political meetings were held in Bloemfontein due to its relatively central location. Soccer was no different, and in 1928 African soccer officials met there and decided to form regional football associations. In 1933 the South African Bantu Football Association appeared with affiliated associations from the Transvaal, Orange Free State, Natal and Northern Cape. In the Western Cape black soccer became organized later.

Coloured leagues emerged in the 1920s, but it was only in the 1960s that African soccer began to develop in Langa. Langa was an old township and rugby was played there from at least the 1920s, however, the Coloured labour preference policy that operated in the Western Cape limited opportunities for black sporting competitions unless resources could be mustered for travel. From the 1960s, however, Africans began to arrive in the Western Cape in far greater numbers. Immigrant workers and those from the Orange Free State and Transvaal who came to work at the vineyards or in military camps formed soccer clubs during the Second World War, and township soccer began to appear by the 1960s. The white superintendent of Langa promoted the game as he had been a Western Province soccer player (Dyasi, 1983: 21).

Many white officials viewed soccer as an ideal game to market among blacks, particularly for migrant mineworkers. While rugby was played at many mission schools in the Eastern Cape, soccer was promoted at Zonnebloem College, the school established by Governor George Grey to educate sons of African chiefs. The son (or grandson) of Ndebele chief Lobengula played centre half for Zonnebloem in 1905–7 and was club secretary there (Couzens, 1983). At Amanzimtoti Institute (later Adams College) American Board missionaries promoted soccer. Couzens (1983) suggests they did so because they had no interest in rugby, but the development of American football was not yet complete and the number of deaths and severe injuries attributed to the rugby-influenced style of play at northeastern American universities (Black and Nauright, forthcoming; Oriard, 1993) must also have influenced the decision to steer away from rugby and promote soccer instead.

Soccer came to Johannesburg from Natal where it gained in popularity during the 1890s. Early black clubs developed in Ladysmith and Pieter-maritzburg after men there witnessed soldiers playing the game during the 1890s. The Rainbows club from Ladysmith dominated early competitive matches to such a degree that they changed their name to the Invincibles (Couzens, 1983). For many years, however, soccer competed with stick-fighting for dominance among urban migrant workers. According to Reverend G. M. Sivetye,[1] in 1896 many African workers went to Durban following a rinderpest epidemic and a significant number of these became domestic servants, 'to re-establish their manhood after working as servants for white women during the week, would form themselves into bands of amalaitas on Sundays and go stick-fighting' (Callinicos, 1987: 216; Couzens, 1983: 201). Concerns about the perceived violent nature of stick-fighting led many Durban businesses to promote soccer among their workers. Revd Sivetye related that:

> Many European gentlemen who were in business soon saw the need of having football played by their workers because it kept them in Durban. They didn't go home during weekends. They used to play in Durban. That is why some firms always took those who could play. (Quoted in Couzens, 1983: 202)

Although Johannesburg and the surrounding mines became the centre of missionary and liberal focus in the twentieth century through the BMSC, the Bantu Sports Club, the Helping Hand Club for young women and other initiatives, missionaries also actively promoted sport for Africans in other cities. In 1916 the Durban and District African Football Association (DDAFA) was founded. Migrant workers based in Durban who had been educated on American Board Mission (ABM) stations formed clubs and began to play soccer in the early twentieth century. American Board missionaries played a prominent role in the early administration of the DDAFA. Association meetings were all held at the ABM Church Hall in Beatrice Street, Durban. The first President of the DDAFA was D. Evans (1916–23), a white man who came from Johannesburg to manage the Somtseu Road Men's Hostel for migrant workers. After Evans resigned in 1923, black men ran the DDAFA, opening the way for links with other African-run associations in Natal and the rest of South Africa (Magubane, 1963). The links to concepts of civilized behaviour and 'respectability' are also evident in early African initiatives to form clubs. Charles and William Dube, brothers of John Dube, first ANC President and founder of Ohlange Institute modelled on Booker T. Washington's Tuskeegee, were early leaders in the organization of soccer in Durban (Couzens, 1983).

African and Indian workers in Durban formed football teams in the 1880s and 1890s, with worker teams playing against school teams from Adams College and Ohlange. Indians are recorded as playing soccer in Pilgrim's Rest in the Transvaal as early as 1875, and Indians formed the first soccer club, the 'Prides of India', in Johannesburg in 1886, the same year the city was first settled. Club members worked in hotels and boarding houses (Callinicos, 1987: 216). With the opening of the railway line from Johannesburg to Durban in 1895, many more Indians came to the interior and they formed soccer teams such as Hindu Natalians, Star of India, Pirates and Western Stars. In 1896 these clubs formed the Transvaal Indian Football Association (Couzens, 1983).

Magubane provides a list of 21 clubs affiliated to the DDAFA in 1923. The names reflect a preoccupation with proving toughness, with clubs named, for example, Wild Savages, Rebellious, Wild Zebras, Natal Canons, Lions, Vultures and Assegais. Tennis clubs, conversely, were named Daffodils, Morning Stars, Primroses and Winter Roses. Magubane attributes this to the feminine and upper crust background of tennis players, and the need for clubs dominated by male workers to evoke images of 'viciousness, fury, and savagery' (Magubane, 1963: 12). As football became more established by 1925, some changed their names to less violent ones. The Fight-for-Evers changed their name to Jumpers, and Wild Savages re-named themselves Mountain Blues, for example.

As with the Dube brothers in Durban, leaders of the game for Africans in Johannesburg were closely linked to political elites and were members of the educated class of Africans. Dan Twala, a leading force behind the organization of soccer in Johannesburg, was the nephew of R. W. Msimang, one of the four lawyers who founded the ANC in 1912. Twala first played organized football at Lovedale, run by the American Board Mission, in the early 1920s. At Lovedale teams were arranged by dormitories that were divided by ethnicity or region of origin, though a school-wide team played other schools (Couzens, 1983).

For educated black men like Twala, sports administration provided one of the few outlets, outside of work on joint councils or local advisory boards dominated by whites, for African men to practise leadership skills. Despite many domestic and migrant workers taking to soccer in Durban, the DDAFA's early administration was run primarily by educated Africans such as Albert Luthuli, later President of the ANC and winner of the Nobel Peace Prize in 1961. In 1932, Luthuli, then Vice-President of the DDAFA, declined the office of President due to his duties as secretary of the Natal Teachers Association but remained keenly interested in the sport. Magubane (1963) identified 31 leading DDAFA administrators for the period of 1924–32. Six DDAFA administrators were ANC members, with two serving on joint councils and fourteen on local advisory boards. At this stage, the ANC was very much an elite organization of educated Africans who opposed segregationist practices, but it was not very radical in its approaches to white officialdom. At an administrative level during the 1920s and 1930s, soccer overlapped with other political and social activities of urbanizing educated black elites. Jeffrey (1992) shows that in Top Location at Vereeniging, early teams such as the Transvaal Jumpers (1933) were formed by educated African men who had been exposed to the game in an organized form in mission schools.

Many of the Johannesburg elite also took to soccer, but the early organization of soccer on the Witwatersrand was largely undertaken by the gold mines. By the early 1920s the Witwatersrand District Native Football Association (WDNFA) had been formed mainly for mine teams. Couzens (1983) claims that the spread of soccer on the Rand largely developed out of the recruiting of migrant labour from Natal. Mine owners benefited from the spread of soccer as it detracted from work-related grievances and occupied many miners' thoughts about their leisure time. Mines, and other businesses after them, recruited good soccer players and offered them the better jobs available to blacks, in order to attract other workers and to keep current workers entertained at weekends. Many leisure time activities were tried in the mines with the help of Ray Phillips and other American Board missionaries in attempts to 'moralize' leisure time, but only soccer and movies had long-term success. The WDNFA fell away during 1928 and 1929; it had not been successful in organizing black soccer in the mine locations and townships. As a result, the Johannesburg municipality made BMSC secretary Sol Senaoane the director of 'Native Recreation' for the city. With the assistance of Graham Ballenden, the Johannesburg Manager of Native Affairs, Ray Phillips, Senaoane, R. W. Msimang (an ANC leader) and D. M. Denalane of Robinson Deep Mine, the Johannesburg Bantu Football Association (JBFA) was formed in 1929 (Badenhorst, 1992b; Couzens, 1983). The involvement of Ballenden and Senaoane demonstrates the close control over the JBFA's organization that the Johannesburg municipality had from the outset, though with assistance from 'respectable' Africans, such as Msimang, and Senaone through his links to the BMSC.

The JBFA claimed 153 senior clubs and 282 junior clubs as members by 1937 (Thabe, 1983; Callinicos, 1987), and by 1948 it had 218 affiliated senior clubs (Badenhorst, 1992b). The success of the JBFA led to the formation of the Bantu Sports Club (BSC) by the BMSC in 1931 on twelve acres of land that had been donated by accountants Howard Pim and John Hardy in 1925. The BSC had a stand that seated over 2000 spectators with total seating for 5000, two soccer fields and several tennis courts (Archer and Bouillon, 1982; Couzens, 1983). The BSC's grand opening demonstrated its links to 'respectability' as a cricket match between a black and a white team took place in the presence of the Mayor of Johannesburg (Couzens, 1983).

The building of the BSC allowed the JBFA to collect gate-money at matches and revenue was shared between the football association and the club. In 1932 the BSC lowered entrance fees to attract more spectators without consulting the JBFA or the municipality. The JBFA in protest moved their matches to the Wemmer Sports Grounds controlled by the Johannesburg City Council (JCC) (Badenhorst, 1992b). In March 1933 Dan Twala led a number of teams out of the JBFA, forming the Johannesburg African Football Association (JAFA) that reformed the defunct WDNFA in 1932.

George Thabe, former soccer administrator and compiler of *It's A Goal! 50 Years of Sweat, Tears and Drama in Black Soccer* argued that the 'split became the festering sore that would malign the body of Black organized football for about 40 years' (Thabe, 1983: 6). The two leading newspapers serving black readers, *Umteteli Wa Bantu,* established by the Chamber of Mines in 1920 to combat ANC influence in educated African circles, and *Bantu World,* devoted much space to the split and arguments from both sides during March 1933. White officials condemned the split which they argued was indicative of African behaviour. Ray Phillips stated in a simplistic and determinist analysis that the formation of the JAFA was 'of the same divisive nature which has resulted in the formation of 294 Separatist Churches' (*Umteteli Wa Bantu,* 25 March 1933). As Badenhorst (1992b) demonstrates, white officials were upset at the show of independence the JAFA reflected, even though they frequently paid lip-service to African initiative and progress.

Twala, Denalane and others who supported the JAFA left the JBFA because matches were moved away from the BMSC to the municipal-controlled Wemmer Sports Grounds. JAFA members argued that the municipality wanted to monopolize and control soccer (*Umteteli Wa Bantu*, 4 March 1933). The JAFA began with Denalane as President, prominent Alexandra businessman R. G. Baloyi became the Vice-President with Twala as Secretary. Twala later became President and held the position for twenty years.

The JAFA administration was all-African and centred on townships and the mines and the division between the JAFA and JBFA was based on whether African officials or white municipal officials would control soccer's administration and organization. The involvement of businessmen as prominent as Baloyi, suggests that money could be made from a successfully run competition, however, the Non-European Affairs Department (NEAD) of the JCC refused to allow the JAFA access to municipal grounds. As a result, the JAFA found itself restricted to the two fields at the BMSC. Eventually some of the mines allowed JAFA matches to be played on their vacant land. JBFA expansion was assisted by access to grounds under city control, however, its management was poor and financial statements and annual reports stopped appearing by the early 1940s, suggesting general apathy on the part of the municipality, other than in its attempts to marginalize independent African initiative in the JAFA. Though the JBFA remained the larger organization, in 1942 several clubs went over to the JAFA whose administration was much more efficient (*Bantu World*, 16 March 1940; 30 May 1942). In response the NEAD tried to exert greater control over the JBFA, but funds continued to disappear and financial statements and annual reports were virtually non-existent. The NEAD also contributed very little to assist the JBFA with the improvement of playing fields that were constantly in poor playing condition (Badenhorst, 1992b).

Similar to concerns that led to the formation of the JAFA, in Natal obstacles to the formation of a provincial-wide association were hampered by Pietermaritzburg African soccer officials' objections to the DDAFA being run by a white man. Durban and Ladysmith joined together in 1920 to form the Natal Native Football Association (NNFA), but Pietermaritzburg only agreed to link with the rest of Natal in 1925 after Evans had resigned as DDAFA head. In 1930 the DDAFA sent a letter to all provincial associations urging the formation of the South African African Football Association (SAAFA). This was done after the DDAFA had been offered a trophy worth £100 to be the property of a national association (Magubane, 1963). Transvaal and Natal became the nucleus of the Association and they first played for the Deans Shield in 1932. Significantly, the NNFA and the SAAFA, like the JAFA, were African-controlled organizations, though Magubane (1963) pointed out that they were not adverse to accepting assistance from whites genuinely interested in African recreation.

The administrative organization of black soccer associations as with white South African sporting associations and wider South African society, has been highly centralized with small numbers of officials holding wide powers. Sport and political organizations in black and white South African societies have historically been the positions that have bestowed the greatest prestige within local and national communities. Black officials ran their organizations and meetings with strict attention to protocol. Meetings were nearly always held in English, thus linking officials with respectable status. The use of English also meant that only a small percentage of Africans who became involved in sport could serve on association executives, as most Africans did not speak English. Although the prestige associated with sports administrative positions led to numerous political battles, and sometimes to splits within associations, the relative stability in administration allowed many black sporting organizations to survive the onslaught of apartheid and its many disruptive relocation policies and social restrictions. Magubane (1963) identified 30 administrative offices within the DDAFA. Between the years of 1924 and 1960 only 103 men held these positions, an average turnover of less than four men per position over a period of 36 years, or an average of nine years per office. Only five of the 103 served less than three years, while 52 men occupied office for more than 10 years (Magubane, 1963: 26). The contributors to Thabe's commemorative history show that other associations experienced similar administrative stability to that of the DDAFA (Thabe, 1983).

The opportunity to become a sports official provided one of the few avenues for political and administrative achievement for educated blacks. Additionally, patronage or ownership of leading local clubs provided a chance for men to gain substantial local reputations and importance, when local political opportunities were limited by the segregation and apartheid states. Leading men became patrons of local soccer clubs in Top Location, Vereeniging, and maintained leadership positions through soccer after Top Location residents were relocated to Sharpeville (Jeffrey, 1992). Several anthropology studies in the 1950s and early 1960s found that wealthy African, Coloured and Indian men held administrative posts or ran sporting clubs in various South African cities (Kuper, 1965; Magubane, 1963; Patterson, 1953; Wilson and Mafeje, 1963).

Soccer matches allowed team patrons, and club and association officials, to present themselves in large public forums as leading men of the community – an opportunity only matched by local and national political leaders in times of mass protest or crisis. In Langa, Wilson and Mafeje argued that the possibilities 'for leadership among Africans is very limited and office in almost any sort of organization is a source of social prestige . . . to most Africans office in almost any organization carries prestige. . . . People in Langa cling to positions as tenaciously as if they were careers' (Wilson and Mafeje, 1963: 145).

By the 1940s, soccer was on a solid footing with associations throughout the country, and moves beginning towards inter-race competitions and international tours, though black soccer players and teams were excluded from competing with whites. Prestige was not the only benefit soccer officials received from being involved in administration. Thabe, who lived in the wealthy Dube area of Soweto, for instance, was known to have made a large portion of his personal wealth through sports and sports promotion (Archer and Bouillon, 1982). Businessmen, such as Baloyi and James Moroka, donated trophies that in essence were forms of sponsorship of competitions. Their close connections to soccer could not have hurt their other business enterprises.

Despite splits between various associations, soccer clubs and competitions, as Callinicos has pointed out, 'brought together many people – migrant workers, clerks, factory workers, people of different language groups and backgrounds – to help form a new culture of the city' (Callinicos, 1987: 217). Whereas stick-fighting had its origins in rural culture, soccer was the sport of the city and became the largest social sporting activity among urban blacks by the 1930s. The JAFA with fewer clubs than the JBFA ran a well-organized competition from the BMSC, and by the 1940s had attendances of up to 10,000 spectators for Sunday games, attracting domestic labourers and mine workers to its matches (Badenhorst, 1992b).

As the JAFA successfully continued as an independent association, the Johannesburg municipality increased its attempts to marginalize the association. In a deliberate destabilizing move, officials decided to locate a municipal beer hall across from the BSC in the early 1940s. Additionally, an adjacent area of vacant land allowed Shebeen owners to sell stronger concoctions to those attending matches. Beginning in Durban in the early 1900s, municipalities began to set up beer halls under their control where Africans could drink legally in the city. Cities then used some of the revenue to finance their small contributions to the development of African townships. The beer sold in beer halls was weak and drinkers were limited in the amounts they could purchase, so many women – the traditional brewers in rural African society – set up Shebeen shops close to beer halls to maximize their profits. African women fought against beer halls and rioted in Durban to keep men out of the halls (La Hausse, 1990). Although they could not prevent halls being established, many sought to profit from the restrictive drinking rules within the halls by supplying stronger brews. The strategy involved risking arrest, but women brewers merely built fines into their brewing costs. Police constantly went on raids to stamp out the illicit liquor trade, even interrupting soccer matches by chasing spectators across the playing fields. In one such raid in Johannesburg three players were killed by stray bullets (Badenhorst, 1992b).

While liquor laws were enforced, the effort of police to stamp out the trade was never uniform and officials did not want, or did not have the will, to eliminate completely the illicit liquor trade. While social control of blacks and the establishment of 'proper' behaviour among urbanizing Africans were important aims of white officialdom, outlets for non-political release of energy were also deemed crucial to the survival of white minority rule and an orderly society. As a result, officials tried to manoeuvre blacks into 'respectable' activities, but not at the expense of completely destroying black popular cultural activities.

The end result of the location of ready supplies of alcohol near football grounds in Johannesburg was a rise in violence between spectators, and by spectators against referees and players. Though assaults had always been a part of organized soccer, they reached new levels in the 1940s. As with rugby in the Coloured community of Cape Town, and with white rugby fans in the Transvaal, occasional violence was a part of the spectating culture of soccer. White officials argued that this demonstrated African and Coloured excitability and the uncontrollable nature of those who were not white. White pronouncements, however, failed to take into account the realities of urban working-class existence, and violent incidents among white spectators and players such as the 1949 Ellis Park incident discussed in Chapter 4.

African men who ran the JAFA or the DDAFA in the 1930s and 1940s were doing exactly what white missionaries and officials argued that blacks ultimately should do, which is to manage their own affairs in a 'responsible' manner. The rejection of white 'guidance' came at a high cost, however, as such responsibility was always to be located in some unidentifiable future rather than an actually existing present. Local white officials seemed unprepared to accept a large responsible association run by Africans, and, rather than encourage its success, worked hard to destabilize it. Despite the municipality's attack on the JAFA, and its failure to do much for the JBFA, both associations continued to grow in the 1940s. By 1943, for example, the JAFA had over 1200 players and 89 affiliated clubs and used ten fields to run matches (Badenhorst, 1992b). The growth of black soccer led to expanded competitions and to a strain on facilities. Black urbanization greatly accelerated in the 1940s and major soccer matches became a central focus of urban black popular culture, particularly in the Transvaal and Natal.

MOVES TOWARDS PROFESSIONALISM AND SPECTACLE
IN THE 1940s AND 1950s

Thabe states that the 'years between 1942 and 1954 were the most eventful in the history of Black football in the Transvaal' (Thabe, 1983: 7). In this period inter-district competitions were popular with matches attracting crowds of several thousand spectators. Club football also grew dramatically with intense rivalries between clubs developing. Clubs such as Transvaal Jumpers, Orlando Pirates, Moroka Swallows, Hungry Lions, Naughty Boys, the Evergreen Mighty Greens, Pimville Champions and others became household names in the townships surrounding Johannesburg and nearby towns. Leading clubs usually played friendly matches against other top clubs while local associations ran competitions in townships such as Orlando (part of what later became Soweto) and Alexandra.

Often clubs would play each other in special matches for a prize, with 'Ox Competitions' being most popular in the 1940s. Joel Mojapela from Vereeniging, also called 'Chamdos' Molafu, who was originally from Basotholand (later Lesotho) began the Ox Competitions. He organized matches between leading Johannesburg clubs such as Moroka Swallows or Orlando Pirates and teams from Basotholand. The matches took place in Vereeniging at the USCO Klip (Wireworks) Ground. Thousands of spectators attended each of these well advertised matches with the winning team taking a prize ox that they slaughtered or sold for profit (Thabe, 1983: 11). Although matches between top teams began to take place across regions and between cities, players remained rooted in local communities in this period.

Although much impetus for the growth of soccer came from white officials and black educated elites, spontaneous soccer matches and competitions also sprang up from urban black working-class settlements. Small-scale matches for money frequently took place in urban townships by the 1920s. In Doornfontein, a poor black working-class area in Johannesburg, matches for small money stakes were commonplace. One yard would challenge another yard for a stake of a couple of pounds.[2] Local teams combined later to form a local club called Rangers. Rangers then challenged teams from other black residential locations in Johannesburg (Couzens, 1983). Throughout the period from 1920 to 1960, players commonly represented their own street, yard or section within a township, thus players had close links with supporters and local communities.

Even though authorities constantly worked to limit access to playing fields, new clubs continued to appear, both teams registered with associations and independent teams. In 1947 Johannesburg's estimated population of 380,000 Africans had access to just 30 football pitches, only five rugby fields and 26 tennis courts (Archer and Bouillon, 1982). Unofficial matches, and matches between streets and yards, took place on any of the rare open spaces that were available. Alexandra had three squares and Number Two square became the township's main soccer ground and political meeting place. In Pretoria, Sundowns, formed in the early 1960s, had to bribe the caretaker of the bus depot so that they could train on the lawn there (Dassie, 1996). Leading Johannesburg teams developed a reputation for being the best in South Africa, forcing top teams from other centres to travel there for the best competition. The Transvaal Jumpers took on extra road work training when playing leading Johannesburg sides in the 1940s and, once they dominated the Vereeniging competition, the Jumpers began to play at the Wemmer Football Ground against leading JBFA teams such as Orlando Pirates, Naughty Boys and Moroka Swallows (Jeffrey, 1992).

Despite general success, the JAFA struggled from 1944 when it began to lose access to mining grounds and, more acutely, from 1947 when it lost 48 teams because mine owners insisted that mine-based teams play in a mine-controlled competition. Even with these temporary set-backs, the JAFA grew during the 1940s, with 22 teams in its main Saturday league competition and 106 in five divisions in the Sunday league by 1946 (Badenhorst, 1992b). With the association in trouble and restricted to four grounds for 92 clubs in 1947, the JAFA sought NEAD assistance which, not surprisingly, was refused. The NEAD was in the process of negotiating for the takeover of the BSC. The municipality gained control of the BSC in 1951, and the JAFA was then forced to pay a large share of gate money to the municipality and restricted to using the grounds for only six months a year. The JAFA tried to amalgamate with the JBFA, but obstacles such as municipal influence and use of grounds made this impossible. The JBFA split in the 1950s with new associations formed such as the Moroka/Jabavu Association, the Orlando and Districts Bantu Football Association, Pimville Association and Western Native Townships Association (Badenhorst, 1992b). With amalgamation unlikely, Twala and others began to turn their attention towards professional soccer as a solution to divisions in African soccer.

By the 1950s regular competitions expanded throughout the country. In the Transvaal, the Transvaal Bantu Football Association ran several competitions including the Transvaal Challenge Cup and the Senanoane Cup. The Transvaal Jumpers dominated these competitions between 1947 and 1953 (Ramokhoase, 1983: 39). As the Jumpers became too good for their Vereeniging opponents and began to play in Johannesburg on a regular basis, the club assisted in the spread of soccer's popularity between towns. Other teams such as the Hume Zebras from Germiston, led by Albert 'Hurry Hurry' Johannsen before he went to play for Leeds United, and Pretoria Home Stars also succeeded during the 1950s, thus showing that Transvaal soccer talent was not the preserve of Johannesburg and Vereeniging-based players and clubs. The success of non-Johannesburg clubs also fuelled thoughts of establishing a professional soccer league.

Along with soccer, boxing is the other sport with mass popularity in black communities within South Africa. Nelson Mandela and several other black male political leaders were noted for their boxing skills in their youth, and many stars in other sports have also participated in boxing. Many soccer players trained with boxers to increase their fitness as few safe opportunities for training activities existed in the townships (Jeffrey, 1992). Many black rugby players also participated in boxing either in training or in competition (Nauright, 1997). The Transvaal Fast XI began in Sharpeville in the 1950s as a team of boxers. As one of the former players stated, 'All of us were boxers. We were just training for boxing, not training for football. We were not so much interested in football. What makes us good is that we were fit all the time' (Jeffrey, 1992: 75). Other clubs at the time did not train on a regular basis and played soccer more as a part-time activity at weekends.

GOVERNMENT RESPONSES TO SOCCER AND URBAN AFRICAN LEISURE

While soccer in particular, and sports in general, became almost universally popular among urban blacks in South Africa, mine officials in the 1940s and the government by the 1950s, began policies of promoting 'tribal' recreational activities and of 're-tribalization'. Mine owners organized collectively as the Chamber of Mines, along with their recruiting agencies, faced a crisis in the 1940s as attacks on the migrant labour system appeared in wider society, and many South African Africans moved into the manufacturing sector, which offered higher wages and better working conditions. In attempting to halt such criticism, the industry argued that a fundamental difference existed between the vast majority of their workers and urbanized Africans. They promoted an idealistic and noble African culture that was being lost and that should be preserved. They railed against the problems of rapid urbanization. As a result, mine owners established more recreational facilities in the 1940s and early 1950s, though they did not all encourage soccer or other 'European' sports. While the government pursued the 're-tribalization' of African urban culture after 1948 (Archer & Bouillon, 1982), Badenhorst (1992b) demonstrates that the policy had its origins in the crisis faced by the gold mining industry in the early and mid-1940s. Victorian ideas of racial degeneration, combined with concerns about the subversive nature of urban culture luring too many potential migrant labourers to the city, combined into a potent force for attempts to shore up rural African society in the 1940s and 1950s.

In the 1950s, the NP government sought to halt the success of African urbanization and the development of African urban culture through policies that focused on 're-tribalization'. The government officially promoted and encouraged 'traditional' sports such as stick-fighting or *amalaita* contests (see La Hausse, 1990), and organized 'tribal dancing'. *Amalaita* contests in Johannesburg attracted up to 2000 spectators, while in Cape Town up to three-quarters of the spectators were whites. *Amalaita* and organized dancing became part of government strategy to market an idealized 'native' culture both internally and overseas for white consumption. In order to sell their vision of apartheid the NP's strategy was predicated on trying to demonstrate the cultural otherness/differentness of Africans that needed protecting in their own 'homelands'. The government funded African 'tribal' dance troupes to go overseas, for example (Archer and Bouillon, 1982). Though *amalaita* is still practised, government support for it and other 'traditional' activities, failed to make any significant in-roads into the popularity of soccer.

The government and big business interests were actively involved in the process of trying to 're-tribalize' African popular culture from the 1950s. In addition to the promotion of *amalaita* and 'tribal' dancing, large capital interests (or the government) bought up black newspapers, thus limiting the ability of educated blacks to work independently and to disseminate particular world views. Discussion in previous chapters shows that papers such as *Imvo Zabantsundu* and the *Bantu World* had a long history and were important sources of social information for urban and mission-educated black elites. Up to the end of the apartheid era there were no commercial newspapers, radio or television networks controlled by blacks. After *Imvo*, founded in 1884, Sol Plaatje published *Koranta ea Becoana* in 1901 in Tswana and English. *Ilanga Lase Natal* appeared in 1903 for Zulu readers with others soon following these early initiatives. Numerous black groups established newspapers before 1930 but all faced economic problems or political suppression. *World* and *Umteteli wa Bantu* discussed sporting events frequently and commented on any crises in major sports, especially in soccer, though the general tenor of both papers remained conservative and focused more on social events rather than major political issues.

A number of radical papers appeared in the 1940s and early 1950s such as the ANC's *Inkundla ya Bantu* (1946), *Torch* (1946) and *Spark* in 1952. The government banned all these publications in 1960 under the Riotous Assemblies and Suppression of Communism Amendment Act of 1954 which allowed for the banning of any publication deemed to incite hostilities between racial groups. A 1956 amendment to the Act widened the powers of the original Act (Merrett, 1994b).

Established by two white men in 1931, the Bantu Press began publishing the *Bantu World*. The Bantu Press gradually cornered much of the black press market adding *Imvo*, *Ilanga* and the *Evening Post* in the 1940s. Through money supplied by Anglo-American, the Argus Company gained a controlling interest of Bantu Press in 1950 and totally owned it by 1963. These black papers lost most political content by the 1960s, other than reference to homeland politics. Exceptions appeared in the magazine *Drum* and the *Golden City Post* both set up by Jim Bailey, son of South African Associated Newspapers owner, Sir Abe Bailey. The major Afrikaans press group, Afrikaanse Pers, established *Bona* to counteract the success of *Drum*. *Bona* was published in Zulu, Xhosa and Sotho and distributed free to black schools. As part of its attempts to marginalize opposition media, the Department of Information tried to buy out *Drum* in 1977, the same year that it banned the *World*. The Department failed and briefly set up *Hit* and *Pace*, the latter through a front company. The English-language press exposed the Department's role, forcing it to sell *Pace* to the Argus Group. In 1980, the Argus Group established the *Sowetan* (Tomaselli and Tomaselli, 1987).

South African Associated Newspapers set up the *Golden City Press* in early 1982. The paper tried to reproduce the sex, violence and sensationalist format of the 1950s but had financial problems. The paper then turned into 'a Kaizer Chiefs propaganda sheet' that attracted much township attention, which allowed it to survive (Tomaselli and Tomaselli, 1987: 49). A new Friday edition focused on horse racing interests and by the end of 1982 the *Golden City Press* outsold the *Sowetan*. In early 1983, the paper appeared (after a short closure) as the *City Press*. The *City Press* and the *Sowetan* remain the dominant newspapers in the black market along with the *New Nation* established by the Catholic Bishops Conference in 1986. Significantly, *City Press*, *Drum* and *True Love* were sold to Nasionale Pers in April 1984 (Tomaselli and Tomaselli, 1987). Nasionale Pers was the voice of the Cape NP, and fought to win over support from sections of the black community in the 1980s in attempts to reform apartheid while trying to maintain NP political power.

As Tomaselli *et al.* (1987) show in their study of the South African press, the black press in the 1970s and 1980s was highly opposed to apartheid, but through its ownership and ultimate white editorial control, the papers did not criticize the capitalist system. Black editors often avoided conflict by concentrating on crime, sport and funerals. When they challenged the capitalist system, or went too far in their anti-apartheid comments, white business interests, or the government, stepped in to limit or eliminate oppositional news. These practices meant that black sport, especially soccer and boxing, received even greater coverage and sensationalization than might otherwise have been the case. Black sporting stars achieved celebrity status in the black print media, especially those playing for the elite Soweto teams of Kaizer Chiefs, Orlando Pirates, Moroka Swallows and Jomo Cosmos. The reporting of sport, however, did not evolve into a large-scale criticism of the apartheid system or capitalist-driven sport, though when events moved beyond the sporting field, such as during the last English rebel cricket tour led by Mike Gatting in early 1990, critical coverage appeared.

THE RISE OF PROFESSIONAL SOCCER IN SOUTH AFRICA

In 1948 the first move towards non-racialism and ultimate national unity in soccer began. A. J. Albertyn, vice-president of the South African Coloured Football Association travelled to Johannesburg to address the SAAFA and arranged a friendly match between the two associations for Cape Town. In May 1950, in Cape Town, the two organizations agreed to form the Federation of South African Football Associations, and a further meeting in Durban in 1951 brought in the South African Indian Football Association, thus forming the South African Soccer Federation (SASF) (Couzens, 1983).

The SASF drew together all black soccer groups into a single national union in 1952 and became a non-racial federation by 1963, with a membership of 46,000 players, while the whites-only Football Association of South Africa (FASA) claimed 20,000 (de Broglio, 1970). The SASF applied for affiliation with FIFA in 1955, on the basis of being more representative of South African soccer players than the all-white FASA, but its application was rejected because it did not control all soccer in the country. The FASA offered SASF affiliation with non-voting powers, so that a unified body could then be affiliated to FIFA, but officials rejected the plan. When South Africa left the Commonwealth in 1961 and became a Republic, the FASA lost its imperial connection to the English FA. Though FIFA did not accept the SASF, it suspended the FASA in 1961, soon after the English FA withdrew support. Sir Stanley Rous, president of FIFA and a supporter of FASA, came to South Africa to investigate the situation and subsequently reinstated FASA in 1963. In 1964, however, FIFA expelled South Africa at its Tokyo Congress which was attended by several newly-independent African countries. The government responded by issuing banning orders, and putting George Singh, the SASF representative who led the campaign for recognition and FASA expulsion from FIFA, under house arrest.

In 1959 some white players broke away from the amateur FASA to form a whites-only professional competition called the National Soccer League (NSL). In response to the League and calls for a black competition, the SASF began a professional competition in the same year called the South African

Soccer Federation Professional League (SASF-PL). Leading clubs, such as Orlando Pirates and Moroka Swallows, joined the SASF-PL from the outset. Between 1962 and 1966 three professional soccer teams, Cape Ramblers, Mother City and Ocean XI, were formed in the Western Cape and affiliated to the SASF-PL, demonstrating the league's emerging national links. FASA, with government assistance, created black affiliated associations and SASF-PL teams found themselves excluded from municipal grounds. FASA also established a professional competition for Africans called the National Professional Soccer League (NPSL). The white association had much greater access to capital, and to municipally-controlled grounds, which put it in an advantageous position in the 1960s. As a result of being excluded from municipal grounds, Pirates and Swallows eventually left the SASF-PL and joined the NPSL, spelling the end of the SASF-PL. The white NSL also split, with some clubs joining the SASF-PL and others the NPSL.

The NPSL with large African support for Pirates and Swallows, attracted greater sponsorship and became the dominant professional league in the 1970s. In 1985 a split occurred which led to the formation of the National Soccer League (NSL). Kaizer Motaung, Abdul Bhamjee and Cyril Kobus led an attack on George Thabe stating that he and the NPSL frustrated the clubs. Sponsors immediately supported the NSL, forcing the NPSL to survive without major sponsorship. Although Bhamjee and Kobus were later accused of stealing millions of rands from the NSL, the league remained dominant in the 1990s. For the 1996–7 season, the NSL began a Premier League of eighteen teams on the model of leagues in England and Italy. At the next level two regional leagues operate, one along the coastal region and one inland.

Top international and club matches draw massive crowds, particularly at Soweto's First National Bank (FNB) Stadium, also called 'Soccer City', which has a capacity of over 80,000. A number of important matches are also played at Ellis Park Rugby Stadium which holds crowds of up to 70,000. The FNB Stadium opened in 1989 when Kaizer Chiefs and Moroka Swallows met in the Castle Challenge Cup Final. Further development of the FNB stadium is planned that will increase its seating capacity to 120,000; the headquarters of the NSL and the SAFA are located at the stadium. The entry of South Africa into international competition in 1992 has led to a devoted following for the national team 'Bafana Bafana', though many club jealousies among fans had to be overcome. The success of the national team in gaining widespread support has been aided by South Africa's victory in the 1996 Africa Nations Cup, which it hosted, and its qualification for the 1998 World Cup in France.

Soccer's popularity has led to a number of continuing problems in the game; corruption charges are rife and tensions run high when leading teams play. In March 1996 a match between Kaizer Chiefs and Sundowns in the

Coca Cola Challenge Cup was called off with Chiefs leading 2–0. A Chiefs supporter injured a Sundowns player by hitting him with a thrown apple. The player had to leave the field and Sundowns, who had used all their substitutes, had to play with ten men. The Sundowns players refused to continue (http://www.aztec.co.za/biz/soccer/scandal.html). During late 1996 the Pickard Commission of Inquiry investigated claims of corruption, and the use of drug money to run the club, levelled against Kaizer Chiefs, as well as other problems in professional soccer. The Commission reported in early 1997 with the recommendation that Soloman 'Stix' Morewa, the head of the NSL, must resign or be replaced, and found that Morewa had misused funds.

While corruption exists in soccer, it is not clear that soccer bosses have been any worse than administrators in some other team sports. Nevertheless, the appointment of the Commission suggests that the government is serious about the policing of professional sport in South Africa. In addition to problems surrounding administration and spectating, South Africa is rapidly following the rest of Africa in being a net exporter of top quality professional football players. The best players from the national team play in Europe. South African teams also import a number of players as well, particularly from the poorer southern and central African nations. For the 1995 season, Orlando Pirates signed a one million rand sponsorship deal assisting the club in signing three West African players. In 1996 players in the NSL came from the following 23 foreign countries: Angola, Brazil, Burkina Faso, Burundi, Cameroon, Chad, Croatia, England, Ireland, Greece, Kenya, Lesotho, Liberia, Malawi, Mozambique, New Zealand, Nigeria, Tanzania, Scotland, Swaziland, Zaire, Zambia and Zimbabwe.

THE PLACE OF SOCCER IN URBAN BLACK COMMUNITIES

While rugby remains popular in the townships of Cape Town, Port Elizabeth and East London and its nearby areas, soccer is overwhelmingly the most popular sport among black South Africans, particularly in the urban areas. Soon after large-scale black urbanization developed, soccer teams and competitions emerged. Johannesburg and Durban have been the centres of soccer's development, though in every city and town, soccer is widely popular.

There are several reasons for soccer's success within black communities. One is the nature of the game itself which allows for an open expression of individual skills which can be readily viewed by spectators. Indeed, white officials attempted unsuccessfully to stamp out what they saw as an overemphasis on individualism in soccer during the 1930s and 1940s. Soccer can be played on any space or open ground with no special equipment needed, and all shapes and sizes can play. Among whites, soccer was played by working-class males and increasingly became identified as a black sport. Thus, blacks' success in soccer was no threat to white culture and interests. White officials promoted soccer among urban blacks in the 1920s and 1930s as an antidote to the possible ills of urban society. Black elites also viewed sport in this light, though sports administration was one key area whereby black men could exercise political, economic and administrative control.

The popularity of soccer ultimately led to national professional leagues being formed in the 1960s. Elite teams became more removed from their local communities as major sponsorship, television and full-scale professionalism appeared in the later 1970s. As in many other countries, the elite teams have gained national followings in South Africa with Orlando Pirates, for example, resembling Manchester United or Bayern Munich in national support. Public announcements made by Pirates are often attended by thousands. In December 1994, 12,000 attended a public Pirates meeting and party at Orlando stadium (*Sowetan*, 5 December 1994). Kaizer Chiefs' national following is such that there are 65 fan clubs located throughout South Africa, while Sundowns have 38 fan clubs. During the 1970s and 1980s certain teams gained reputations and nicknames based on styles of play or dress; for example, Kaizer Chiefs' supporters in the 1970s began to dress like Kaizer Motaung, the team's founder, and Chiefs' fans became known as 'The Hippies' as they wore Afros and bell-bottomed trousers (Mlokoti, 1996).

Most townships appear to stop when a Soweto derby takes place between Pirates and Chiefs, with matches between the two clubs outdrawing the national team for attention in the mid-1990s. Andrew Muchineripi described the rivalry in November 1996 in the *Weekly Mail*, 'in South Africa when Chiefs and Pirates meet, no matter what the competition, Soweto and most of Johannesburg's townships come to a standstill. A Soweto derby usually has all the ingredients of a cracker: Pride, passion, skill and flair'.

The popularity of soccer in the townships provided a unique opportunity for political leaders to address mass audiences without the necessity of trying to obtain a police permit, which for many anti-apartheid groups was not likely to be granted anyway. Even before apartheid, political leaders had links with soccer. Many ANC elites were involved in soccer administration and James 'Sofasonke' Mpanza, leader of the Orlando squatters movement of 1946, had played soccer with Revd Sivetye at Adams College. Mpanza was called 'Magebula' by Orlando residents for his work in 'turning the sods' on ground for houses in Orlando and Moroka. 'Magebula' as a name then became synonymous with Orlando Pirates (Couzens, 1983). Local elites such as R. G. Baloyi and James Moroka also used their sponsorship of soccer and other activities to lift their personal and political profiles. Baloyi was prominent in

Alexandra Township politics in the 1930s and early 1940s, and both he and Moroka were active in national political issues through membership of the ANC and other organizations. George Thabe used his position as a soccer administrator to secure the position of chairman of the Vaal Triangle Community Council in 1977. According to Jeffrey (1992: 87) 'his status and control originated from his role in football administration and it is not surprising that there was a good deal of overlap between local government and football'. Thabe's chief local political rival on the Community Council, Knox Matjila of Evaton, was also a rival of Thabe's in football. The two had a falling out in the mid-1970s as Matjila tried to take control of the SANFA from Thabe. In 1981 Thabe resigned from the Vaal Council after being defeated twice in succession for chairperson by Matjila (Jeffrey, 1992).

During the 1970s and 1980s groups such as the Black Consciousness Movement led by Steve Biko and the United Democratic Front (UDF) often used soccer matches to address audiences (Lewis, 1992/3). In the 1970s, leaders spoke at a number of matches from the middle of crowds. Through hiding in the crowds and using a portable amplifying system, messages could reach thousands while speakers could avoid police detection, and during the 1980s the UDF also utilized this strategy. Founded in 1983, the UDF was an umbrella organization for hundreds of groups aligned to the ANC. The organization of the UDF made it impossible for the government to round up the leaders as it had done to the ANC in 1963.

While mass rallies were held throughout the 1980s, the state of emergency from 1986 until 1989 made it more difficult for the UDF to hold large meetings. As a result, soccer matches and other public events provided the opportunity for political organization and speech making. Significantly, the ANC held mass rallies at the FNB Stadium upon the release of its political prisoners in 1989 and 1990. These initial rallies were held in front of almost 90,000 people. Ironically, the South African Communist Party also held its first legal rally at the Bank's stadium in May 1990. To mark his inauguration in 1994, President Mandela attended a soccer game played at Ellis Park between South Africa and Zambia, the latter under its long-time leader Kenneth Kaunda being a staunch supporter of the ANC and home to many ANC people in exile.

Added to the overtly political uses of soccer, have been discourses that support individual freedom, team spirit and reward for hard work, as evidenced in Castle beer advertisements of the early 1990s. Castle advertisements depicted the game as representative of the spirit of the 'New South Africa'. One shows a young black star player who has the opportunity to play in England, but who cannot go because he cannot afford it, so a white team-mate leads a campaign to raise the money. Desiree Lewis (1992/3) argues that the advertisement 'is an appropriation and transferral of the liberatory meanings of soccer. The advert is an index of the pervasiveness of soccer's emancipatory meanings' (p. 13). Lewis argues that the structure of the game allows soccer to be represented as emancipatory, even though such representations can be captured by breweries and other companies. Soccer throughout its history in South Africa has been a signifier for 'respectability', African initiative, political struggle, individual freedom, escapism and capitalism through its pervasive role in urban black communities.

NOTES

1. Reverend Sivetye was interviewed by Tim Couzens in October 1978, three months before his death at the age of 95. Sivetye taught and played soccer at Amanzimtoti Institute in the early 1900s.
2. A yard consisted of a number of shacks usually sub-let by owners or renters of property stands in mine locations or townships to various families or individuals for small rents.

6

'NO NORMAL SPORT IN AN ABNORMAL SOCIETY': APARTHEID, THE RISE OF NON-RACIAL SPORT AND INTERNATIONAL BOYCOTT MOVEMENTS 1958–90

Mr Chairman and Gentlemen, politics are already in sport, they are there in the colour bar, they are already there in the policy of the S.A. Olympic Committee to bar non-white athletes from international competition. It was not you, Gentlemen, who brought politics into sport, in fact you are trying to get politics out.

Alan Paton, Opening Address to the Conference of National Sporting Bodies Convened by the South African Sports Association, 1959.

Much has been written on the movement to isolate South Africa in sports (de Broglio, 1970; Hain, 1971; Harris, 1972; Kidd, 1988; Lapchick, 1975; Nauright and Black, 1994, 1995, 1996; Newnham, 1975; Ramsamy, 1982; Thompson, 1964, 1975; Woods, 1981), however, it is important to revisit the contours of protest and debate. This is particularly so in the light of some comments about the relative success of the sports boycott. Harvey and Houle argue that the 'anti-apartheid movement had been the most effective social movement in sport to date' (1994: 348). Additionally, the sporting boycott needs to be assessed in the context of post-apartheid sporting structures and social identification with sport.

International protest against South Africa was very minimal before the late 1950s. There was little public opposition to the exclusion of Maoris by the NZRFU, for example, when it selected a team to go to South Africa in 1928. The best New Zealand player of the day, and some still argue of all-time, George Nepia, was excluded only because he was Maori. Small protests appeared when another all-white All Black team went to South Africa in 1949, but again the voices were few and not followed by large groups of people. As apartheid became entrenched in the 1950s and with the passing of intensive racist legislation in the early 1950s, such as the Group Areas Act, the Population Registration Act, various measures to control the sale of 'European' alcohol to blacks and extensions to the pass laws, more organized international protest began to appear. From the 1950s, sport began to be viewed as an area where pressure could be exerted on white South Africa.

While rugby and soccer emerged as the dominant sports among white and black communities, and sport developed along segregationist lines prior to the apartheid era, most former colonial societies moved towards integration, if slowly, after the Second World War. South Africa went the opposite direction, however, as the segregationist policies of the first few decades of the twentieth century were hardened under apartheid. It is impossible to understand the current problems in South African sport, the sports boycott movement, and the continued underrepresentation of black athletes in many sports, without a detailed examination of government and labour policies that affected black sporting and recreational activities during the periods of segregation and apartheid.

We have already seen that government forces progressively relocated black communities during the early 1900s to new urban and peri-urban locations out of immediate white view and away from white areas as part of the 'sanitation syndrome'. By the late 1930s, it was evident that black labour was a necessity for industrial expansion and that it was impossible to stem the flow of migrants moving to urban areas. White discourse of the period constantly evoked fears of black swamping of whites, and the 1929 election was fought and won on this very issue.

In order to avoid such 'swamping', many whites demanded further restrictions on urban blacks, and the location of blacks in specific areas or zones that were as far removed as possible from white areas. Black slums represented a form of social life that dominant white classes, conscious of their own modernity and 'civilization', did not want to see. The residents of the northern suburbs in Johannesburg, for example, led a decade-long campaign from 1935–45 to have Alexandra Township removed so that mine, industrial and domestic workers travelling to the township for weekend entertainment would not cross their properties or walk through their suburbs (Nauright, 1992). In essence, the black influx of the 1930s and 1940s undermined white images of the city and their sense of urban orderliness. 'Order' and 'control' were the common watchwords of white discourse about South African society in general, and black society in particular.

The continual influx of workers from the countryside to the city led the NP government after 1948 to embark on policies of influx control in its attempts to control migration. White fears centred on the 'uncontrolled' nature of black urban behaviour and culture that differed from their own. By the 1940s, the nature of the South African economy shifted towards manufacturing which showed a tremendous increase in jobs during the decade. Many Africans, therefore, could work for better wages and in improved conditions in comparison with jobs in the gold mines, and, in order to retain and attract workers, the gold mining industry devised entertainment attractions such as organized football and movies.

The rise of non-racialism and the greater organization of blacks across supposed 'tribal' and racial lines exacerbated government fears of 'swamping' and of miscegenation (interbreeding). White responses to rapid black urbanization, from the government to English-speaking white liberals organized in the SAIRR, insisted on the need to 'protect' traditional African recreational practices, and to prevent the degradation of African or 'tribal' culture and customs that urbanization appeared to threaten. British imperial policy fostered a 'divide-and-rule strategy', one with which Afrikaner intellectuals had no problem. Indeed, German *volkekunde* provided the model for Afrikaner anthropology and sociology, as it stressed the essentialist origins of different human societies based on common language and folk customs. Non-racialism in sport and other spheres of social life contradicted the aims of apartheid policies during the 1950s and 1960s. This chapter examines white responses to the development of black sport, the moves towards non-racialism in sport, and local and international protests against racially-based sport during apartheid.

APARTHEID AND SPORT

As several authors have pointed out, there was no official apartheid policy that banned inter-racial or non-racial sport (Merrett, 1996; Roberts, 1988). Several policies, however, worked in conjunction to prevent racial mixing in sport except on very rare occasions. Mixed sport could be played on private grounds if no spectators were present, separate facilities were used, no alcohol sold and no socializing occurred after the match. The Aurora Cricket Club in Pietermaritzburg managed to compete in the 'white' Pietermaritzburg Cricket Union between 1973 and 1978 before going over to a non-racial competition (Merrett, 1988). In other cases any white sportspeople who wanted to play non-discriminatory sport had to leave the establishment and go to non-racial competitions, thereby giving up representative sport and any hopes of playing for the national team. As a result, only a handful of top level whites left the establishment, though there were some notable exceptions, like André Odendaal in cricket and the Watson brothers in rugby.

After the Second World War, white South Africans continued to participate in the Olympic Games and other international sporting events, while blacks were not allowed to represent the country. Indeed, the NP government did all in its power to ensure that there would be no mixing in sport. In 1956, Theophilus Dönges, Minister of the Interior, stated the government's position. He argued in *Die Burger* that:

> Whites and non-whites should organize their sporting activities separately, there should be no inter-racial competition within South Africa, the mixing of races in teams should be avoided, and sportsmen from other countries should respect South Africa's customs and she respect theirs (quoted in *Race Relations Survey*, 1958: 9).

Additionally, he suggested that the government supported 'legitimate non-European sporting activities', but that sport had to follow the wider policies of apartheid and mixed-race teams would not be allowed. While this policy statement marked an important shift in government policy and involvement in the policing of sporting activities, some mixed sporting contact and matches occurred in the late 1950s. Yotham John Muleya defeated world-class white runner Gordon Pirie in a three-mile special invitation race in Harare (then called Salisbury, Southern Rhodesia), which was the first opportunity in this period for a black South African to race against a white one. Significantly, the race took place outside South Africa.

In the late 1950s many English county and test cricketers spent time coaching in South Africa. While in the country, they played a few matches against Coloured or African cricketers. In one match that included Fred Titmus, a d'Oliveira-led team played a close match against the whites, which led to publicity and then to the ending of such matches (d'Oliveira, 1969). This contact with English cricketers led to a professional contract for d'Oliveira who went to play in England from 1959. While the coaching no doubt helped black cricketers as well as white, it did little beyond giving a small handful of blacks a chance to play overseas. By 1960, then, the government officially discouraged black and white contact in sport, though no official legislation existed that specifically banned mixed or non-racial sport. Other laws such as the Group Areas Act and Separate Amenities Act, however, usually worked to keep black and white sportspeople apart.

The government only reacted in any significant way to the issue of sporting competitions after initial calls for sporting boycotts, the acceptance of the mixed race South African Table Tennis Board and the expulsion of the all-white body by the international association in 1956. In addition, the non-racial weightlifting body applied to the International Olympic Committee (IOC) for permission to compete in the 1960 Olympic Games in Rome.

The South African Sports Association (SASA) was formed in 1958, initially with eight national organizations, and its first initiative was to ask the South African Olympic and Commonwealth Games Association (SAOCGA) to insist that all its affiliates provide fair membership based on equality for all (Roberts, 1988). SASA, unable to win concessions locally, went directly to international bodies in attempts to win recognition of the right for black South African sportspeople to compete internationally. It approached the IOC in its attempts to have all South Africans given the right to compete in the Olympic Games in 1960 and beyond, only doing this after organizing a meeting of all national sporting bodies. Of all the white bodies invited, only the South African Tennis Union indicated a willingness to attend; every other one ignored the invitation (Roberts, 1988). SASA was thus forced to take their cause to the international level as white sports officials refused to hold discussions on an equal basis.

SASA was assisted in its aims by the greater centralization of broad protest movements against apartheid. By the early 1950s the ANC Youth League had manoeuvred the ANC into more active protests, with mass protests against pass laws and other apartheid legislation occurring on an increasing basis throughout the decade. The South African Congress of Trade Unions was created in 1955 and the ANC-led Congress Alliance formed in 1956 when the Freedom Charter was proclaimed calling for a non-racial South African society.

The NP government and the South African press categorized all attempts by black sportspeople to gain recognition and international acceptance as attacks on white sport. Captain G. H. F. Strydom, National Party MP, stated that assaults on white sport amounted 'to a declaration of war against White civilization in South Africa' (Merrett, 1996: 147). Indeed, the war and siege mentality was common in Afrikaner and later broad white South African discourse. The view of most white South Africans might be summarized in the foreword of Paul Dobson's book *Great Moments in South African Sport*:

> There is much to glory in and also much cause for sadness and nostalgia. Those good old days when South Africans were honourable combatants on the world's playing fields are no more.
>
> Opportunity will return and then above all memory of what has happened will be important, as we shall need the traditions of the past to build proud performances in the future. Our day will come again. (Dobson, 1988: 8)

Dobson's book refers to 23 'great moments' in South African sport, all of them discussing white South African successes. This was the continued state of thinking of most whites in 1988, the time when initial negotiations for sporting unity were being launched.

The government's response to SASA criticism was similar to that launched against other anti-apartheid groups during the 1950s. Officials raided its headquarters and seized papers in April 1960, and in 1961 banned Dennis Brutus, then executive secretary (Roberts, 1988). Brutus was subsequently arrested, released, shot in the back (allegedly trying to escape according to white officials) and finally forced into exile. For most activists like Brutus in the early 1960s the choice was between death, long-term gaol sentences or exile. As a result of government action, SASA officials broadened their attack, forming the South African Non-Racial Olympic Committee (SANROC) in 1963 with Brutus as President. As the name suggests, SANROC's immediate target was racially-based international sport and it fought to eliminate all racially-based organizations from international sporting competition. With government pressure on Brutus and others so strong, the organization fell apart within South Africa, but re-emerged in exile in 1966. The government never formally banned SANROC, though its leaders were banned, arrested and harassed. The conservative nature of international sporting bodies, plus the greater significance of team sports played against old imperial rivals, meant that the government initially did not see SANROC as a major threat.

The divisions created by segregation and apartheid fostered a deep hatred of white sports among many blacks, manifested in support for foreign teams who played against the Springboks and, significantly, in a movement to generate equality of opportunity in sport for all South Africans whatever their racial background. It must be remembered, however, that the majority of blacks were not involved in organized sport and, outside of soccer and boxing, most sports among blacks were dominated by the educated, Westernized elite. The paramount discourses surrounding the sports boycott movement were in effect not all that radical, and amounted to demands by educated blacks for inclusion within the dominant sporting structures.

The years between the late 1950s and 1990 marked a struggle between those attempting to eliminate white South Africa's international sporting contacts and those who tried to maintain those contacts. Those who supported the maintenance of international sporting contacts refused to understand the level of hatred that developed among those not allowed to represent South Africa internationally. To play at the highest levels, black South Africans had to go overseas if they could. International sporting bodies, dominated by members from Europe and North America, only recognized white South African national associations as official ones by the 1950s.

International sport was developed at a time when white-dominated countries of Western Europe and the USA created empires throughout the world with native peoples accorded unequal status. This white male 'old boys' world order has dominated modern sport for most of the past century.

Inequalities based on race and gender were maintained under the guise that sport is apolitical, and any attempt to change sport is merely bringing politics into sport. Thus, the non-racial sports movement faced difficult odds both inside South Africa and internationally.

Stoddart refers to the wide-ranging influence of sport in the informal authority systems of Empire, and that crucial to the success of sport was that 'despite considerable evidence to the contrary, sport gained a reputation as an egalitarian and apolitical agency which alone transcended the normal sectional divisions of the colonial social order' (Stoddart, 1988: 651). In South Africa, the rigidity of the social and political systems of segregation and apartheid frustrated this aim, and led to the politicization of sport rather than the opposite.

As the spectre of apartheid invaded all areas of South African society in the 1950s, calls for boycotts and sanctions against South Africa began to appear in the international community. Additionally, the struggle against apartheid and white domination of the black majority gathered force during the 1950s as the ANC and the PAC launched passive resistance campaigns. In sport, blacks began to resist continued divisions and many began to call for non-racial sports, whereby anyone could be selected for any team based on merit and not on the basis of race. The first priority, however, was to create unity across sporting organizations from the various disadvantaged communities in South Africa.

CRICKET: LIMITED PROTEST IN THE 1950s AND 1960s

After the Second World War, within black and liberation politics, alliances were made between Africans, Coloureds and Indians (with the support of a few whites) and this gradually appeared in cricket. From 1945 the South African Cricket Board of Control (SACBOC) worked to reunify black cricket, first through an umbrella body and inter-race tournaments (the first was at Natalspruit, Johannesburg, in March 1951). This initially involved Indian, Coloured and African boards, with the 'Barnato Board' (SACCB) changing its name to the South African Malay Cricket Board and joining other groups in inter-race tournaments in 1952. Racial classification was increasingly ignored, and from 1958 the SACBOC operated as a unified body and by 1961 was organized purely along provincial lines. Players often led the push for integration, against conservative officials eager to maintain their own administrative positions.

The Malays who abstained from the vote on the united body in 1958 (d'Oliveira, 1969) joined the SACBOC soon after, while the Africans, who voted for unification, soon broke away as the South African African Cricket

Board (SAACB). The SAACB's position reflected the difficulties for non-racial sport that divide-and-rule strategies created, as its officials were suspicious of Indian and Coloured bodies and more comfortable with a role as the protégé of the white South African Cricket Association, a position it occupied for a decade.

The opinions of black cricketing officials were relatively conciliatory when compared with opinions of other black sportspeople during the late 1950s and early 1960s. SASA, for example, viewed the SACBOC with scepticism. In 1959 the SACBOC made plans to invite to South Africa a strong West Indian side to be captained by Frank Worrell. Although supported by some, including West Indian cricket writer and Marxist intellectual C. L. R. James, SASA condemned the tour as unhelpful to the cause of black cricket development and ultimately supportive of apartheid.[1] Conditions for the use of the white cricket ground of Kingsmead in Durban for one tour match included the erection of temporary dressing rooms and toilets so that 'black' people would not 'contaminate' white facilities (*Post*, 4 May 1969). Although black sporting organizations raised over £5000 to cover expenses, and the government approved of the tour as the West Indians were only to play black teams, the tour was cancelled as a wide range of black political figures spoke out against it.

Basil d'Oliveira, by then the best black cricketer, angered by the cancellation, stated that he was 'particularly sad that they should be restricting the development of sport because they insist on mixing it up with politics. The ways of politicians, black and white are a mystery to me . . .' (d'Oliveira, 1969: 38). D'Oliveira's reaction and the calls for cancellation are representative of the two dominant views that emerged in the debates over international sporting contacts during the 1960s, and which continued up to the early 1990s. D'Oliveira's position was indicative of those who advocated the supposed 'bridge-building' possibilities of sport, dominant among whites and some black sportspeople. On the other hand, SASA and its successor SANROC pushed for boycotts, while the internal organization of non-racial sport in South Africa under the South African Council of Sport (SACOS) adopted the slogan of 'no normal sport in an abnormal society' during the 1970s.

The SACBOC's aims in the 1950s were limited, and moves toward supporting boycotts developed slowly within black cricket and rugby circles. In 1955 the SACBOC applied to join the ICC who, in return, asked it to prove its ability to conduct tours and attract sponsors (Odendaal, 1977). The SACBOC's request for a match against the 1956–7 MCC tourists, which white officials rejected, would have merely restored the position of 1892, when limited matches against touring teams were arranged for black teams in the Cape Colony.

Limited international contact opened for black South African cricketers, but only within a segregationist framework. India and Pakistan, two obvious links for Coloured and Indian cricketers, refused to tour South Africa in opposition to apartheid. In 1956, however, the Kenya Asians lost a three match series 2–0 to a team captained by d'Oliveira that included Salie Abed, thought by experts who saw him play to be one of the best wicketkeepers in the world. In 1958 a black South African team visited East Africa and Rhodesia (Zimbabwe), beating Kenya (three times), Uganda, Tanganyika and Zanzibar, as well as a Rhodesian Indian XI. This tour was to be the only international tour by a representative black cricket team in South Africa's history. Tom Reddick described d'Oliveira in the Hartleyvale (Cape Town) test of 1956 as 'a really good player' (*South African Cricket Review*, 1956: 11). However, much comment still dwelt on solidarity between the white groups, 'until the Afrikaner takes his place on our cricket fields no Springbok team can be said to be truly representative of our country's cricketing ability' (*South African Cricket Review*, 1956: 34). In 1959, a South African cricket magazine carried a front page picture of d'Oliveira above the ironic caption 'South African cricket captain' (Reddy, 1959).

Abe Adams explained the situation of black cricket in the 1950s and early 1960s succinctly, 'All cricket under the aegis of the SACBOC is played on matting over gravel pitches. They do not possess one ground which is even remotely up to international standard.' (Reddy, 1960: 3.) Denied access to Newlands and other top quality pitches, d'Oliveira recalls the 25 pitches at the Cape Town municipal ground, where Coloureds had to play, whose outfields overlapped one another (d'Oliveira, 1969: 22). Lenasia, Johannesburg's Indian township, had pitches evocatively named 'Gravel 1' and 'Gravel 2' (Odendaal, 1977: 237). Ray Robinson, writing in 1949, described pitches that 'no first class player would normally have set foot on, even if his life insurance was doubled' (d'Oliveira, 1969: 34). It is therefore amazing that Ivor J. 'Sakkie' Abrahams, called the 'prince of batsmen' and widely regarded as the greatest of all black South African cricketers (d'Oliveira, 1969: 34), Dol Freeman, d'Oliveira and others could score half-centuries and centuries with regularity on such pitches. There was clear understanding in black cricket circles that, without clarity in the law, government bodies that invoked 'tradition' maintained sporting apartheid to protect white cultural separateness and power (Hain, 1971).

From 1950 onwards, SACBOC endeavoured to develop ties with India and Pakistan. Financial problems thwarted a tour of India that the ICC would have probably vetoed in deference to SACA. Pressure from SACBOC, and later SASA, to recognize the position of black South African cricketers caused India, Pakistan and the West Indies to question the position of white South

Africa in the ICC, thereby creating, for the first time, cracks in its traditional imperialist and patronizing assumptions. This division was to characterize the ICC from the late 1950s onwards. Appeals to the MCC in the early 1950s were ignored and no challenge was made to SACA. Despite demonstrations against the 1960 South African cricket team in England, and pressure on New Zealand from within South Africa to cancel its 1961–2 tour, traditional imperial sporting ties persisted (Odendaal, 1977).

During the mid-1960s a few white cricketers were growing increasingly worried about the loss of long-standing ties with the white Commonwealth nations, and the effect this would have on their sporting careers. The NP government's insistence on cricket following 'traditional policy', and its attacks on critics, essentially prevented such cricketers from reaching their desired goal of broadening South Africa's international cricket links. At this stage of South Africa's cricket history, the basic issue (as in other sports) was that of mixed national trials. Although master of the ambivalent statement and policy of variable interpretation, the South African government was consistent in its rejection of mixed trials. In May 1970, when the South African cricket tour of England was cancelled, Prime Minister Vorster made it clear that cricket relations with the rest of the world were white relations (Lapchick, 1975). While the loss of any sporting contact was a blow to the apartheid regime, Vorster and the NP leadership were not that concerned about the cancellation of cricket tours or, as we will see, the expulsion of South Africa from the Olympic movement, when other international sporting opportunities remained, especially in the Afrikaner 'national' sport of rugby.

The opinion of blacks on segregated international sport was illustrated at the Johannesburg test match in December 1957, between South Africa and Australia, when black spectators booed the South Africans. This match occurred just before the start of the famous Treason Trial which attempted to convict many anti-apartheid leaders (including Nelson Mandela) of crimes against the South African state, so black opposition to the white team should not have been surprising. In response to local black hostility, the Transvaal Cricket Union threatened to raise the price of tickets (a common strategy in the 1990s) or to exclude blacks altogether (Lapchick, 1975). At Johannesburg black spectators were corralled in a wire netting compound; at Newlands, in Cape Town, in space under the trees with a separate entrance (d'Oliveira, 1969: 32).

Attempts to prevent the 1960 tour of England were mirrored by small demonstrations in England, marking an early international protest movement against South African racially-based sport. Charles Fortune described one gathering condescendingly, as 'a tattered and bleak little conglomeration of chilly looking adolescents . . . no more than the cats-paws of certain churchmen who seized on the visit of the cricketers as an opportunity to gain for themselves some public notice' (Fortune, 1960: 2). This shows an inability to understand that the old realities of imperial sporting culture were beginning to crumble. In addition, the statement appeared shortly after the Sharpeville massacre. Louis Duffus argued that protests against the tour marked the introduction of politics into South African cricket and he labelled protesters as 'sinister, ignorant and illogical' (Duffus, 1969: 164). The use of the term 'politics' became common in white South African discourses on sport and the beginnings of sporting boycotts. Racial segregation and internal and international responses to it were brushed aside by white writers and just called 'politics'. As the *Reader's Digest* celebratory history of white South Africa put it in 1981, in reference to (white) 'Sporting Life':

> Today more than 90 varieties of sport are played on a national basis by millions of South Africans of all races. For some it began as, and remained, a form of recreation; for others it was a driving need reflecting their determination to keep South Africa in the forefront of sporting nations. More would have made it to the very top *but for the intrusion of politics* and, in recent years, the exclusion of South African sportsmen [sic] from the world arena. [emphasis added] (Joyce, 1981: 135)

While opponents of white South African sporting organizations' policies of segregated sport were denigrated for their 'introduction' of politics into sport, it is clear that politics had always played a part in the exclusion of the majority of South Africans from non-racial sporting activities, and it merely took several decades for opposition to galvanize in order to mount a challenge against segregated sporting structures, as the case of black cricket associations suggests.

Few of the early sporting organizations promoted unity among black South African groups, but rather organized along segregated lines of African, Coloured, Malay and Indian. Despite this, seeds of non-racialism appeared as early as the 1890s in the SACRFB under the influence of Bud Mbelle (see Chapter 2). It was not until the late 1950s that black sporting officials and sportspeople began to unify their organizations, and promote non-racialism as an ideology for the ultimate means of playing sport in South Africa. The appearance of the mass democratic movement actively campaigning against apartheid in the 1950s clearly affected all areas of black society including sports. Many ANC leaders, for example, were keen athletes and many black politicians had historically played sport or supported, administered or patronized black sporting teams and associations. Nelson Mandela, for example, had played rugby and was a keen boxer in the 1940s and Albert Luthuli was a soccer administrator in the DDAFA in the 1930s.

The non-racial sports movement was morally powerful, and helped to cause the isolation of South Africa from international sport since racially-based selection was out of step with an international mythical/political ideology about the universality of sport and sporting opportunities. Ultimately, it was white South Africa who was judged to be out-of-step with global ideas and processes, though it took the non-racial sports movement over ten years of struggle before the real impact of the sporting boycott hit white South Africa. Initial successes occurred in Olympic sports and the Olympic movement itself, while the white old boys' imperial network fought to maintain contact in the face of the socialist and newly independent developing world nations' support of sporting boycotts.

SASA, SANROC AND INTERNATIONAL SPORT

Soon after the government began to make pronouncements about sporting policy and tradition, SASA began to target international isolation as a way to pressure the government for changes to segregated sport. Other developments in the 1950s also worked to harden the attitudes of black sportspeople. After Jake Ntuli won the British Empire flyweight boxing title in 1951, the government banned any international boxing contests involving blacks from being held in South Africa. In 1955, blacks were excluded from the new Free State rugby stadium on the grounds that tensions between white and black spectators would arise during international rugby matches. In 1957 a mixed table tennis team represented South Africa in the world championships in Sweden, but in 1959 the government withdrew the players' passports rather than allow such a situation to happen again. The ANC Youth League also mobilized support behind SASA's call for protests against the 1960 New Zealand rugby tour of South Africa, in which a racially-selected New Zealand team would play the Springboks and white provincial teams. As early as 1956, Trevor Huddleston identified the potential power of possible sporting boycotts in isolating South Africa's apartheid regime. Author and leader of the Liberal Party, Alan Paton, opened SASA's inaugural conference of National Sporting Bodies in Durban in 1959.

The difficulties faced by non-racial organizations in isolating white South African sport are illustrated in the fight to have South Africa expelled from the International Amateur Athletic Federation (IAAF). The Marquis of Exeter headed the IAAF in the 1960s and older IAAF member countries were granted eight votes while newer members (developing countries) were only granted two. This was done in an attempt to maintain Western control over the association. In 1964, the IAAF discussed the South African issue at its Tokyo Congress. The Marquis of Exeter decided the matter would be investigated and held over to the 1966 meeting. At that meeting, South Africa was left off the agenda and attempts to bring up the issue for debate were refused. The president allowed one question on the issue, to which he replied that great progress was being made and the matter should be held over again. The recalcitrance of Western IAAF officials continued through to 1968. At this meeting in Mexico a white South African was elected to represent Africa on the IAAF's executive. This time, however, the outcry was so great that the Sudanese representative had to be chosen as a replacement (de Broglio, 1970).

As for the Olympic Games, SANROC was in a strong position since the selection of white-only South African Olympic teams violated the IOC's Olympic Charter, which banned the exclusion of athletes based on race, religion or politics. Despite this provision, the IOC turned a blind eye to South African selection, as long as serious international protest was not readily evident. In the mid-1960s, the IOC consisted of 74 life members, over 30 of whom were from Western Europe (most were aristocrats), while only six were from Africa (two of these were a white South African and a white Kenyan). The IOC's first black member was Ade Ademola of Nigeria, only chosen in 1963. Reg Honey, the South African on the IOC, was also life president of the South African Olympic and National Games Association (SAONGA).[2]

In 1959 the IOC ignored SASA's attempts to force South Africa out of the 1960 Rome Olympics unless racist selection practices changed. The IOC appeared to accept Honey's word that discrimination was not practised, despite the weight of evidence Brutus supplied on behalf of SASA (de Broglio, 1970). IOC member Alexei Romanov, from the Soviet Union, formally brought up the issue at an IOC meeting in May 1959. Honey, in an amazing statement, replied to Romanov's charges against South Africa saying, 'I would like to state firmly and straight that I object, and my country objects to general allegations that South Africa displays racial discrimination, there is no evidence, none at all' (quoted in Quick, 1990: 22). SASA attempted to work with SAONGA to end racially-selected teams, offering to join SAONGA officials in forming a non-racial association (Macintosh et al., 1993).

The issue of South African participation in the 1964 Tokyo Olympics surfaced at the IOC meeting in Baden-Baden in October 1963. The IOC demanded that SAONGA abide by the IOC's policy of non-discrimination in selection, and obtain a commitment from the South African government to change racial policies in sport. SAONGA responded by picking several black athletes for the Games leading the IOC to drop its second condition. The government responded, however, by announcing the prohibition of mixed teams representing South Africa in international sport. As a result, the IOC barred South Africa from the 1964 Games.

While SAONGA worked to find a solution that would be acceptable to the IOC, other developments appeared that heightened protest against South Africa in sports. The formation of SANROC and the subsequent arrest and shooting of Brutus focused greater attention on the issue. SANROC, re-organized in exile, was aided by the formation of the Supreme Council for Sport in Africa (SCSA) in December 1966. The SCSA consisted of 32 African nations and led attacks on racist sport in South Africa and Rhodesia. Despite the formation of the SCSA and pressure from SANROC, the IOC still hoped for a compromise solution in 1967 that would allow South Africa to participate in the Mexico City Games of 1968. This occurred in part through the willingness of SAONGA to field a team consisting of 50 per cent black competitors for 1968. SCSA, however, in its first move told the IOC that its members would boycott the 1968 Games if South Africa participated. This prompted an angry response from the President of the IOC, Avery Brundage, who stated that the Games would go on even if only he and South Africa were present. The IOC remained hopeful of policy shifts from the South African government as Prime Minister Vorster looked to expand South Africa's international role. In April 1967, Vorster announced that South Africa could send a racially mixed team (selected in separate trials) to Mexico, so that the country could 'play its rightful role in world affairs' (Guelke, 1986: 127).

The IOC sent a three-man fact finding committee to South Africa in September 1967. The committee consisted of Lord Killanin (future IOC President) as Chair, Ade Ademola of Nigeria and Reginald Alexander, a white Kenyan. The committee reported that progress was being made and hoped that a mixed team would be sent to Mexico. The IOC voted in early 1968 with 36 members in favour of South African participation, while 25 were opposed. Prior to the Games, the IOC reversed its decision in the face of threatened boycotts by African-American athletes, the Soviet Union and SCSA member states. The IOC argued that they could not guarantee the safety of the South African team and withdrew the invitation.

In 1970, South Africa was finally expelled from the Olympic movement for violating the Olympic Charter. White South Africa was denied access to the Olympic Games after 1960 and an integrated team was finally allowed to participate only in 1992 in Barcelona, once a non-racial national Olympic committee was in place. As a result of South African exclusion, the NP government supported the establishment of the South African Games in 1969 to compensate white athletes for missing out on the Olympics. International athletes were invited but only a small handful from West Germany, New

Zealand and Britain competed. Separate games for black athletes began in 1970, but these were boycotted by most black sportspeople and spectators.

While the Olympic ban was important in the context of international politics, boycotts of traditional sporting competitions by traditional rivals did more to damage the psyche of white South Africans. While the government argued that the attack on South Africa in the Olympic movement was part of a Moscow-inspired communist plot against South Africa, it was harder to argue that when cricket and rugby relations came under attack. Two events were crucial in the initial moves against racist international sport – the d'Oliveira affair and the postponement of the 1967 All Black rugby tour of South Africa.

THE D'OLIVEIRA AFFAIR

The MCC's attitude concerning the d'Oliveira affair of 1968 was one of ignoring the realities of apartheid in South Africa. It tried not to embarrass the South African government while maintaining contact through international cricket channels. Peter Hain described the MCC's approach as one of 'feudal absolutism' (Hain, 1971: 105) that came out of the imperial inheritance. Billy Griffith, MCC Secretary, believed that South Africa was too important to be left out of world cricket, that South African teams abroad would play anyone, that within South Africa teams were subject to the law (which he like so many others confused with government policy), and that there was no colour bar in the constitution of SACA (d'Oliveira, 1969). The MCC frequently referred to 'traditional links' and 'essential communications' in justifying its approach. Dennis Brutus made use of these bland phrases after the election of Sir Cyril Hawker as President of the MCC, asking him if his position as Chairman of Standard Bank had anything to do with these traditional links and communications.[3]

An MCC call for volunteer stewards to protect the threatened 1970 South African cricket tour of England evoked a colonial image of loyalists putting down an uprising of dissident natives. Lord Monckton, quoted in the *Guardian* of 6 December 1968, described a Conservative Cabinet as a group of left wingers by comparison with the committee of the MCC (Lapchick, 1975: 254). Right-wing British support for the South African status quo was plain to see, and later manifested itself in the prosecution of Peter Hain for his role in the 'Stop the Seventy Tour' campaign, and in the public statements and government policies of Margaret Thatcher in the 1980s.

The problem for more rational right-wing elements was that continued support for the remnants of imperialism threatened the unity of the contemporary Commonwealth, and confounded the MCC's claim that it was acting in the long-term interests of cricket. English-speaking South African cricketers blamed the NP government and the 'stench of politics' (*South African Cricket Annual* 15, 1968: 5). These cricketers seemed oblivious to the fact that segregationist politics had governed the game since the end of the nineteenth century. Wilfred Wooller, for instance, a pillar of the British sporting establishment, clearly articulated traditional attitudes when he wrote to Brutus, 'We have no sympathy with your cause in any shape or form and regard you as an utter nuisance . . . I personally suspect your motives and your background'.[4]

The traditionalist view that cricket (and rugby) relations between South Africa and the white Commonwealth should remain unchanged frequently called on images of the Second World War. Wilfred Isaacs mentions his fighter pilot experience and the bonds of friendship created by that conflict in justifying the organization of tours in his name to England.[5] John Vorster's bitter claim that the 1968 MCC team's visit to South Africa was that of his political opponents was extraordinarily misdirected, given the effort the MCC had made to keep his country in the international fold (*Survey of Race Relations*, 1968: 300). In his supposed last minute plea to persuade the New Zealand Rugby Football Union (NZRFU) to cancel the 1981 Springbok tour, New Zealand Prime Minister Robert Muldoon evoked strong imperial memories when he discussed the role of New Zealand and South Africa as allies in war (Nauright and Black, 1995, 1996). What these attitudes did not consider was the role of Afrikaners in the war. Prime Minister Vorster himself served time in prison for opposing the war effort. Many Afrikaner nationalists openly supported the Nazis while others refused to come to the aid of 'die Engelse'.

In an attempt to head off momentum gathering for a boycott, SACA set up a trust fund of R50,000 to come out of tour profits that would help black cricket. SACBOC predictably spurned the offer as a bribe, but the SAACB accepted the money to fund a schools' week. By 1970, with the advent of isolation, some of the SACA establishment began to realize that South Africa's 'customary way of life' was ruining its international cricket future, and there was a need to 'modernize our way of thinking' (*South African Cricket Annual* 17, 1970: 7). SACA's decision to invite SACBOC to nominate two names for consideration for the Australian tour was vetoed by the South African government on 26 March 1971, which led to a walk off of cricketers at the Republic Festival match and trial at Newlands on 3 April 1971. For the first time a significant body of white South African cricketers had accepted that 'merit [should be] the only criterion on the cricket field' (*South African Cricket Annual* 18, 1971: 53).

Clearly by the early 1970s, South Africa was out of step with its old imperial partners and the loss of sporting ties emerged as one of the most potent psychological pressure points in international campaigns to oppose apartheid. Imperial links involving common ideology and long-standing relationships gave way to commercial expediency. The significance of cricket within white society, and the willingness of many leading English, Australian and later even some West Indian and Sri Lankan cricketers to travel to South Africa in return for handsome payouts, led government and big business to underwrite the cost of 'rebel' tours. Thus, during the period of isolation, South African cricket fans still saw the likes of Graham Gooch, Geoffrey Boycott, Greg Chappell and Alvin Kallicheran play against their national cricket team.

Supporters of the status quo and entrepreneurs found common cause in defying international sanctions and, at the same time, internal protest continued. In sport this was aided in March 1973 by the formation of the South African Council of Sport (SACOS), which at the time was one of the few effective voices of opposition to the apartheid regime (together with the emergent trade unions, the universities and the churches). Non-racial sporting competitions developed, attracting a handful of white players who gave up potential fame in white sport in the hope of contributing to the foundation of a democratic, liberated South Africa. Despite its early success in the Western and Eastern Capes, SACOS failed, however, to organize non-racial sport in any comprehensive way across South Africa. Nevertheless, SACOS combined internal pressure with SANROC's external pressure to steal the sporting initiative away from the imperial old boys' network and the apartheid state. The initial aim of SACOS was to have non-racial sporting bodies accepted by international organizations, but it evolved rapidly into an important voice against apartheid sport (Roberts, 1988).

The South African government and the opposition United Party, who between them controlled all but one seat in Parliament in the 1960s, debated the d'Oliveira issue, and the possible results of allowing Maoris to tour South Africa as part of an All Black touring side. Leaders of both parties had seen the country suffer as a result of the NZRFU's decision to cancel the 1967 tour of South Africa, and hoped an accommodation could be reached to restore normal rugby relations. The debate centred on whether a Maori or two touring South Africa, and competing against white rugby sides, would threaten the very foundations of apartheid. Hardliners saw Prime Minister Vorster's decision to allow Maoris to tour, if they were genuinely selected, as the beginning of the end of their system and way of life.

Led by cabinet member Albert Hertzog, son of former Prime Minister General J. B. M. Hertzog, four MPs left the National Party to form a new reformed National Party, the *Herstige Nasionale Party* (HNP) in 1969 over the issue of allowing mixed sporting teams to tour, and the compromising of Verwoerd's Christian nationalist vision of South Africa (Nauright, 1993; du Toit, 1991). The Broederbond, though initially divided on the issue, came down heavily in favour of government policy and the HNP was rapidly marginalized through the mobilization of Broeder power (Nauright, 1993). In the 1969 election, the HNP received only 3.59 per cent of the vote, compared with the NP's 54.86 per cent. The fact that such a debate took place, and occupied much parliamentary time, demonstrates the distance that white officials had to go in 1970 before there would be any form of genuinely desegregated sport.

During the 1970s, the government tried to head off additional boycotts through its 'multi-national' sports policy and some moves began to allow blacks to be selected in national teams. Under the multi-national policy, which became official government policy in 1971, South African sports teams could only be mixed in competitions that included foreign athletes or teams. A Broderbond committee, led by Andries Treurnicht, was formed to develop a sporting policy that could be sold overseas, and that would not change the realities of internal sporting practice. In 1976, the policy was extended to club level, though the NP refused to legislate specifically against mixed sport. Each main group had a 'national' team that could compete against other groups, but only initially at this national level.

The policy did nothing to alter apartheid sporting structures and worked to entrench the power of the establishment. Only white-dominated sporting bodies and their black affiliates received government subsidies. Contradictions appeared in central state policy, but much power remained at the local level where white councils controlled access to sporting facilities. Organizations outside white control did not receive money to support sport, from either the central government or local councils, while white bodies, in addition to government grants, received interest-free or low interest loans from local councils (Merrett, 1994a). Thus, for black sportspeople to have access to reasonable facilities, they would have to join a body affiliated to the white controlling body, the latter of which maintained control over official decision-making in the sport. In 1985, the NP announced it would de-politicize sport, thus ensuring the maintenance of white hegemony in sporting structures. With the removal of restrictions, establishment bodies were free to raise their presence in black areas and begin to combat groups like SACOS directly, through their greater access to state and capital resources.

While initially composite 'multi-national' teams were not to be given Springbok colours or status, the official policy by the late 1970s was to begin to include some blacks in national teams. The term 'multi-national' and the differentiation from the Springbok teams meant that such teams were unlikely to draw major segments of the South African population together in support of inter-group 'national' teams. Black athletes began to gain Springbok colours in the late 1970s, however. Vincent Tshabalala, an African golfer, was the first black athlete to receive Springbok colours in 1976, and in 1980 Errol Tobias, classified Coloured, was selected as a Springbok rugby player. Also in 1976, an Indian from what was then Rhodesia, I. Ramabhai, was allowed to play in the South African Open squash championships. These moves were all viewed by local and international protest groups as 'window-dressing', or attempts by sporting bodies and the government to include a small handful of acceptable blacks in order to maintain, or reinstate, international sporting contact and white domination of South African national teams in international competitions.

Tobias faced intense pressure (and threats) not only from people opposed to those involved in white sporting structures, but also from the white South African media and from rugby officials. Broederbond member Johann Claassen, manager of the 1981 Springbok tour of New Zealand, argued that a Tobias request to be considered for the test team in a different position reflected the 'inability of people without proper education to stand up to pressure'. Springbok team member Rob Louw commented that he could not imagine Claassen making such comments about any other team member (Louw, 1987: 148). Louw commented further on white attitudes towards Tobias in the early and mid-1980s:

> All true South African sportsmen have been delighted with the success that Errol had achieved. At the same time, some rather short-sighted people have regarded him as some sort of threat and have tried to play down his achievements. For some time it has been hard to acknowledge that Errol was actually one of the great Springboks. At the golf course overlooking my home, I was once confronted by a prominent local attorney who challenged me, 'I hear you're the father of Errol Tobias' black son' obviously referring to the fact that I am godfather to Errol's son. (Louw, 1987: 149)

Louw suggested that attitudes were changing by 1987, but acceptance by most whites of even one or two blacks in national rugby and cricket teams was reluctant and while only one or two players of colour remained in these teams, whites would find it easier to accommodate blacks in national teams.

Some white sports officials and athletes slowly began to call for more integration. In 1976 leading former Springbok track and field star runner Gert Potgieter called for open athletic competitions at club level, and stated that 97 per cent of sports bodies affiliated to SAONGA had voted to open the Springbok emblem to all races (Mirwis, 1976: 9). At about the same time, however, SARB President Danie Craven stated that the Springbok emblem should be for whites only, as Coloured teams had the Protea and African teams the Leopard, so a composite team should have a 'higher emblem'. Craven argued that he was against discrimination but for tradition (Heilbuth, 1976: 3). He was also widely quoted at the time as saying that there would be a black Springbok over his dead body. Unfortunately for him, this quote was remembered clearly by all those who opposed apartheid sporting structures, and it made unity much harder to achieve (Effendi, 1994).

Rugby writer Derek Wyatt states that in 1980 he asked Craven about black players and their possible contribution to rugby. "'Black players?" he responded, in that famous gravel voice of his. "Black players should stick to soccer, that's their game. We don't want black players in our game. It's our game"' (Wyatt, 1995: 103). Clearly Craven did not hold to this line of thinking completely as he supported the selection of Errol Tobias in Springbok teams during the early 1980s. This is not to say that Craven was a friend of the anti-apartheid movement in sports or, as the 1980 quote suggests, supported genuine de-segregation of rugby. Craven was first and foremost for the preservation of the power structures in the SARB, and for the continuance of the Springboks in regular international competition.

An insight into Craven's mentality regarding the maintenance of sporting contact, can be gleaned from comments years after on the 1981 cancelled match against Waikato in New Zealand. He argued that the New Zealand police should have beaten protesters off the field so the match could go ahead (*The 1981 Tour Ten Years After*). Craven also did not hesitate to support rebel tours and repeatedly argued that protest movements were bringing politics into sport. In 1989 Craven called for the end of apartheid but, in early 1990, he reiterated his support for rebel tours and refused to bring rugby into the sports moratorium then advocated by the National Sports Congress as part of the negotiations for unity in sports (Beattie, 1991). Craven did, however, challenge the government on occasion and also criticized the Broederbond and NP for bringing politics into sport. It seems clear that Craven's attitude, like many other white sports administrators not in the Broederbond, was short-sighted and meant doing whatever it took to maintain some form of international sporting contact without openly challenging government policy in any significant way.

While sporting isolation was nearly complete by 1971, rebel tours continued to bring quality cricketers to South Africa as did the South Africa Games in Olympic sports. In rugby, however, only Australia of the 'traditional' leading rugby nations broke off official contact, while New Zealand, England, Scotland, Wales, Ireland and France continued to play against South Africa into the 1980s.

BLOODSHED AND BROKEN DREAMS: SPRINGBOK–ALL BLACK RUGBY, BOYCOTTS AND THE CRISIS OF WHITE SOUTH AFRICAN IDENTITY

While much has been written on the moves to isolate South African sport and the relative success of sports sanctions, this literature, for the most part, has focused on the Olympics and cricket, missing the most crucial point of sporting pressure as it impacted on white identity. As we saw in Chapter 4, rugby was the one common point of cultural convergence in white South African culture and identity, particularly the Springbok emblem worn by the national team. The Springbok emblem and the success of the national team in international rugby predated apartheid, and the symbols of the white nation invented by Afrikaners such as the flag and the white anthem *Die Stem van Suid Afrika*.

In order to understand the relative impact of sporting sanctions on the white psyche and will to resist the ending of apartheid, we need to examine the parameters of international rugby relations. To white South Africans, matches against arch-rivals New Zealand and the British Lions, and tours of New Zealand and the British Isles were of most significance. The first large-scale protest against a South African team touring abroad took place during the Springbok tour of Britain and Ireland in 1969–70. While the protest movement was significant in mobilizing international support against South Africa, protests against the Springboks were constructed as being led by anti-authoritarian radicals. Even in rugby accounts of the mid-1990s there was an unwillingness to see what lay behind such protests, so they were seen only as being against sport, as shown in Greyvenstein:

> With demonstrators chanting messages of hate from the terraces and with tin-tacks and smoke bombs on the playing fields, Dawie de Villiers and his Spring-boks completed their tour of the United Kingdom in the winter of 1969/70 under conditions no South African team must ever be subjected to again.
>
> The tour will be remembered for the Springbok's dignity and restraint under pressure and provocation, and for moral courage and determination of their opponents and hosts who refused to be intimidated by the most violent campaign ever to be conducted against a group of sportsmen. It will be remembered, also, for the brave and patient British police-force who bore the brunt of abuse even more directly than the Springboks. Whatever convictions motivated the demonstrators were obscured by their uncouth behaviour; the slogans devalued by their spitting and cursing (Greyvenstein, 1995: 168).

Thus those who fought so hard to eliminate apartheid in sport and in society are branded a group of spitting uncouth radicals in celebratory rugby histories which do nothing to challenge the beliefs of rugby supporters. Given the nature of the game of rugby, and its attendant mysogynist culture, it is ironic that demonstrators are labelled 'uncouth' or denigrated for swearing.

Trade between South Africa and New Zealand has always been minimal and other than a common political connection through the British Empire and Commonwealth to the early 1960s, the nations have had little reason to be closely connected other than through rugby. New Zealanders and white South Africans have a strong sense of each other's geography and history, and this is filtered through the rugby context in the potted histories given in tour programmes. In both countries writers and players have commented that the pinnacle of any man's rugby career is when he has the opportunity to play in a Springbok–All Black match.

Rugby relations between South Africa and New Zealand since the 1920s, however, have been a persistent source of debate, especially in New Zealand. The origins of these debates are rooted in the two countries' differing experiences of race relations. New Zealand's general policy approach, since the Treaty of Waitangi of 1840, attempted to include Maoris within a wider, albeit white-defined, society, while South African racial policies in the twentieth century have been based on principles of racial segregation and white domination. In 1921 the Springboks played the Maori All Blacks (winning by a point). The emerging difference in racial attitudes was summed up after the match by a South African reporter, named Blackett, who was 'sickened' at the sight of white New Zealanders cheering for Maoris against members of their own race (Nepia and Maclean, 1963: 26). Here we can see the strength of a white imperial brotherhood in operation, but the Afrikanerization of rugby had not reached the levels of the 1940s and 1950s. The exclusion of George Nepia in the All Black touring party of 1928 was seen as a given and not even debated in the New Zealand press, who only lamented that a white Nepia could not be found. Nepia finally went to South Africa as an 'honorary white' tour commentator in 1970, when Maoris were included as members of an All Black touring side.

Exclusion of Maoris from tours of South Africa sparked little controversy in New Zealand before the Second World War. After the NP set about implementing their apartheid policies, however, sporting contacts began to be questioned by a few New Zealanders. This took several years to develop as there was no protest during the 1956 Springbok tour of New Zealand. It seemed as if the whole country united behind the single goal of defeating South Africa to avenge the humiliating defeat of 1949. In those days before television and close links between New Zealand and the outside world, awareness of South Africa was largely confined to its status as a rugby power and an ally in the British Empire and in the war (Pearson, 1979; Phillips, 1987; Roger, 1991).

When debate developed in 1959, it centred on the exclusion of Maoris from trials for the proposed 1960 All Black tour of South Africa and the NZRFU's complicity with South African requests that they be excluded, rather than the internal racial policies of the South African government. The slogan protesters developed was 'No Maoris, no tour', and anti-tour petition drives were organized in New Zealand by the Citizens' All Black Tour Association (CABTA) and by groups within South Africa, including SASA. Thousands of South Africans and New Zealanders petitioned the New Zealand government to cancel the tour, with CABTA obtaining over 162,000 signatures out of a total population of less than two million adults. Still, New Zealand's Prime Minister Walter Nash decided not to interfere with the decision of the NZRFU on the tour, confirming his Labour Party's then policy of 'non-interference' with sporting bodies (Sorrenson, 1976: 53). This non-interference stand of the Nash and subsequent New Zealand (and British), governments meant that rugby relations survived much longer than those in other sports. While South Africa was effectively removed from most international sports by the early 1970s, rugby relations continued with only a few interruptions into the 1980s.

In explaining the resilience of rugby in resisting political efforts to isolate South Africa, we have to examine the historical connections between elite male groups, the historic political conservatism of the International Rugby Board (IRB) and its members such as the NZRFU. The NZRFU and SARB were adamant that tours between the two countries should continue even as popular protest increased dramatically in the 1970s and 1980s. Protests in New Zealand increased sharply after the South African police massacred peaceful protesters at Sharpeville on 21 March 1960. In protest over the killings, the New Zealand Cargo Workers' Union passed a resolution strongly condemning the loss of life, and urged that the situation 'now makes it imperative that no New Zealand team at all should go to a country with such a black record of mass murder' (*Cape Argus*, 24 March 1960). Despite the growing domestic protests and emerging international opposition resulting from Sharpeville, the NZRFU went ahead with the 1960 tour.

One final reason why the NZRFU and SARB were reluctant to stop tours was that they turned in massive profits, as the All Blacks and Springboks filled every ground on which they played. In an era when the sport received little direct money from the government, such money was seen as vital to the development of the game. Finally, through its complicity in selection policy it is hard to conclude that the NZRFU was anything less than racist in its own attitudes.

From 1960 onwards, the South African government realized the threat protesters in New Zealand could pose to future rugby relations. In addition, after South Africa was barred from the Olympic Games in 1964 and 1968, and expelled from the Olympic movement in 1970, the continuation of international rugby tours became a crucial element in South Africa's international sports and broader political strategies. Both the ruling NP and the opposition United Party rationalized expulsion from the Olympics as part of a Moscow-orchestrated communist onslaught. Both parties, however, viewed international rugby (and to a lesser degree, cricket) as an integral part of white South Africa's historical and cultural ties to European 'civilization'.[6] As a result of these developments, New Zealand was targeted by both the South African government, the international sports boycott movement, and non-racial South African sporting organizations in exile as the key to successful sports boycott strategies.

South African Prime Minister Hendrick Verwoerd, the architect of apartheid, chose to keep quiet during the run-up to the 1965 Springbok tour of New Zealand, refusing to comment on whether Maoris would be excluded from future tours to South Africa. But, during the tour he stated that all future teams touring South Africa would have to abide by South Africa's 'local custom'. It was clear to New Zealanders that this meant no Maoris. Prime Minister Keith Holyoake subsequently announced in his Parliament that New Zealand could not 'be fully and truly represented by a team chosen on racial lines' (*NZ Hansard*, 7/9/65: 2527). As a result, the NZRFU called off the proposed All Black tour of 1967, the only time that they followed the general wishes of a New Zealand government in preventing tours. Significantly, it was a National Party conservative government that the NZRFU listened to. In 1973 and 1985, they were to oppose the Labour government, thus forcing the government to face the political fallout caused by a tour cancellation.

In 1968, two years after Verwoerd's assassination, Prime Minister Vorster dramatically decided that, rather than face the possibility of no further tours of South Africa by the All Blacks, he would allow the NZRFU to send Maoris on forthcoming tours. This step was the first real attempt by the South African government to alleviate international pressure in the sports arena, and heralded a myriad of mildly reformist measures over the next twenty years. Consequently, in 1970, the NZRFU sent a team that included three Maoris and one Samoan to South Africa.

Protests against the 1970 tour in New Zealand, and again against the proposed 1973 Springbok tour of New Zealand, were partly motivated by concerns that Christchurch might lose its bid to host the 1974 Commonwealth Games and that New Zealand would be ostracized in international sporting and diplomatic circles. These concerns arose, in part, out of New Zealand's record of support under its National Party for South Africa in international organizations. New Zealand's record on United Nations' resolutions against

South Africa in the 1960s was regarded by non-white Commonwealth states, among others, as clearly supportive of South Africa, as it voted against or abstained on nearly every resolution that condemned apartheid (Sorrenson, 1976: 39–42). New Zealand also staunchly defended South Africa at the IOC meeting that expelled it from the Olympic movement. In addition, African Commonwealth leaders used Australia's new tough stance on sporting contacts with South Africa to pressure the New Zealand government to take a similar stand against competition with South Africa until racial discrimination in sport was abolished.

In 1969, South Africa sent one of its most senior diplomats, P. H. Philip, to New Zealand to serve as Consul-General. Philip distributed much pro-government information on South Africa, wrote numerous newspaper columns, and spoke to countless groups during his tenure, which lasted until 1976. He also hosted numerous social functions to which many All Blacks and National Party MPs and Cabinet ministers were invited. Commentators at the time pointed out that he was a very senior diplomat to be sent to such an unimportant country as New Zealand, with whom South Africa's economic relations (and strategic links) were 'insignificant' (Sorrenson, 1976). Vorster's government, however, clearly thought the maintenance of rugby links with New Zealand was important both for white support at home, and from the standpoint of international relations and attempts to combat growing sanctions movements.

Despite its expulsion from the Olympic movement, and banning from most other international sporting organizations in the 1960s and early 1970s, South Africa remained firmly entrenched on the IRB, along with other white-dominated countries (New Zealand, Australia, England, Scotland, Ireland, Wales and France). To the government and many white South Africans, sporting isolation could be tolerated as long as rugby could still be played. Norman Middleton, President of SACOS stated in 1976 that:

> It has to be realized that to genuine Afrikaners – the NP is substantially Afrikaner from top to bottom – rugby of all sports has a mystical significance and importance. I don't think that the Government could care less about such sports as cricket and soccer. They don't really mean much to the true Afrikaner.
>
> Therefore the expulsion of the country from international competition in these sports doesn't mean too much. BUT RUGBY IS DIFFERENT. RUGBY IS THE AFRIKANER'S SECOND RELIGION. (*Daily News*, 2 September 1976, emphasis in original)

Springbok–All Black rugby was again threatened in 1973. A proposed tour of that year was cancelled by the newly-elected Labour government headed by Norman Kirk. Kirk's initial policy was one of non-interference, but he commissioned a police report on the possible levels of protest during a South African tour. The police report stated that more than 10,000 demonstrators could be mustered in the major cities of Auckland, Wellington and Christchurch if the Springboks toured. In addition, the police stated that the tour would 'engender the greatest eruption of violence the country has ever known' (Sorrenson, 1976: 61). This report, combined with threats from black Commonwealth countries to boycott the 1974 Christchurch Commonwealth Games, eventually forced Kirk's hand. The NZRFU, for its part, left it to the Prime Minister to determine the fate of the tour, calculating that he (and not they) would be stigmatized by a decision to cancel. An attempt by SARB to include token blacks in the tour party was exposed on the eve of the tour, and Kirk was finally forced to call it off. Subsequently, in 1974 he reversed Labour's historic position, stating that any team representative of any sporting organization which practised apartheid at any level would not be welcome in New Zealand.

Politically, the cancellation of the rugby tour proved damaging to the New Zealand government. The new, populist National Party leader, Robert Muldoon, had made rugby relations with South Africa a campaign issue in the 1975 election, and Muldoon's use of rugby prompted cartoonists to portray Muldoon and SARB President Danie Craven as running mates during the campaign. Although the Springboks did not immediately come to New Zealand, the All Blacks toured South Africa in 1976. As international outrage mounted over the juxtaposition of the All Black tour with the Soweto student uprisings, 22 African countries boycotted the 1976 Montreal Olympics in protest against New Zealand's participation. Within South Africa, the tour allowed whites to focus on rugby, which helped to divert attention away from the student revolt. The South African media gave the tour prominent coverage and match results made front page headlines. The Olympic boycott allowed the South African media and government to portray African opposition as a continuation of the communist-inspired plot against white South Africa, and to hold the New Zealanders up as friends and allies against a supposedly unfair international attack.

In 1977, the Canadian government's effort to avoid a repeat boycott at the forthcoming 1978 Edmonton Commonwealth Games, again over New Zealand–South Africa rugby links, led to the adoption by the Commonwealth Heads of Government of the 'Gleneagles Declaration on Apartheid and Sport'. The Gleneagles Agreement called on all Commonwealth governments to discourage sporting contacts with South Africa (Macintosh, Greenhorn and Black, 1992; Nauright and Black, 1994; Payne, 1990). Spearheaded by the Canadian government and orchestrated by the Commonwealth Secretariat, it subsequently emerged as perhaps the most important international landmark in generating more comprehensive sports sanctions. Muldoon's agreement to Gleneagles facilitated the success of the Edmonton Games, but the Agreement was framed in such broad principle that considerable manoeuvrability remained for Muldoon if he thought it politically expedient at home not to act against South African links.

SHOCKING TWO NATIONS: THE 1981 SPRINGBOK TOUR OF NEW ZEALAND

In 1981, New Zealand society was split and shaken by a Springbok rugby tour. Many New Zealanders questioned themselves, and debated and fought with others including members of their own families, as massive demonstrations greeted each match. An opinion poll taken in New Zealand during the tour showed that 49 per cent opposed the Springbok presence, while 42 per cent favoured the tour. The crisis point in the tour was on 25 July when hundreds of protesters occupied the rugby stadium in Hamilton, forcing the cancellation of the second match of the tour.

South Africans viewed this incident live on television, and whites must have been rudely awakened to the depth of animosity felt by many New Zealanders towards 'their boys'. Images of the New Zealand police beating protesters and fortress-like rugby stadiums behind barbed wire 'shocked the nation' in South Africa (*Eastern Province Herald*, 31 August 1981). The South African government was openly hostile to television in the 1950s, 1960s and early 1970s. Dominant thinking in the government and Afrikaner nationalist circles was that television would erode the cultural differences apartheid sought to construct, and also threaten the society from without with American liberalism and promotion of racial contact (Nixon, 1994). The government reluctantly allowed television in under the tight control of the state-controlled South African Broadcasting Corporation (SABC). Limited programming was shown in the late 1970s and 1981 heralded the first overseas rugby broadcasts. The live broadcast of anti-apartheid protesters confirmed the government's worst fears, as it was difficult to censor live broadcasts from overseas.

Confronted with such dramatic levels of hostility for the first time, the Springboks returned from New Zealand with 'more enlightened views on race' and began to question the necessity of many apartheid laws (*Sunday Times*, 11 October 1981). The 1981 tour also caused political tension as the liberal opposition party, the Progressive Federal Party (PFP), opposed the tour, making it an election issue.

From 1981 until 1992 no official rugby tours between South Africa and New Zealand took place and South Africa was effectively isolated from playing IRB countries after an England tour of 1984. In 1982, the

Commonwealth Games Federation adopted a Code of Conduct which gave the Gleneagles Agreement clear and tough guidelines in the context of the Commonwealth Games (New Zealand and Britain abstained on the code). Subsequently, in 1985, the NZRFU announced plans to mount another All Black tour of South Africa. However, this time, the recently elected Labour government of David Lange vigorously opposed the tour. It was finally cancelled when New Zealand's High Court granted an interim injunction in *Finnigan* v. *The NZRFU*, a case brought by Auckland lawyers representing a rugby club member, in which they argued that the tour would be contrary to the NZRFU's statutory commitment to promote and foster the game in New Zealand.

Despite the cancellation of the 1985 tour, secret negotiations were held behind the scenes to arrange for top New Zealand rugby players to tour South Africa. Louis Luyt, President of the Transvaal Rugby Football Union, invited 30 New Zealand players to visit South Africa as individuals who would then play South African teams. The players secretly left New Zealand to the embarrassment of the government, the SARB, the NZRFU and the IRB, all of whom denied prior knowledge of the tour. That Luyt and some New Zealand players and officials would go to such lengths to arrange a tour provides clear evidence for the strength of South African–New Zealand rugby ties. Even the opposition PFP supported the tour, contrary to their stand on the 1981 tour, once plans were revealed, only lamenting the way in which it had to be arranged (*Cape Times*, 16 April 1986). The tour was sponsored by *The Yellow Pages* to the tune of R2.5 million and rumours abounded that the players were paid R110,000 each, though tour manager Colin Meads only admitted years later that players were paid. Such expenditure on sports tours to try and outmanoeuvre the international boycott movement was not unique, though clearly contrary to the laws of the IRB.

The New Zealand 'Cavaliers' tour was significant in that the Springboks won the series by three matches to one and it did much to shore up white South African confidence in the midst of economic recession, rising black protest, an accompanying State of Emergency, and increasing international isolation. In 1987 the first Rugby World Cup (RWC) was held and the All Blacks, including several former Cavaliers, swept to victory.

The success of New Zealand only a year after the 1986 tour precipitated comments on the relative strengths of the All Blacks and the Springboks, with many articles and letters to editors lamenting the fact that the 'true world champion' could not be decided in a subsequent match between the two teams.[7] Craven argued, however, that the effects of isolation had eroded the Springboks' ability to compete against the top sides of New Zealand, France and Australia.[8] Wynand Claassen added to Craven's opinion in 1991 after

South Africa was not allowed to play in the second RWC, stating that the exclusion 'should have made us come to terms with the fact that the Currie Cup is no longer sufficient to keep our rugby on a strong footing or to keep our top players sharp, ready and able to take on any country in the world right now. . . . We simply cannot afford to wait one day longer to get our rugby house in order' (*Star*, 6 October 1991). Craven, realizing the Springboks' coming isolation, tried to arrange a tour by the Australian Wallabies, but the Australian government would not allow a tour. Craven then tried to arrange a rebel tour that resulted in a World XV coming to South Africa for the SARB centenary in 1989. South African Breweries, a major sponsor of 'official' and rebel white sports in South Africa, and of international sport in the new South Africa, funded the World XV. Initially a Welsh team was to come with players being paid, but a full side could not be recruited. Welsh players who came as part of the World XV were paid between £20,000 and £30,000 each (Wyatt, 1995).

Despite concerns about the readiness of the Springboks to return to their former glories, the opportunity to resume international rugby contacts was grasped immediately by rugby officials in late 1991 and 1992 as SARU and the SARB agreed to form the new amalgamated entity, the South African Rugby Football Union (SARFU). Single test matches with New Zealand and the 1991 World Cup Champions the Australian Wallabies were hastily arranged for August 1992 to mark South Africa's return to the international fold. The symbolism of rugby in the context of rapid political changes, however, went counter to the hopes of the ANC who thought that the return of international rugby would merely placate recalcitrant whites.

In effect, the Springboks were excluded from major international rugby from 1982 onwards; however, on close inspection the time South Africa was not able to play top quality teams was very short compared with other sports. Tests were played against 'South America' in 1982 and 1984, though the teams were essentially the Argentinian test side led by Hugo Porta. In 1984 the Springboks played England, and in 1986 the rebel New Zealand 'Cavaliers', which included many All Blacks who subsequently helped New Zealand win the first RWC in 1987. South Africa was, however, not allowed to play in the World Cups of 1987 and 1991, and soon after 1987, negotiations were underway for rugby unity.

South Africa was thus isolated for a period of about six years, though tests were played against invitation 'World XV' teams after 1986. So why was the rugby boycott so limited? Test series between New Zealand and South Africa, the Lions and South Africa, and South African tours of Britain, in particular, were large money spinners for the rugby unions involved. The 1976 All Black tour of South Africa set a record for profits for tours during the apartheid era, while the NZRFU's refusal to cancel the 1981 tour was partly based on hopes of similar profits. The lure of profits quickly brought South Africa back into the international sporting arena by mid-1992. The outcomes of South Africa's 'return' and the new sporting structures of 'unity' will be analysed in the final two chapters.

<h2 style="text-align:center">ASSESSING THE IMPACT OF SPORTING SANCTIONS
ON SOUTH AFRICAN SOCIETY</h2>

While many authors have discussed the relative success or failure of sanctions both in general and in the specific South African case, few have attempted a detailed analysis of sporting sanctions. A measurable impact of sports sanctions is hard to determine as it is not possible to quantify an exact effect. It is possible to suggest, however, that the psychological impact of sporting sanctions had perhaps the most potent role in undermining white South African confidence and complacency. In particular the postponement and cancellation of rugby tours hit white society at its core.

The expulsion from the Olympic movement and many of its attendant international bodies could be explained as part of a 'communist'- led plot to undermine South Africa. The cricket boycott, while important, was felt most keenly in the English-speaking white community. The massive amounts of money poured into 'rebel' tours by Anglo-American, South African Breweries and other companies, who received tax breaks for their efforts, also meant that a semblance of top-level international competition could be maintained, or at least legitimated to white South Africans starved of international sporting and other links. Top South African cricketers such as Clive Rice, Jimmy Cook and Alan Donald had careers in English county cricket which South African fans could follow.

In rugby, however, the situation was different. Up to the end of the apartheid era the IRB's list of full members was South Africa, New Zealand, Australia, England, Scotland, Wales, Ireland and France – all white Western nations with whom South Africa had a long and prosperous relationship in rugby union. The postponement of the planned 1967 All Black tour precipitated the first reforms in apartheid and unleashed a slow, but ever increasing flow of government reform. The cancellation of the 1985 All Black tour, the victory over the rebel New Zealand 'Cavaliers' in 1986, and the barring of South Africa from the inaugural RWC in 1987 combined to force rugby officials to seek negotiations and contributed to a massive public outcry at the exclusion. Rugby officials met with the non-racial SARU and the ANC in Harare in 1988, a move which led President F. W. de Klerk to brand Danie Craven and Louis Luyt of the SARB as traitors to white South Africa.

By 1989, sporting officials were well ahead of politicians in negotiations for a new non-racial order, though not all non-racial sportspeople agreed with the negotiation strategy. SACOS, in particular, clung to its slogan of 'no normal sport in an abnormal society', but it lost ground rapidly to the new National Sports Congress (NSC). The NSC was established in 1989 to oversee negotiations for sporting unity that would bring about non-racial sport in South Africa. SACOS suffered because it had been outmanoevered, and it had never really expanded successfully from its Western Cape and Port Elizabeth power bases. Many African sportspeople saw SACOS as a Coloured organization that had done too little to develop non-racial sport in other parts of the country, but it was hampered by the incredible restrictions of apartheid and a lack of a large resource base. Despite that, many aligned with the NSC believed their criticisms of SACOS to be legitimate and their move to a negotiated settlement timely.

ANC officials supported the moves to sporting unity, as they quickly identified a return to international sport as a key arena from which to reach out to whites who were afraid of some kind of cultural swamping in a non-racial South Africa where everyone had the vote. While negotiations for unity were difficult, and a long process involving the efforts of hundreds of sporting officials, many sporting organizations agreed on unity by the end of 1991. After the unbanning of the ANC in 1990 and the release of long-term political prisoners, the international sports boycott was speedily (and some would argue unjustifiably) abandoned. In his rush to get all the world to his hometown Olympic Games in Barcelona for 1992, IOC President Juan Antonio Samaranch announced the recognition of the new National Olympic Committee of South Africa (NOCSA) in July 1991. With NOCSA and South Africa officially back in the Olympic movement, it was difficult for other international associations to resist the urge to re-establish links with South Africa.

In November 1991 the South African cricket team went to India on a hurriedly arranged tour as a replacement for Pakistan, and in March 1992 South Africa made a full return to international cricket by participating in the Cricket World Cup in Australia and New Zealand. The World Cup coincided with a whites' only referendum on negotiations called by State President de Klerk and is discussed further in the next chapter. Finally, in July 1992 South Africa played single test matches in rugby against the old enemy New Zealand and 1991 RWC champions Australia. So in the short space of four years, South Africa went from sporting division at home and isolation abroad, to unity at home and full international interaction in global sporting competitions. The cycle was perhaps completed when Samaranch announced the appointment of former SANROC leader and NOCSA President Sam Ramsamy to the IOC in 1995. As Booth (1995) argues, unity has not meant the real empowerment of black sportspeople. In many cases, black sports officials became ceremonial figureheads, often on large salaries, alongside a core of old establishment officials who called on their supposed expertise to maintain key administrative positions.

South African sport was divided until the late 1980s between democrats, with a non-racial vision for society, and the establishment, with a self-serving and limited understanding of the role of sport in a changing and rapidly globalizing world. Gone were the days when sport was a white old boys club of Europeans, North Americans, Australasians and southern Africans. In international terms change was reflected in support for and against the sports boycott of South Africa. The ultimate effectiveness of the sports boycott was to force white sporting officials to move ahead of politicians in the latter part of the 1980s, as various piecemeal attempts by whites to stave off boycotts failed to achieve the compromises necessary for the continuance of international sport. SANROC and SACOS took the lead in pressing for international isolation of white South African sport. As SANROC was based in London and SACOS was centred among Coloured intellectuals in the Western Cape, however, little successful sporting development among blacks took place in the 1970s and 1980s that did not occur within the established white structures, to which some black associations affiliated, or in autonomous or local leagues in areas outside the Western Cape. SACOS sport was well developed in the areas around Cape Town by 1990, but it was quickly outpaced as other officials raced past them in the negotiation process. Traditional links, previously for white South Africans only, had been restored but the ideological bond was now sealed by commercialism rather than racial superiority and political, social and economic power.

THE LIMITS OF RACE-BASED PROTEST

A final comment on the struggle for non-racial sport must be made here. This has to do with the limitations of protest based primarily on racial inclusion. Many of the problems that SACOS had in organizing non-racial sport, outside of Western Cape townships, stemmed from its inability to command resources and loyalties across a wide political spectrum and geographical space. Although many involved in the non-racial sports movements were genuinely interested in altering the fundamental class and gender structures within South African society, many campaigned primarily on the issue of merit selection – that is on a liberal doctrine of inclusivity.

The results of sporting 'unity' in the New South Africa demonstrate the limits of the non-racial protest, as many non-racial leaders quickly accepted posts in new sporting structures – which resembled the old ones – and quickly became enmeshed in the global sports power system. Sam Ramsamy who led SANROC after Dennis Brutus, for example, now sits on the IOC, the very organization that had to be cornered into banning white South African teams from participating in the late 1960s. This is not to suggest that the non-racial sports struggle was a failure or did not pressure the South African government in significant ways. The movement was, perhaps, the most successful at bringing international action against apartheid structures in South African society. The non-racial sports movement, however, was unable for a variety of reasons, both of its own making and beyond its control, to generate alternative structures or models for sport within South Africa, especially in disadvantaged communities. As a result of the failings of SACOS in creating a mass sporting base, and with SANROC still in exile, many black sports officials with the support of the ANC, sought to place sport at the forefront of negotiations for a non-racial society in the late 1980s, attempting to create a new unified national identity and to reconcile whites who were afraid of black domination.

NOTES

1. Letter from Dennis Brutus (SASA) to Rashid Varachia (SACBOC) dated 28 February 1959; and to West Indies Cricket Board of Control dated 20 March 1959 in the Brutus Papers, Borthwick Institute, University of York, England (CAS MF 15 and Box II).
2. The name of the association was changed after South Africa became a Republic in 1961 and was expelled from the Commonwealth and the Commonwealth Games Association.
3. Letter from Dennis Brutus to Sir Cyril Hawker, chair of MCC Council, 29 May 1969, in the Brutus Papers.
4. Letter from Wilfred Wooller, Glamorgan County Cricket Club secretary to Dennis Brutus, 31 December 1968 in the Brutus Papers.
5. Letter from Wilfred Isaacs to Dennis Brutus, 26 May 1969 in the Brutus Papers.
6. For examples of this, see Republic of South Africa, *House of Assembly Debates (SA Hansard)*, 8 February 1967, 924–936.
7. Of the leading All Blacks in the RWC winning side, only David Kirk and John Kirwin did not tour with the Cavaliers.
8. *Cape Times*, 22 June 1987. Craven stated that 'We need overseas tours to maintain our high ceiling. . . . We are losing out on international competition and it has affected our rugby.'

7

SOUTH AFRICA IN UNION? SPORT, 'UNITY', IDENTITIES AND THE RAINBOW NATION

Our young democracy witnessed the ability of sport to act as a catalyst to bring people together, share excitement and build a nation.

> South African Minister of Sport, Steve Tshwete, commenting on South Africa's victory in the 1995 Rugby World Cup. (South African Press Association, 22 June 1995)

The Springbok reminds me too much of the old South Africa when the race wars were everywhere including on the sportfields; when blacks were pointedly excluded from being part of that world, part of the camaraderie of the Springboks.

Both the flag and the national anthem of the past regime forced us out of South African citizenship.

> Aggrey Klaaste, *Cape Argus*, 10 October 1995

As the post-apartheid period began and South African sport became unified, South Africa rapidly returned to the international fold in sport and other activities. At the time of unity, two paths appeared possible among those interested in South African sport. The first was that of developing the underused resources of the majority of the population, particularly in sports that had historically been dominated by whites such as cricket, rugby union and Olympic sports. The legacies of segregation and apartheid were indeed great. The people of Uitenhage near Port Elizabeth, for example, had one soccer and one rugby field to serve its population of 250,000 in the early 1990s. The other path, advocated by many senior sports administrators and sponsors of elite sport, was to race headlong into full international competition in all sports as soon as international bodies reinstated South Africa. While the first option deserved praise as it would have given sport a mass base and worked to increase participation, the latter won out as the global capitalist sports system is too powerful for nations such as South Africa to resist. Additionally, Mandela and the ANC invested sport with the role of reaching out to worried whites who feared what majority rule would mean to their 'way of life'. As the opening quotes to this chapter suggest, though, the legacy of sport as a racist activity from the apartheid era meant that the transition to unifying sporting structures was not as simple as the ANC might have hoped.

Already set in motion was a massive struggle which was being waged against apartheid sport, as those opposing the NP government increasingly identified international sporting links as an area of vulnerability, where white South Africans would feel the pain of isolation perhaps more intensely than in any other sphere. Equally, white sporting and governmental officials identified international sporting contacts as crucial in their efforts to shore up white angst over the increasing pace of internal and international protest in the period from the mid-1960s through the late 1980s. As a result of these divisions, segregation and the separate structures of 'establishment' and non-racial sporting competitions, the possibility of drawing South Africans together through sport appeared a daunting task in the early 1990s.

Two events occurred which were crucial to this process of 'nation-building' through sport. Perhaps ironically, though, each involved a sport that was entrenched in white power circles – the 1992 Cricket World Cup and the 1995 Rugby World Cup, the latter hosted by South Africa. In addition to these events, however, were many others that rapidly reincorporated South Africa in international sporting structures, and were promoted in the process of 'nation building'. One further event involving the national soccer team also played a significant role, as the team won the Africa Nations Cup in early 1996. This chapter, and the next, explore the significance and meanings of these events and South Africa's return to international competition in other sports.

While many have rushed to embrace sport as a unifying force in the new South Africa or Rainbow Nation, a strong reactionary undercurrent remains among whites as shown in responses to a series of rugby test match defeats to historical rivals New Zealand during 1996. While other events are discussed, the spectre of rugby union, the sport that did the most to divide South Africans in the long-term, being promoted as the one to unify the country is analysed in greater detail through the events of the return to international rugby in 1992, the 1995 Rugby World Cup, and the 1996 New Zealand tour of South Africa. The prospects for unity and the problems of division caused by the past are nowhere more evident than in rugby union. Rugby, however, is but one sport in a host of popular sports in South Africa that have become unified and reorganized in the new nation. First, it is important to discuss briefly the unity process.

THE NATIONAL SPORTS CONGRESS AND MOVES
TOWARDS SPORTING UNITY

The process of sporting unification has received much attention in the 1990s (Baxter, 1994; Booth, 1992, 1995; Guelke, 1993; Hendricks, 1994; Kidd, 1991) as academics sought to explain the transformation from racial to supposed non-racial structures. Serious negotiations were underway by 1988, and in 1989 a small group of non-racial sports leaders came together to form the Interim National Olympic and Sports Congress. In April 1990, the National Sports Congress (NSC)[1] was formally established and soon after they added 'Olympic' to their title in hopes of gaining IOC recognition. Splits in the non-racial sports movement emerged in this process as SACOS refused to join the NSC, who did not recognize it as the official sports body of the liberation movement. In exile, divisions emerged within SANROC as early as 1987 as its chairman, Sam Ramsamy, stopped referring to SACOS as the authentic sports wing of the liberation struggle while others remained faithful to it. The Interim NSC met with SACOS in Cape Town during April 1988, and again in East London in December 1988. SACOS wanted to maintain its authority for non-racial sport in urban areas and to restrict the Interim NSC to rural areas.

Between 1988 and 1990, the NSC worked out a number of development programmes and moves towards unity with several South African sporting organizations (NSC Secretarial Report, April 1990), thus gaining the initiative from SACOS who maintained their stance of 'no normal sport in an abnormal society' and refused to negotiate with white bodies prior to the ending of apartheid. The NSC group decided not to wait on political leaders but to forge ahead, while SACOS would not budge until apartheid was over and its legacy addressed in wider society. The NSC and white bodies quickly out-manoeuvred SACOS and, as a result, the sporting boycott disappeared rapidly in the first few months of 1992, with South Africa appearing in the Cricket World Cup, returning to the Olympic movement and international rugby.

Despite its relative position of strength by 1992, the NSC was very weak before the Mike Gatting-led rebel tour of English cricketers that began in January 1990. The NSC through its links to the ANC-aligned Mass Democratic Movement mobilized thousands to protest against the tour. The NSC called for a moratorium on international tours and succeeded in forcing the abandonment of the Gatting tour. The sports moratorium was organized to be a total embargo on sports tours by teams, or individual sportspeople, to or from South Africa during the negotiation period. The moratorium followed UN resolutions passed in 1977 and 1985 that formed the International Convention Against Apartheid in Sport. The NSC agreed that the lifting of the moratorium was not necessarily contingent on a wider political settlement, but viewed the two as linked (NSC, 1991).

This position, however, was a key departure from the SACOS line of 'no normal sport in an abnormal society', led to splits between NSC and SACOS supporters and ultimately to the incorporation of non-racial structures within establishment ones, with the NSC as an overall umbrella body for sport. The SACU argreed to support the moratorium in June 1990 and through the mediation of Steve Tshwete, the ANC's spokesperson on sport, the SACU and the South African Cricket Board (SACB) amalgamated to form the United Cricket Board of South Africa (UCBSA) in June 1991, becoming the first sport to achieve formal 'unity'. While the formation of the UCBSA was achieved satisfactorily at the time, the broad aims of achieving significant change at grassroots level out of sporting unity was not realized. As Booth (1992: 190) points out, the 'unity' achieved in most sports over the ensuing twelve months was a 'sham', particularly at provincial level. The moratorium was short-lived as the sporting boycott effectively ended once President de Klerk announced the repeal of major apartheid legislation in mid-1991, thus allowing international bodies to rapidly reintegrate South Africa into international sporting structures without waiting for truly non-racial negotiated sports structures to emerge.

International sporting politics and economic imperatives rapidly drew South Africa back into the international fold. The IOC readmitted South Africa on 9 July 1991, though at the time the newly formed National Olympic Committee of South Africa (NOCSA) did not form a national Olympic committee under the IOC Charter. NOCSA had to accept the IOC's offer of reinstatement or see the offer go to SANOC, as it was told privately by IOC officials. As part of an arrangement that brought IAAF President Primo Nebiolo onto the IOC in March 1992, South Africa, only one month after unity negotiations in athletics, was hastily admitted back into the IAAF so that its track and field athletes could compete in Barcelona. Some international sporting bodies even readmitted South Africa before unity was achieved in that sport (Booth, 1992).

Under the new sporting structures in South Africa, sport is ostensibly run on a non-racial basis. The National Sports Council, which essentially functions as the NSC did in the transition period, organizes sport under the ultimate direction of the Department of Sport and Recreation (DSR). The National Sports Forum operates with representation from the NSC, the DSR and NOCSA. The Forum, initially chaired by Mtobi Tyamzashe, the Director General in the DSR, is a central body of nine members that decides in confidential meetings on the funding of sporting organizations. The philosophy of the DSR and its related bodies was stated in a DSR 'White Paper' of 1995, which is summarized below.

Under the ANC's Reconstruction and Development Programme (RDP), sport is listed as one of the key programmes for developing a new society. The RDP states that:

> Because of apartheid, sport and recreation have been denied to the majority of our people. Yet there can be no real socio-economic development without there being adequate facilities for sport and recreation in all communities. The RDP wants to ensure that all people have access to such facilities. Only in this way can all peoples have a chance to represent their villages, towns, cities, provinces or country in the arena of sport and to enjoy a rich diversity of recreational activities. (*The Reconstruction and Development Programme*, 1994: 9)

The RDP specifically states that sport and recreation should 'cut across all developmental programmes' (*RDP*, 1994: 72). Sport is also discussed as a significant part of youth programmes in urban areas. Under the ANC government, sport for the urban poor is embedded in an old liberal ideology which stresses the benefits of recreation in combating juvenile delinquency, and as a method of social control in densely populated areas.

The government's priority, however, is to provide housing, services such as electricity and running water, and primary health care to millions, and it has been forced to rely on sporting organizations and the private sector to build many of the necessary sporting facilities to ensure the RDP in sports succeeds. Additionally, the ANC has tried to support sporting organizations in their bids to host major international sporting events, seeing it as an opportunity to generate a climate of change. Unfortunately, the sporting organizations only see development as a necessary burden to bear so that international contact is maintained. The argument many use is that the money generated from hosting international events will provide additional resources for building new facilities that would not otherwise be available. Mandela and Sport Minister Steve Tshwete have commented repeatedly on the vital role sport has played in nation building. While specific events such as the cricket World Cups of 1992 and 1996, the Rugby World Cup of 1995 and the Africa Nations Cup of 1996 have been important moments in building broader identities, it is necessary to unpackage such events in the context of transition.

THE 1992 CRICKET WORLD CUP AND THE WHITE REFERENDUM

As formal political negotiations progressed between the NP government and the ANC, South African sporting organizations began to achieve unity. As a result of unity in cricket and the scrapping of major pieces of apartheid legislation, South Africa was admitted to the Cricket World Cup held in

SUMMARY OF THE DSR WHITE PAPER

The successful implementation of the unity process in South African sport, our country's re-admission to international sport, the important role for South Africa in the Supreme Council for Sport in Africa and the newly created statutory sport structures at Provincial level necessitated a reappraisal of the role of the DSR in the provision of sport.

The previous government narrowly focused on only a support service for the promotion of sport and recreation. The present DSR has redefined this role and its main focus is to play the role of provider of sport and recreation. For this policy to succeed, the DSR will closely co-operate with the NSC, the NOCSA as well as with the national sport and recreation federations and the statutory Provincial sport and recreation structures.

The divisiveness which characterized South African sport in the past was a direct result of the apartheid system that portrayed our athletes as racial and ethnic categories and which ascribed the differentials that emerged between black and white. With the emergence of a new democratic dispensation, the time has come to entrench this new democratic ethos in sport as part of the transformation process for the upliftment of the quality of life of all South Africans.

Sport is a factor in the national endeavour of the Government of National Unity to redirect the fortunes of a reconciled people into channels of peace and prosperity. It remains unsurpassed as a bridgehead because it speaks a simple practical language.

The White Paper is aimed at a structural strategy of taking sport and recreation to all the people – young and old, male and female, rural and urban, including disabled and handicapped. Under the banner of 'Getting the nation to play' it is intended to positively redirect the massive latent talent available whilst encouraging current elite performers to realise their potential.

The availability of physical resources constitutes a central component in providing for sport and goes hand in hand with human resources. . . . There are serious backlogs in the availability of basic sports facilities. In this regard the DSR will endeavour to provide funds within the parameters of its budget. However, other sources of funding, e.g. local government, the private sector, the education authorities and other central government institutions have a meaningful role to play in this regard.

The time is long overdue to provide a coordinated sport scientific support service to our sportspeople. If we wish to compete successfully in sport, our athletes, trainers and coaches should have such a service at their disposal.

In summary, therefore, the DSR's priorities for the 5-year period ending 1999 are as follows:

1. Identification of stakeholders in sport and agreement of roles between the State and the Sports Movement, to ensure efficiency in the delivery of sport.
2. Creation of basic, multipurpose facilities in disadvantaged areas.
3. Upgrading sports administrators' levels of expertise from club level upwards through the development of volunteer corps training, and staff teaching.
4. Promotion of health consciousness via theme campaigns aimed at specific interest groups.
5. Identification of talent especially via mass participation programmes.
6. Investments in the preparation of sportspeople for competition via the establishment of sports support services, i.e. sports information, technological support, drug testing and the establishment of a central elite sports academy and provincial grassroot academies.
7. Institution of appropriate affirmative action controls aimed at redressing racial, gender and demographic imbalances, as well as narrowing the gap between able-bodied and less able sportspersons.

(Adapted from Sports Information South Africa, Department of Sport and Recreation (1995), 'Summary of the Department of Sport and Recreation's White Paper')

Australia and New Zealand in February 1992. South Africa's cricketers became the first to return to official international competition in November 1991 when India hastily organized a tour for South Africa, to replace Pakistan who had withdrawn at short notice due to threats by anti-Muslims.

Just prior to the beginning of the World Cup, State President F. W. de Klerk called a referendum for white voters to decide whether or not to continue the negotiation process already underway. De Klerk sought a mandate that would enable him to marginalize right-wing dissent and give him and the NP the power to move towards a new constitution. The NP cleverly used the surprise success of the cricket team in its advertisements for a 'yes' vote on continuing negotiations. NP advertisements asked voters a number of questions including, 'Aren't our sportspersons on the playing fields of the world?' in seeking continued support from whites. As the campaign reached its climax, the South African cricket team awaited the result prior to their semi-final match against England. A 'no' vote probably would have seen the team forfeit their match and return home. Fortunately for the negotiation process and the cricketers, the vote was in favour of negotiation by a two to one margin with only one region, the far northern Transvaal, voting against.

Many credited the cricket team's success as having an influence on the vote, as did the announcement that the All Blacks and the World Cup champions the Australian Wallabies would play rugby test matches against South Africa later in 1992. The return of South Africa to international sports was a tangible carrot where immediate results could be readily seen.

NOSTALGIA, WHITE SUPREMACY AND THE ELLIS PARK RUGBY TEST MATCH OF 1992

Despite the apparent will among whites to negotiate for a new political dispensation, the historic rugby test match between South Africa and the All Blacks of 15 August 1992 demonstrated the persistence of white South African racist and racially-based nationalistic cultural values. For many other South Africans, it symbolized continued white arrogance and unwillingness to compromise. The events surrounding this first official test match for eleven years, between the world's two historically dominant rugby-playing countries, illustrate the strength of white cultural identity in the face of potentially dramatic political changes. The match came only a few weeks after the 17 June Boipatong massacre – yet another case of black protesters being shot in a South African township.[2] Despite the return of international sport and the end of most economic and cultural sanctions, the old regime maintained its position of strength throughout the formal political negotiation process which included the continued harassment of the opposition.

The ANC, hoping to gain a measure of white trust and win at least some moral backing, decided in the late 1980s to negotiate for sporting unity, and by 1992 it also supported the planned short rugby tours by New Zealand and Australia. The ANC almost withdrew its approval of tours after Boipatong, but decided to go ahead if certain conditions were met by South African and overseas rugby officials. These were that the visiting teams go to Boipatong, that a minute of silence be observed before the tests, and that the white South African flag and the white national anthem, *Die Stem van Suid-Afrika*, not be played officially at the test matches in Johannesburg and Cape Town. The latter two conditions were agreed to, but TRFU President Louis Luyt broke the agreement at the first test in Johannesburg. Luyt arranged for the anthem to be played officially, since the majority of fans were waving the flag and singing the anthem vigorously as they eagerly awaited the match. White rugby supporters' actions on the day demonstrated their strength of attachment to their cultural identity and their reluctance to make concessions to the ANC at the cultural level. The behaviour of the overwhelmingly white rugby crowd led to major discussions in the South African press, and the near cancellation of the following week's test match against Australia. The history of white rugby crowd behaviour, such as the treatment of blacks outside Ellis Park in the 1960s and 1970s, must be remembered in this context.

The 1992 Johannesburg crowd reveals how dominant cultures have to reconstitute themselves and reassert their cultural beliefs and values in the face of losing the very power that made them hegemonic in the first place. Rugby for whites in the 'new South Africa' can be viewed in a contested state between its historical position as central to the dominant culture, and its potential new role as a form of resistant white culture as new hegemonic structures develop in the South Africa of the 1990s. As Peter Donnelly notes, 'The basic defining condition for transformation in cultural forms such as sport is transformation in the larger society' (1993: 139). White South Africans certainly have been facing dramatic changes with their loss of political power and as economic rationalization became the order of the day by the early 1990s. White concerns led Mandela and the ANC leadership to take a conciliatory line towards whites that left much of their cultural identity intact.

In discussing white identity in a changing society, the sociology of nostalgia allows for a greater understanding of how many white South Africans are coping with the monumental alterations to their society. Whites have used history and nostalgia to create a sense of cultural security during a loss of political, and possibly cultural, power. The 1992 rugby test match with New Zealand, and the aftermatch responses, represent a strong residual cultural *laager*[3] mentality held by many white South Africans fearful of losing their 'way of life'. Although it appears on the surface that white behaviour changed between 1992 and the 1995 Rugby World Cup, little altered in the rugby culture itself or in its position in white society. Emerging criticism of rugby in 1996, after a series of Springbok defeats by the All Blacks, demonstrated that cultural identification and nostalgia for the 'good old days' remains powerful.

The siege mentality of many whites, locked behind their security gates or in their rugby stadiums, and their attachment to invented cultural traditions may well strengthen in coming years, particularly if rugby stadia remain as strongholds of white cultural activity and group cultural expression. It is clear that some whites are asserting their historical cultural values, rather than embarking on a path towards cultural assimilation or the creation of a new national culture for the new South Africa, though publicly the identification with new symbols and an expanded definition of 'South African' appears readily evident. Many whites are trying to create a cultural 'security-blanket' around which they and their children can maintain as much of their former lifestyles and cultural practices as possible, while showing outward loyalty to the new South African nation.[4] This is done largely through broad attachment to Western international popular and high culture while asserting patriotism to South Africa. As long as the New South Africa remains recognizable in many forms to those educated and enculturated in the old, this trend will continue.

The support of President Mandela for the 1995 Rugby World Cup allowed whites to mask their cultural insecurity a little better and to adopt the new flag as an additional cultural symbol. Despite the numerous public pro-nouncements on the wonders of the Rainbow Nation and unity through sport, many whites remain deeply concerned about the prospects for a post-Mandela ANC-led South Africa.

There appear to be three groups emerging among white South Africans: those who have made the transition to the new political order; those who state in public that they have made the psychological change, but who privately confess to each other they have not; and those who remain defiant. That such groups should appear is not surprising given the history of de-segregation in other societies such as the American South and Rhodesia/Zimbabwe. Attachment to cultural symbols may continue, or reappear, in ways similar to the use of the old confederate flag and the singing of the unofficial southern white anthem 'Dixie' by many white southerners in the United States. White southern Americans' identification with their cultural symbols persists 30 years after desegregation and the legal end of discrimination. In Zimbabwe, some whites, known as the 'When We's', cling to the past days when they controlled the country as Rhodesia. Some of these make annual pilgrimages to the grave of Cecil Rhodes for whom their old country was named. In contexts such as these, we need to examine how dominant groups cope with challenges to their cultural, political or economic power.

As the Zimbabwean case suggests, analysing the collective use of nostalgia can assist us in developing a conceptual framework to understand what otherwise can appear on the surface to be racist or sexist responses to challenges to an established social order. Nostalgia also helps link group with individual identity, as remembering past events operates at individual and societal level. As Kathleen Stewart states, nostalgia 'in positing a "once was" in relation to a "now" creates a frame for meaning, a means of dramatizing aspects of an increasingly fluid and unnamed social life' (1988: 227). Taking the concept further, historian David Lowenthal argues that nostalgia 'can also shore up self-esteem, reminding us that however sad our present lot we were once happy and worthwhile. . . . nostalgia is memory with the pain removed. The pain is today' (1985: 8).

In times of rapid social, cultural and political shifts, people frequently draw on elements of their past cultural identity in order to cope with societal changes. They often retreat into nostalgic recollections and reconstructions of a happier past time when their world was more stable and organized (Davis, 1979) and when they had more individual or collective power. As DaSilva and Faught argue, 'Nostalgia requires a collective emotional reaction toward, if not an identification with, a symbolization of the past' (1982: 49). For white South Africans, nothing has symbolized the success of their collective past more so than the Springbok emblem worn by white national sporting teams, and closely identified with the national rugby team. An informant of Vincent Crapanzano (1986) reported on the relationship between rugby and white longing for the past:

> We've got to live now and plan a future for our children, but instead we live our past over and over again. A little while ago there was a program on television, the *Springbok Saga*, about our glorious rugby tradition. . . . Whenever things get rough for us, we look to the past. We're out of international rugby now, and so we create a glorious tradition and watch it on television. (Crapanzano, 1986: 49)

Crapanzano, though criticized for some of his methods, argued perceptively in his astutely titled book about whites, called *Waiting*, that whites – victims of 'social entrapment' were caught between the knowledge that government policies were unworkable and the fear of giving up power to the majority. As a result, the knowable past is longed for as opposed to the uncertain future.

As white South African leaders negotiated the transfer of political power, the question of cultural integrity remained a worry for many whites. As Donnelly (1993) shows, the question of who has the power to determine what constitutes the dominant culture, and whose interests that culture serves is a significant part of cultural negotiation in any society. In the old South Africa, white, predominantly Afrikaner and male, authorities largely determined what belonged in the 'national' (read white) culture. Despite ANC assurances that they will protect white culture, some whites fear that black domination will generate similar consequences for them that white domination formally had for blacks. In 1988 the *Financial Mail* published findings of a Human Sciences Research Council Report showing white expectations of black rule in South Africa. The Report found that 89 per cent of whites thought their lives would not continue as before, 83 per cent thought their way of life would not be protected, 86 per cent thought that whites will be discriminated against and 80 per cent thought law and order would not be maintained. These fears existed alongside a white majority belief in the mid-1980s that white rule would end in the near future (Schrire, 1991).

Obviously Mandela understood white fears because he made forgiveness and reconciliation a key part of his strategy in speaking about the new South Africa. Although the immediate post-election signs appeared to be positive, outward manifestations of optimism do not necessarily mean that old beliefs and values will disappear from white consciousness. The victory of a nearly all-white Springbok team in the Rugby World Cup brought a sense of euphoria to many South Africans, as we shall see, though how this will resonate over time is unclear. Elements of what many refer to as 'white arrogance' emerged in some of the post-Cup statements about South African rugby, and racist signs re-surfaced during the All Black tour of South Africa in mid-1996. The fact remains that while the Cup victory was promoted as a victory for all South Africans, little within South African rugby appears different at this stage. White nostalgia and the love for the Springboks may in fact be more important after such a victory than it was even in 1992 or the late 1980s.

A major legacy of apartheid affecting culture in general is that people of different groups were spatially separated and this led to mental and emotional separation as well. Market forces will not immediately thrust all South Africans together in mixed areas. As a result, values and perceptions of many may be slow to change as the continued perceptions of white 'When We's' nearly 20 years after transition to majority rule in Zimbabwe suggests. In addition to spatial separation, the South African state-controlled media repeatedly bombarded whites with images of general black violence in the late 1980s (Posel, 1989) exacerbating white fears of black attacks whether under apartheid or not.[5]

The 1992 rugby test match with New Zealand meant much more than South Africa's return to international rugby. It demonstrated that many white South Africans' attachment to their 'national' identity was as strong as ever. As we have seen and many have argued, rugby has been an integral part of white South African culture and identity for the past several decades (Archer and Bouillon, 1982; Claassen, 1985; Nauright and Black, 1996; Woods, 1981). One concern for many whites in the early 1990s, however, was over the survival of rugby as a dominant cultural form in post-apartheid South Africa. Rugby, and other elements of white culture, faced a battle of legitimation within wider society as traditions surrounding it, and other white cultural forms, had excluded black South Africans in the past.

Rugby has changed in recent years to adopt a dynamic marketing strategy and has been moving more towards the American sporting model with concentration on profit and elite level competitions. The new governing body, the South African Rugby Football Union (SARFU) signed a marketing deal with Mark McCormack's International Marketing Group in 1992. Under the deal, national rugby team members received money from marketing scheme profits. In 1995 after the RWC, rugby union rapidly moved to professionalism with provincial and national team players signing formal playing contracts and being openly paid for playing. The emblem of Lion Lager, one of South African Breweries' leading products, now appears with the Springbok emblem on national team jerseys.

South African rugby magazine *Rugby 15* interviewed several former Springboks in 1992 and many were against the commercialization of the emblem 'especially seen in the light that Springbok Rugby has been built up over 100 years by many famous Springboks; they played for the love of the game and got nothing for their efforts' (*Rugby 15*, 1992: 20). This statement ties into the notion of 'sacrifice' for the game and society which has been an important feature of white South African culture, thus former players are venerated while current players are seen as greedy and less virtuous by comparison. Such perceptions are not unique to South Africa. A recent study of the decline of professional tennis points to spoiled and greedy players and excessive money in the game as part of the sport's problems (Jenkins, 1994). Of course, former Springboks have been rewarded in other ways for their efforts as playing top level rugby often led to successful political or business careers (Nauright and Black, 1994). The 1995 IRB decision to allow the full professionalization of rugby union, plus the US$550 million ten-year deal with Rupert Murdoch's satellite TV station for the Super 12 competition between South African, New Zealand and Australian provincial teams, plus a tri-nation test series beginning in 1996 has taken the issue of money and commercialism in rugby to new levels.

Added to concerns about over-commercialization, in 1991 the South African Rugby Football League was established to promote amateur rugby league. League promoters stressed the excitement of the game and that it was less dangerous than rugby union. Several rugby union clubs in the Transvaal, upset with the rationalization policies of the TRFU joined the league body in 1991 (Griffiths, 1991). The establishment of amateur rugby league, and its attraction as a means to resist rationalization of the supposedly amateur rugby union, may add further to the potential crisis in South African rugby and support the findings of Donnelly and Young (1985) on the success of American football in England, and the growth of rugby union in the United States, as subcultural activities of cultural alternatives and resistance. It remains to be seen whether amateur rugby league will ever pose a serious threat to a now professional rugby union in South Africa, especially in light of the 1995 RWC victory by South Africa and the massive television deal with Murdoch. As Murdoch also now controls most of global rugby league it is possible that future plans may involve greater development of the game in southern Africa, but this will surely not be done at the expense of elite rugby union. By 1997 Australian Rules football also received support as an alternative to rugby.

Another issue also worried white South African rugby supporters in 1992 and 1993. The Springboks were simply not as good as they were before rugby sanctions restricted international rugby contact. Such fears were proven in losses to New Zealand, Australia, France and England in 1992, and the loss of a test series to Australia in 1993. The vaunted Springboks even lost to a Buenos Aires side during their 1993 tour of Argentina. These performances were a far cry from those of 1900 through to 1955 when South Africa did not lose a single international test series anywhere. White South Africans up to the 1980s had been used to front page headlines such as 'Springbok's Finest Hour' (*Sunday Times*, 26 June 1960), 'Boks Pulverise the French' (*Sunday Times*, 17 July 1967), '"Wonder" Boks Shatter The All Blacks' (*Sunday Times*, 26 July 1970) and sports page headlines such as 'The Superboks!' (*Sunday Times*, 9 November 1980, p. 38; all articles collected in Greyvenstein, 1989). By the 1990s, white rugby supporters thus faced threats to their game and its standard, in addition to the wider changes emerging in South African society.

ISOLATION, NEGOTIATION AND THE RETURN OF INTERNATIONAL RUGBY

In negotiations that led to the New Zealand and Australian tours, SARFU, the New Zealand and Australian rugby unions agreed to conditions laid down by the ANC so that short tours could take place. The South African flag was not to be displayed in an official capacity, the national anthems would not be sung officially and a minute of silence for the victims of violence was to be observed. The government response was that it was 'saddened' that the national flag was not to be displayed, but called for the 'greatest circum-spection' in dealing with the issue. The official opposition Conservative Party, however, called for rugby fans to bring as many flags as possible to the All Black match to display their national culture and heritage (*Citizen*, 17 August 1992). The actions of Conservative Party members and other white political groups on the right clearly fuelled the issue by promoting flag-waving.

It would be wrong to assume, however, that the conservatives somehow manipulated the crowd into behaving the way that they did. After all, the beloved Springboks were playing their historical enemy, the All Blacks, in an official test match on South African soil for the first time in sixteen years. It had also been eleven years since the two teams last met officially. The pinnacle of rugby careers in both countries was to play in a series against the other (Claassen, 1985; Nauright and Black, 1994; Woods, 1981). The last series with the All Blacks that were really devoid of political controversy were in 1949, when the Springboks swept the All Blacks in South Africa, and 1956 when New Zealand won a hard-fought home series with the country apparently united in the single purpose of beating the Springboks (Roger, 1991).

The 1992 match provided an opportunity for years of frustration to be released in a celebration of white culture and joy at the return to the international fold in general, and specifically to playing the All Blacks again. The ANC may have miscalculated in supporting international rugby before the elections, as white fans were not interested in thanking the ANC, but annoyed at what they believed was the open involvement of politics in rugby. Finally, the match with the All Blacks played on nostalgic recollections of white fans. The 1992 test was staged at the only time in history that neither team could claim to be world champions, even so, this was the Springboks against the All Blacks, just like 'the good old days'. As white reactions during and after the Ellis Park match suggest, white rugby fans felt tired of being dictated to by black politicians, whom they used to arrest or kill for challenging their system. They were sick of feeling that their dominance was disappearing, even though they knew it must, and asserted a collective resistance to this process.

The point here is to try and understand the meanings underpinning the outpouring of emotion expressed by the rugby fans. Ellis Park can be viewed then as a site or space for cultural resistance. The stadium itself is an icon symbolizing the power of the white South African culture, economy and of white South African planning and engineering, as well as reportedly being the largest rugby stadium in the world. The first test played at Ellis Park was in 1928 between South Africa and New Zealand. The old Ellis Park stadium saw eighteen test matches from then until 1976, with 90,000 present for the 1955 match between South Africa and the British Lions. The new Ellis Park symbolizes the power and grandeur of capitalist growth in South Africa and is viewed as a monument to white South African power and culture. Thus, it symbolizes for many whites the success of their culture and a space which they can control, at least when their Springboks play rugby. Furthermore, both the old and new Ellis Park grounds were the scenes of Springbok and Transvaal victories over the best teams in international rugby (*Shafto*, 11 September 1970). Ellis Park along with other test match venues like Loftus Versfeld in Pretoria and Newlands in Cape Town are thus tangible icons reminding whites of a nostalgic and successful past. Ellis Park is now a contested symbol, however, since NSL matches began to be played there in the 1980s due to a period of financial crisis for the TRFU. Thus, the stadium itself is a space where all of the strains between the old and new South Africa are visible with each rugby or soccer match played there. Retreat into myth and nostalgic recollections should not be unexpected given the levels of assault on old, economic, political and cultural values of many white South Africans and the playing of soccer on a hallowed rugby ground.

APARTHEID OF THE SOUL?
RESPONSES TO THE WHITE CROWD'S BEHAVIOUR

The pre-match events of the Ellis Park test received tremendous media coverage during the following week. The immediate response of the ANC was to question future support for tours, given the blatant refusal of the TRFU and the fans to respect the request for a minute of silence and to not play the national anthems. Many white responses to what they termed a dictatorial attitude on the part of the ANC were hostile to criticism of the fans and even the TRFU. SARFU officially apologized for the singing of the anthem, stating that it did not authorize the playing of any anthems before the start of the test. Luyt, however, refused to apologize, stating that he and his TRFU would not 'be threatened by anybody and I don't care if certain people, not having rugby at heart, feel upset about my decision'. Luyt responded to ANC criticism by asserting that symbols such as *Die Stem* and the national flag were still officially recognized as part of South Africa until abolished by a new government (*Citizen*, 17 August 1992). The conservative English-language daily, the *Citizen*, concurred with Luyt in its editorial on the issue. It stated that only when a new anthem and flag are chosen should the official flag and anthem of the day be abolished. The editorial went on to condemn the political wisdom of breaking the agreement not to play the anthem, but then also criticized the ANC for threatening to withdraw support for future tours which had already been arranged.

If we examine the discourse of reports and editorials appearing after the match, we gain a deeper understanding of the tenacity of white South African identity and the defence of white culture in the face of perceived dictates of the ANC. Most South African newspapers are owned by three groups of white capitalists. The two main English-language daily newspapers serving the white community in Johannesburg, the *Citizen* and the *Star*, were filled with articles and editorials in the week following the test. Responses in the English-language press demonstrate that English-speaking as well as Afrikaner whites feel strongly about their culture. In addition, some people in both groups were tired of the ANC 'dictating' to them.

The more conservative *Citizen* ran reports and editorials that nearly all supported the actions of the crowd. Headlines such as 'Anthem brought a lump to throat', 'Good sense' and 'We've had enough' dealing with editorials and letters were meant to reinforce the crowd's resistant actions. The general tone of the *Citizen*, defending those singing the white anthem, was defiant towards the ANC. The *Citizen*'s editorial on the test supported the singing and flag-waving arguing that, 'Whites had had enough of being dictated to by the ANC on sport, the anthem and the flag' (20 August 1992). The editorial went on to declare that the failure to observe a minute of silence was 'unfortunate' and in 'poor taste', but stopped short of outright condemnation.

The *Star* presented a more balanced view with headlines such as 'Anthem discord' and 'Most South Africans did not have lump in throats', alongside 'Singing a sign of Patriotism'. The *Star*'s editorial of 17 August concentrated on the failure of the TRFU to honour its agreement with the ANC, arguing that the flag is 'another highly emotive symbol' and the singing of the anthem could not be expected to stop whenever large crowds of whites are gathered. *Star* political editor, Shaun Johnson, published a long report on the match on 17 August. He argued that the fans were encouraged in their behaviour by the Afrikaans press and that they were determined to make a political point. He also spoke of 'liquored-up' fans who sang 'F... die ANC, f... die ANC'.

Such behaviour reflected white annoyance with the power of the ANC to dictate conditions under which international rugby could be played, and frustration at the process of negotiating the transfer of power to a group that white South Africans had been taught to think of as 'communists' and 'terrorists', who wanted to destroy white South African society. It is not surprising that a sporting event was the site of open demonstration of white hostility. By its very nature sport posits an 'us' against a 'them', and fosters a site where racism, if not inevitable, is certainly possible. In South Africa, specific sports have been viewed as characteristic of white and black culture, therefore racism in the suggestion of which sports members of certain groups should play is also prevalent (Archer and Bouillon, 1982; Lewis, 1993).

The language used in both the *Star* and the *Citizen* reinforced cultural assumptions about blacks shared by many whites. In defending South African policies, the government and big business in South Africa stressed ways that black South Africans were advantaged through white benevolence. Advertisements showed how black South Africans were better off than blacks in other African countries and how whites funded African education. One, depicting a young black girl, stated, 'Without us, Miriam Kabako would be an illiterate, hungry, cold little girl' (Frederikse 1986, 16). The paternalist 'civilizing mission' preached by British imperialists was alive and well in the self-promotion of white South Africa, and of the necessity of continued white positions of significance in the new South Africa. One report on Luyt's approval of the ANC's decision to allow the match against Australia to go ahead quoted his praise of the ANC's 'adult' and 'responsible' behaviour (*Star*, 20 August 1992).

White assignment of status to blacks has a long history in South Africa. Segregation and apartheid discourses assigned blacks the position of 'children' who were often 'irresponsible'. Now, by responding in a way acceptable to whites, in this case by allowing Australia's rugby tour to continue, blacks could be patronizingly given the title of 'adult'. White self-delusion could then logically be extended to the thought that whites were 'giving' the government over to the majority, who were viewed as becoming 'responsible'. These attitudes fit the NP's strategy of portraying ANC leaders as more respectable than the 'radicals' in the townships who were perpetuating violence. Even before the release of Mandela, government controlled television began to de-racialize violence and promote a difference between responsible and irresponsible blacks (Posel, 1989), similar to the attitudes of white liberals in the segregation period.

In addition to domestic reports, the *Star* carried views from the British press on 17 August. The story focused on the British media's joy at South Africa's return to international rugby. Such coverage reinforced white South African links with an international white-dominated cultural community, and shows that sporting ties with historic rivals were welcome despite any internal problems. The international media also continued to refer to South African national teams as the Springboks, despite modifications of the emblem worn by South African sporting teams, and attempts to change the name of national teams. Such reports helped solidify white South Africans' attachment to one of their most revered historic symbols.

What of the black response to the controversy? Clearly, the Springbok emblem, the flag and the white anthem are all symbols of racism and white domination in the eyes of many South Africans who were victims of the apartheid system. Harry Hendricks, a leader in the non-racial South African Council of Sport (SACOS), states that as early as the 1930s, Coloured rugby fans in Cape Town cheered for visiting international sides due to the exclusiveness of white rugby (Hendricks, 1994). The ANC and many black sporting officials feel that they have done much more than their share in negotiating new sporting structures in South Africa. Steve Tshwete, the ANC's leading negotiator in sports talks and now the Minister for Sport, was so upset by the actions of the crowd that he preferred that the subsequent match against Australia be cancelled. This was strong action from the man seen in a teary embrace with cricket captain Kepler Wessels, when the white players of the South African cricket team defeated Australia in their first match of the 1992 cricket World Cup. The pictures of that embrace were shown all around South Africa and were influential in coaxing white voters to opt for continuing negotiations in their referendum of 17 March 1992.

Despite Tshwete's initial attitude, the ANC voted for the Australian match to go ahead under assurances from the Western Province Rugby Union and SARFU that there would be no repeat of the, Johannesburg incident. Joe French, president of the Australian Rugby Football Union informed Tshwete that they would call off the tour if the ANC withdrew its support (*Citizen*, 19 August 1992), thus showing whites that the continuation of international rugby depended on the benevolence of the ANC. This dependence frustrated many whites; those who had always supported political changes to maintain international sporting contacts felt that the ANC was interfering with sport in much the same way that the NP government had done in the past. Others, used to being in a dominant position, were angered at being 'dictated' to by an ANC they had been taught in school, by the government and through the media to hate as 'the communist and terrorist enemy' (see Evans, 1989; Frederikse, 1986; Posel, 1989).

The spectre of whites clinging to public and group displays of white culture and expressions of identity in the early stages of post-apartheid South Africa should not be surprising. South Africa's return to international rugby was marred by the actions of a white crowd, vilified for asserting its identity in the face of a society changing faster than many could follow or comprehend. In times such as those in South Africa of the early 1990s, it is important not to just condemn behaviour, but to try and understand why individuals and groups behave in the way that they do. While right-wing groups exploited the situation by urging fans to wave flags and sing *Die Stem*, it was clear that those attending the match were overjoyed at the return to international rugby and the prospect of playing the All Blacks. Springbok–All Black rugby presented whites with a cultural event entrenched in social and individual memories which provided comfort as political power was being negotiated away.

SPORT, SYMBOLS AND REALITY IN THE NEW SOUTH AFRICA

Aftermatch responses demonstrated that many whites in 1992 were not about to give up their privileged position in all spheres of society if their cultural expression was threatened by perceived dictates from the ANC or anyone else. Mandela, Tshwete and other ANC leaders realized the significance of rugby to whites, and targeted rugby as an area where whites could see that majority rule meant the survival of white culture, rather than its further demise through continued international sanctions. While many whites remained wary of the ANC and felt like they were being dictated to for a change, they also remained firmly attached to their culture which could provide them with a 'safety blanket' to face the new South Africa, while not giving up everything of the old South Africa.

It may be accurate to label resistant whites as 'conservative' or 'racist' as some have done (Booth, 1992; 1995), but such labelling does not fully explain how and why many white South Africans responded to change in ways such as those demonstrated during and after the Ellis Park test. In the current context of a new political dispensation locally, and the increasing incursion of globalizing processes, some cultural critics and political theorists, as Jarvie (1993: 61) points out, state that 'local, regional and national communities will hold on even tighter to those symbols, myths, memories, traditions and nostalgia which have helped to define various cultural identities'.

In 1992 white South Africans also protested the conditions under which South Africa was to compete in the Barcelona Olympics. The team was to compete under the Olympic flag and anthem, and with a neutral emblem. White public opinion overwhelmingly condemned such conditions and the local media argued that the Springbok was a 'national' emblem that pre-dated apartheid. NOCSA and the ANC bore the brunt of this criticism. In a *Sunday Times* poll, 7,452 readers supported South Africa's non-participation under such conditions while only 1,553 were in support (Booth, 1992).

The new South Africa is a reality, but for many whites, uncertainty may lead them to cling to a past when they were 'in control', the economy was prosperous for them, and the Springboks struck terror into the hearts of opposing rugby sides. The victory of the Springboks over the All Blacks in the 1995 Rugby World Cup final further strengthened nostalgic notions, as rugby success is at least one way for many whites to link the present to the past, while being concerned about the future. The controversy over the Ellis Park test match, and the behaviour of the white crowd at the match, demonstrated the strength of cultural attachment to the Springbok symbol and the old flag. The debate over the symbols of the new nation was intense, and the final outcome is still not entirely satisfactory with the Protea being used for all teams except the national rugby union team which gets to keep the Springbok. Roger Adams, a sports administrator at the University of the Western Cape, wrote in response to the return of international rugby about what it meant for him:

> 'Our' national rugby team singing *Die Stem* on national television. What a reminder of the minority white dominance and blatant arrogance that prevails in our country. What a flagrant disregard for the emotions felt over apartheid symbols. What a raping of the moral convictions of those who seek an egalitarian society in South Africa. And all of this was happening within a *united* sport structure (emphasis in original) (Adams, 1992: 7).

The apparent change in attitudes by 1995 amazed many observers as rugby crowds appeared to embrace the symbolism of the new South Africa, particularly the new flag. The ANC contributed to this by keeping *Die Stem* as one of the two official anthems and not interfering on the sporting emblem issue in rugby, allowing the national rugby team to retain the Springbok. Mandela's last minute but whole-hearted support for the Springboks in the RWC made many whites genuinely euphoric and stirred feelings of national belonging. The RWC also took place only months after Mandela had assumed power with expectations and concerns from all areas of society at high levels. Former SARFU chief executive Edward Griffiths states that, 'By May 1995, if ever a country was in need of a party, a good time, a reason to celebrate, it was South Africa. In so many ways the RWC was delivered at the right time' (Griffiths, 1996: 51).

ONE TEAM, ONE COUNTRY?
AMABOKOBOKO AND THE 1995 RUGBY WORLD CUP

While finding symbols of unity proved a difficult task, the rugby authorities managed to hang on to the Springbok as the emblem for the national rugby team. This symbol was to appear to the world in the 1995 Rugby World Cup held in South Africa during May and June of 1995. The RWC is rated as the world's fourth largest international sporting event among television viewers, and created an immediate problem for the marketing of the new South Africa globally. Indeed, the RWC was viewed as a precursor to South Africa obtaining the ultimate sporting prize of the Olympic Games, which the city of Cape Town bid to host in 2004. Because of the significance of international sport, particularly in a country like South Africa which needs as much access to international audiences as possible to reinvigorate the economy, the government and President Mandela placed tremendous value on a successful RWC.

Mandela met with leading rugby officials and players before the RWC and pledged full support for the national team and the event, with the concession that the Springbok team to play in the tournament would be the last nearly all-white rugby team to represent the country in a World Cup. Mandela's support allowed the RWC to be marketed across all areas of South African society and the Springboks to be transformed in the 'One team, one country' slogan, a concept developed by then SARFU Chief Executive Officer Griffiths to encourage support among Africans. Mike Tissong, an editor at *The Sowetan* came up with the name Amabokoboko for the team after he saw people watching the opening RWC match on television. He said it was:

> the sort of crowd we usually get when there is a big soccer match on. As I walked by, I teased them that they weren't watching Amabhagabhaga, which is a Zulu nickname for Orlando Pirates. 'You are watching Amabokoboko,' I

shouted. Everyone laughed, so I said we would use that name on the front page if South Africa won. They did, so there it was in the paper and the nickname seems to have stuck. (Griffiths, 1996: 69)

President Mandela went so far as to wear a Springbok cap whilst speaking to a Youth Day rally on the nineteenth anniversary of the Soweto student protests of 1976. Mandela held out the cap at the conclusion of his speech and stated, 'You see this cap that I am wearing? This cap does honour to *our boys* who are playing France tomorrow afternoon' [emphasis added] (SAPA, 16 June 1995). The actual ability of the people to watch RWC matches was highly restricted in that many tickets went to overseas visitors (as part of the agreement between the hosts and the RWC international organizers), and those sold for seeded team matches cost R88 and those for other matches R60, well beyond the means of the overwhelming majority of South Africans. In addition, SARFU sold its 700,000 ticket allocation so that tickets to the final were only sold in packages that included less popular matches early in the tournament (Griffiths, 1996). Tickets for the RWC final were scalped for up to R2000 several days before the match (SAPA, 15 June 1995). To its credit, SARFU made 1000 free tickets available to each match to underprivileged rugby players, though this was made easier with the return of over 400,000 tickets from the overseas allocation. ANC officials and those with the free tickets were, however, almost all of the black attendees at RWC matches.

While the victory of the Springboks over their historic arch-rival in the RWC final sparked a wave of mass euphoria in the country and pronouncements like the one by Sports Minister Tshwete that opens this chapter, others from different perspectives challenged this 'unity' and the means by which it was achieved. Some right-wing whites lost in the quagmire of nostalgia for the old racial order of apartheid argued that the Springboks were 'the Mandela team'. Fred Rundle of the far right-wing Afrikaner Resistance Movement (AWB) argued that 'Mandela is an enemy of Afrikaners. The players have no national pride whatsoever'. In an ironic twist, Rundle stated that 'I wouldn't pay five cents to go to a game. I wouldn't go if you paid me. I support any team that's playing against the Springboks' (Ferreira, 14 June 1995).

Some SARFU officials, those who survived from rugby administration in the old South Africa, appeared to miss the significance of the wide appeal of the team or were not genuinely interested in the costs of this popularity in developing the game in black communities. Before the appointment of Griffiths, SARFU's white officers basically ignored development while Coloured and African officials were assigned positions to deal with development issues. Griffiths (1996) argues that the Coloured officials had been placed in an own affairs section to deal with development, while white officials remained uninterested and went about the business of running real rugby. The attitude of Hennie Serfontein is indicative of white rugby officials' attitudes toward development. Griffiths recounts that:

> Serfontein, who had learned to speak Tswana as a child . . . . As President of a Union [Northern Transvaal] which paid individual players more than R300,000 per year, he would become enraged when the CEO [Griffiths] suggested that his Union, not SARFU, should fund a R90,000 programme for blacks in the far north of his province. (Griffiths, 1996: 201–2)

In 1992, then development officer Ngconde Balfour proposed affirmative action plans to integrate the game at levels below the Springbok team. These proposals were ignored by white officials and only re-surfaced when Griffiths proposed them in order to win broad support for the RWC. Griffiths also announced that 40 per cent of the RWC net profits would go to development of facilities and coaching in underprivileged areas. With such pronouncements and coaching clinics run by the Springboks leading into the tournament, SARFU ensured open ANC support for the national team. The resultant images of the tournament, and its various meanings to the new South Africa, are discussed along with developments in 1996 and early 1997 in the final chapter, which seeks to place sport in the new South Africa within a broader national and global context.

CONCLUSION: A UNIFIED SPORTING NATION?

South African sport has undergone dramatic changes since 1990. All sports have been readmitted into international organizations and competitions, and South Africa participates in many global and regional sporting events. Since the 1995 RWC, South Africa successfully hosted the Africa Nations Cup of soccer which the national team 'Bafana Bafana' won in front of Mandela. In the last netball world cup, South Africa surprised many by making the final against perennial world champions Australia, and Penny Heyns, Josia Thungwane and Heziekial Sepeng were heroes at the Atlanta Olympics. By 1992 about 100 black sportspeople had represented South Africa in all international sports since the late 1970s (Booth, 1992).

In the old white-dominated sports of rugby and cricket, however, little changed at the top by the latter years of the 1990s. By early 1997, Chester Williams remained the only black player to represent South Africa in rugby since its return to international matches in 1992, and 40-year-old Omar Henry (briefly in 1992),[6] Paul Adams in 1995 and Herschelle Gibbs in 1996 have made it in cricket. Perhaps significantly all of these men are Coloured. The cricket development programme, though not without its critics, has begun to make inroads in the townships of Johannesburg and Durban. Rugby, on the other hand, has done very little to implement real township development. While the RWC victory generated a momentary euphoria, and a significant identification of most South Africans with the new Rainbow Nation, this moment was not sustained through 1996. While Mandela and Tshwete continue to promote sport as a significant element in nation building, they dropped their public vocal support for rugby as the promises of SARFU appeared to dissipate. Mandela did not attend a rugby test match in 1996. The final chapter explores how and why this has happened.

Cricket, unlike rugby, has crossed the racial divide for a longer period of time and more successfully. White players, such as Jonty Rhodes and Fanie de Villiers, have been genuine heroes in the townships and in the wealthy suburbs. Soccer remains dominant in the townships, and the appearance of South Africa in the 1998 World Cup in France may have a similar galvanizing effect to that of rugby in 1995. The harsh reality of a South Africa faced with the legacy of apartheid is that sporting equity can only be achieved with much effort and years of hard work.

South Africa has many other pressing problems with between 50 and 60 per cent of the population unemployed, up to 75 per cent of the people living below the poverty line and hundreds of thousands of new houses needed. Malnutrition is rife and the health care system overloaded and underfunded. All of these problems mean that sport cannot receive the energy of the government as a top funding priority. Sport has been used, however, to shore up confidence and generate good feelings, even if temporarily. Additionally, many government and business people believe, or at least publicly argue, that opportunities created by the hosting of major international events will aid in the reconstruction and development of South Africa. The marketing director of American Express in South Africa stated that the RWC had placed South Africa 'on the map' (*Mail & Guardian*, Open Africa Supplement, July 1995: 3), a phrase oft repeated by civic and national boosters in defence of bids to host major sporting events.

South African government officials and sporting administrators have quickly adopted the dominant discourses surrounding sport that seem almost universal, espousing the myths of fair play, the glories of international successes and the way that sport can bring the nation together. Despite this lofty and often glowing rhetoric, South Africans are still divided by the legacies of apartheid, the unevenness of capitalist development and massive discrepancies between the rich and poor. Making the nation through sports in South Africa is not as straightforward as in many other 'nations', as the imagined national community of South Africa means many things to many people, and there is still no image of one South Africa with which all South

Africans can identify, despite the noble efforts of President Mandela. While he has secured respect and support from a large proportion of white South Africans, that support is based on the cult of his personality alone. How successfully he or anyone else can promote identification with the new nation remains to be seen. The final chapter explores reality, representation and the burden of the past in the construction of South African sport in the new nation, and South Africa's position in the global context as it constructs new identities both for local and global consumption.

NOTES

1. The NSC was also for a time called the National Olympic and Sports Congress and the name changed to the National Sports Council under the ANC-led government in 1994.
2. The 1960 and 1976 New Zealand rugby tours of South Africa occurred at the times of the Sharpeville and Soweto massacres.
3. *Laager* is an Afrikaans word which referred to the circular formation of ox wagons used by the Voortrekkers (pioneers) to defend themselves against attack as they moved into the interior of South Africa. Since then it has been used to describe the cultural mentality of Afrikaners as a besieged people surrounded by hostile Africans and English-speaking whites.
4. The use of the term 'security' is significant for most white South Africans who live behind their security fences and are protected by security agencies. In addition, the National Party has recast itself as the party of security, claiming it is the only political force with the power and the will to maintain security in a violent society. Links between 'security' and rugby are also evident. The Eastern Province Rugby Football Union signed a three-year contract with D S Security Company in 1992. D S Security Managing Director, Dawie Sprangenberg, stated 'Nobody can be more aware of the value of security than we are . . . we are proud to be able to offer to EP rugby the support they need to go ahead with their plans, secure in the knowledge that we are behind them every step of the way' (*Scoreboard* April 1992, 2).
5. These images were tightly controlled to show general black violence, but not violence directly linked to one political grouping. The point was to show certain radicals or crowds were volatile rather than blacks *per se* as Posel (1989) demonstrates.
6. Many thought that Omar Henry's selection as a member of the 14 man World Cup squad in 1992 smacked of tokenism. Douglas Booth (1992) asserts that 16 cricketers from the non-racial cricket structures were more meritorious of selection: Mehmood Badat, Vincent Barnes, Yaseen Begg, Jesse Chellan, Alistair Coetzee, Faiek Davids, Nazir Dindar, Iqbal Khan, Mongezi Majola, Mandisa Mali, Hussein Manack, Jack Manack, Mxolisi Matyila, Andre Peters, Naveen Ramnarin and Mohamed Sarang. Alistair Coetzee was, however, a rugby player and not a cricketer.

8

THE BURDEN OF THE PAST: (RE)PRESENTATION, HISTORY, SPORT AND SOCIETY IN THE RAINBOW NATION

Sport has played an important role in the transformation of South Africa.

Winnie Mandela, quoted in the *Sowetan*, 5 December 1994.

We have survived and reached the Cup final because we have played sure in the knowledge that we have the united support of all South Africans. It is impossible to understate the impact this surge of national support has had in our minds. . . . the whole country has pulled us through. In the process, in some small way, we hope Springbok rugby has become an important focus of nation-building. We have set aside the divisions of the past and today embrace all South Africans right across this rainbow nation . . .

Morné du Plessis, Springbok team manager, RWC 1995, 19 June 1995.

There is such a thing as an incurable nostalgia. It provokes skin rash, tics around mouth and eyes, long periods of spiritlessness. The pillow becomes a father-confessor listening to stories of the country of the heart. Ancient flames infest the subconscious. Images scald the eyelids. . . . There must be a song that can still be sung.

Breyten Breytenbach, *Return to Paradise* (1993: 1).

Immediately following the 1995 Rugby World Cup and the success of the 'Amabokoboko', many people could be forgiven for thinking that the image of South Africa as a 'nation', where all identified with the national team and the symbols of the new nation was a reality. The subsequent successes of the Bafana Bafana national soccer team in winning the Africa Nations Cup held in South Africa in early 1996, the excellent performance of the South African cricket team in the 1996 cricket World Cup, and the performances of Hezekial

Sepeng, Penny Heyns and Josia Thungwane at the Atlanta Centenary Olympic Games, appeared to reinforce such notions. Despite all of these athletic achievements and their portrayal in the media, a series of losses against arch-rival rugby power New Zealand saw the return of old South African flags, and charges of racism levelled against a government minister who publicly stated his support for the All Blacks. That such occurrences appeared so soon after a series of 'national' victories demonstrates the tenuousness of a new non-racial pan-South African identity, especially one that is predicated too much on the success of predominantly white teams. This chapter draws on the history and contemporary situation in South Africa in analysing the place of sport in post-apartheid society and prospects for sport in the future.

BETTER LUYT THAN?
THE LEGACY OF APARTHEID IN SPORTS ADMINISTRATION[1]

The ironic situation of sports administration of cricket and rugby in the new South Africa is how Ali Bacher and Louis Luyt[1] have maintained positions of power in the new amalgamated associations. Bacher led South African cricket in the late apartheid years, and Luyt was one of the most powerful rugby officials as President of the TRFU and a member of the SARB executive. As rugby was promoted during and after the 1995 RWC as the sport of reconciliation and for generating a new South African identity, Luyt appeared to take greater and more centralized control of the game. Several controversial dismissals and resignations have occurred while Luyt has been at the centre of SARFU administration. Given his reported track record, though, this should perhaps not be surprising. In 1981, the *Washington Post* (16 August 1981) reported that Luyt paid the Eastern Rugby Union $25,000 in advance of the Springboks being invited to play in the USA, following their 1981 tour of New Zealand. The SARB also secretly helped finance the Eastern Rugby Union to the tune of $50,000 according to the *Boston Globe* (23 September 1981) (Ramsamy, 1982: 64). As we have seen, Luyt was also implicated in the Muldergate information scandal of the late 1970s, and involved in inviting the New Zealand 'Cavaliers' rugby team to South Africa in 1986. Finally, it was Luyt who broke the agreement between SARFU and the ANC not to play *Die Stem* at the Ellis Park test against New Zealand in 1992.

What about Luyt and SARFU's administration in recent years? Several key people in positions of influence or power in SARFU have resigned or been dismissed by Luyt. Ebrahim Patel, former leader of SARU and then head, was forced to resign in 1993 in dubious circumstances. In 1995, prior to the World Cup, Luyt dismissed Janie Engelbrecht, former Springbok star and team manager, because of a feud between the two. After the RWC, Edward Griffiths, architect of the Amabokoboko campaign to gain widespread support for the Springboks in the RWC, was fired by Luyt and replaced with Rian Oberholtzer, Luyt's son-in-law. In 1996, after South Africa lost four out of five tests against New Zealand and one out of two against Australia, long-time Luyt supporter Andre Markgraaff became the Springbok team coach and selector. During the New Zealand series popular Springbok winger James Small was kicked out of the Springbok team for attending a nightclub, not the first time he has had problems with rugby authorities, having been dropped after violent play in the third test in New Zealand in 1994.

In addition to this, one of Markgraff's first crucial decisions was to axe Springbok captain and popular hero François Pienaar (*Star & SA Times*, 16 October 1996: 28). Pienaar had challenged Luyt over contracts of Transvaal players by leading a player strike after the RWC and then signed with the rival World Rugby Corporation before coming back to the establishment. Soon after his removal from the national team, Pienaar signed a contract to play professional club rugby in England. After Pienaar's sacking, Engelbrecht and Griffiths spoke out against Luyt's control of SARFU, stating that he wanted total control of rugby in South Africa. Engelbrecht stated 'He's an autocrat and sometimes he's even worse than that.' Griffiths added that Luyt wanted to be in control and others were too frightened to stand up to him. Indeed, when one executive member of the TRFU dared to oppose Luyt for the presidency of the Union in an open vote, his reward was dismissal from the executive. These actions and others led to an official investigation in 1997.

Added to all the controversy over Pienaar's demise was an attack on Luyt from Natal Rugby Union President Keith Parkinson, angered over the handling of the Pienaar issue and the exclusion of several 'outstanding' Natal players from the Springbok team to tour Argentina, France and Wales. Parkinson withdrew from consideration to be re-elected to the SARFU executive (*Star & SA Times*, 16 October 1996: 1). With Small and Pienaar out and Chester Williams injured, three of the main heroes of the RWC were out of the team in 1996, assisting in rugby's decline since the Springboks won the Cup. In a Currie Cup quarterfinal at Ellis Park, Transvaal was only able to attract 20,000 out of an official capacity of 62,000 for its game against Western Province, while Natal attracted just 22,000 to King's Park (which holds over 52,000) for its quarterfinal against Griquas (*Star & SA Times*, 16 October 1996: 25).

Rugby is not the only sport facing administrative problems in the new South Africa. In football there have been disputes between SAFA and the NSL and leading personalities. In December 1994, Kaizer Motaung, managing director of Kaizer Chiefs, was fined R10,000 for insulting NSL chairperson

Leepile Taunyane by calling him a 'puppet' and stating that the NSL was run by a cartel with a hidden agenda. Journalist Meshack Motloung urged the League to clean up its act, stating that officials 'in high posts in the league must bear in mind that the NSL belongs to the public. It is not their property' (Motloung, 1994: 31). The Pickard Commission report, discussed in Chapter 5, concurred with Motloung's opinion of the need to eliminate corrupt practices from soccer. Despite administrative battles that are increasingly fought out in the media, the majority of reports during 1995 and early 1996 focused on the place of sport in unifying South Africa. Underneath this veneer of national unity existed divisions within specific sports, and among their administrators, waiting to come out once victories turned into defeats.

NOSTALGIA, PLACE AND IDENTITY IN THE NEW SOUTH AFRICA

As of late 1996, the place of sport in the shaping of South African identity appears to have changed little from the days of apartheid. The brief moment created by the RWC triumph in June 1995 faded away as rugby underwent a series of post-Cup crises in 1995 as the sport turned professional. In 1996 matters grew worse in rugby as SARFU administration and power became more centralized than when Danie Craven ran the old SARB. Added to these problems was a string of five successive defeats against the All Blacks and Australia, the sacking of popular players James Small and François Pienaar, and the incredibly white look of the Boks with Chester Williams injured. Even President Mandela lost interest in his 'boys' in 1996, failing to attend any of the rugby test matches against Australia or New Zealand. The white-dominated media slammed finance minister Trevor Manuel for admitting that he cheered for the All Blacks. Worse still for public relations, one Bok selected in 1996 had been charged in the death of a young black man who had worked on his farm.

With all of these subsequent developments, the place of South African rugby appeared in 1996 to resemble its position of 1992, rather than 1995. Even the old South African flags began to appear again at major matches. While the internal wranglings of rugby and other sporting administration are beyond the control of South Africans in general, the responses that these problems generate added to on-field failures have fed the insecurities that many white South Africans still feel about their society and the future.

Ironically, perhaps, whites are not the only ones who are nostalgic for the past. A significant proportion of the Coloured population also feels a sense of nostalgia, if not for the 'good old days' of apartheid, at least for the days when they were in a middle position in society. Some feel that they have gone from being second to third class citizens in the New South Africa (Effendi,

1994). Additionally, the amalgamated sporting structures have amounted to a take-over of non-racial sport by the old white establishment.

Despite all of the difficulties in altering South African sport and nostalgic attitudes, some things have changed since the ending of the sporting boycott. South Africa which has been an exporter of sporting talent began to import sports stars from other countries for the cricket and rugby provincial competitions. Ironically, two of the best imports in cricket were Malcolm Marshall and Desmond Haynes, stars of the dominant West Indies cricket team during the 1980s and early 1990s. Haynes even captained Western Province briefly in 1994. While Alvin Kallicheran played for the Free State in the 1980s after he toured with the rebel West Indies team, the thought of several West Indian stars as regular players in South Africa was unimaginable only a few years before. Kallicheran was a special case. Unable to return home to play after coming to South Africa, he stayed and settled in the Free State. Kallicheran, however, had to obtain special permission to live in the State as those classified as 'Indian' were not allowed to live in the Free State without special permission. By the mid-1990s, however, black people could live anywhere they could afford and many wealthy blacks moved into formerly all-white elite areas.

South Africa is full of ironies both within and outside sport. In early 1993 the media revealed that the former head of the Broederbond, NP Minister of Sport and Recreation and Ambassador to the USA, Piet Koornhof, had a Coloured mistress. The *Sunday Times* (17 January 1993: 3) labelled him the 'Minister of Fun'. In addition to his position as Minister of Sport, Koornhof also served as the Minister of Co-operation and Development which made him responsible for the forced removal of millions of black people. Even more striking, and perhaps the most ironic development in South Africa over the past forty years, is that the grandson of former Prime Minister Hendrick Verwoerd is a member of the ANC.

While Koornhof reinvented himself through a cross-racial relationship, many former power holders of the apartheid era have been reinventing themselves publicly through denying responsibility for their actions under apartheid. In scenes reminiscent of post-Nazi Germany, apartheid was increasingly laid at the feet of a handful of leaders, particularly Verwoerd.

While local developments have been significant in shaping sport in the New South Africa, sport in the country is also firmly entrenched in the global sports system.

SOUTH AFRICA AND THE GLOBAL SPORTS ORDER

A number of scholars have written about the role of globalization in the development of sport in national and local contexts (Bale and Maguire, 1994; Bale and Sang, 1996; Kidd, 1991; Maguire, 1990 1994; McKay, Lawrence, Rowe and Miller, 1993). These studies demonstrate that there is a global sports market and economy that is dominated by major events such as the Olympic Games, the World Cups of soccer, rugby and cricket, the IAAF World Championships and by major national leagues in leading sports. These events draw competitors from all over the world and pit cities and nations against each other in bidding processes to host events that are broadcast to global audiences (Macintosh and Whitson, 1993). Global and national television rights now play a large role in the financing of major sports and their competitions. South Africa is unavoidably linked into this global network and has rapidly sought to become a major player in the hosting of large-scale events by promoting itself as the only country on the African continent with the infrastructure to host such events. International organizations have appeared quite eager to award events to South Africa, as evidenced by the 1995 Rugby World Cup, the 1996 Africa Nations Cup of soccer and the 1999 All-Africa Games. Cape Town was one of the five finalists bidding to host the 2004 Olympic Games. The support of President Mandela has been a crucial factor in South Africa's success, but whether such success will survive in the post-Mandela era is not certain.

Theorists of globalization constantly claim that the nation-state is becoming less relevant in the contemporary world. While this may be the case in terms of production, trade and communication, in sport the opposite seems apparent. International sport is the most significant cultural activity in the construction and reconstruction of national identities in the global age. The media actively utilizes images of the past in constructing national discourses around sport (Maguire, 1994; Nauright and White, 1996). In South Africa, such constructions are difficult given the history of racial division, gender discrimination and group difference and hostility. New images of the nation had to be constructed which would resonate with whites who occupied so many positions of power in the economy and media, and with the African majority who sacrificed so much during segregation and apartheid. Indeed, the focus on international sports was potentially fraught with danger as money devoted to sporting enterprises would not be spent on housing and basic health care and education. The RWC glossed over the problems in the new South Africa as the government and media combined to present the nation and the world 'in union'.

(RE)PRESENTING THE 'RAINBOW' NATION
TO SOUTH AFRICA AND THE WORLD

Shosholoza, the Zulu theme song chosen for the Springbok team during the RWC became immensely popular across all sectors of South African society. The song has a long history, highlighting the plight of migrant workers who travelled to work on the mines in South Africa from what was then southern Rhodesia (Zimbabwe). The original version of the song was probably Ndebele, and points out the mode of transport used and the long distances travelled by migrant mine workers as they passed through the mountains. The original words to the song mean 'We are running through the hills of Rhodesia, we are running swiftly though the hills of Rhodesia'; in the version for the RWC, South Africa was inserted in place of Rhodesia. *Shosholoza* has long been sung by workers to generate a work rhythm during group tasks and to alleviate boredom and stress. In the 1960 and 1970s Lutheran students sang the song as an anthem and audiences at major sports events in South Africa since 1995 have taken on *Shosholoza* as a sporting anthem.[2] Thus, a mineworkers' song sung by miners who marched to their early deaths in the gold mines, was a central cultural element in the presentation of the new and unified South Africa. Organizers of the opening and closing ceremonies also utilized the RWC theme song 'It's the World in Union' to present international and national harmony in their representations of South African culture and that of the visiting nations.

The representation of the 'Rainbow Nation' of South Africa in the RWC ceremonies did little to present South Africa in ways that did not resonate with white rugby supporters. Ceremony architect Merle McKenna, whom Edward Griffiths somewhat patronizingly calls 'a wife and mother from Johannesburg' (Griffiths, 1996: 62), attempted to create a ceremony that would 'make every South African feel proud and that was difficult because we are so diverse' (Griffiths, 1992: 68). While some were happy with the ceremony itself, its success was largely accomplished through the elimination of history from the display. Thus timeless African 'natives' appeared clad in traditional dress, and paraded after the African wildlife segment. South African novelist and University of Cape Town Professor of English, J. M. Coetzee, wrote a detailed critique of the RWC and its representations shortly after the tournament's conclusion. Coetzee acknowledged the brief moment of unity created by the Springbok victory, but looked beyond that result to the entire event which he described as 'a month-long orgy of chauvinism and mime-show of war among nations'. Coetzee argued that the making of history in the new South Africa is so contentious that the organizers decided to be 'history-less'. The ceremonies:

. . . presented a de-historicized vision of Tourist South Africa: contented tribesfolk and happy mineworkers, as in the old South Africa, but purified and sanctified, somehow, by the Rainbow. When it got to the paler end of the spectrum, however, it found that it could not proceed without becoming, intermittently, not only a pageant but an historical pageant as well. And so to the procession of timeless Sotho in blankets and timeless Zulu in ostrich feathers it had to add what looked very much like happy eighteenth-century slaves and slaveowners in knee-breeches, bearing baskets of agricultural produce to the Rainbow feast. . . . (Coetzee, 1995)

Such timelessness and sanitizing of history has become almost universal from historical theme parks that 'recreate' a period of the past for our 'recreation', edification and supposed education, to large, almost universal, theme parks such as Disney World or EuroDisney, where 'all vital and potentially shameful moments in American history' are suppressed (Van Wert, 1996: 189). As Disney World belies the history of the death of thousands of 'Main Streets' in the USA, so too the RWC opening ceremony betrayed the history of the struggle, resistance, capitalist domination, racism, segregation, sexism and apartheid in showing the world a 'happy' and united 'new' South Africa. In the rush to demonstrate 'newness' and harmony, history disappears leaving us with little more than a 'white's own' voyeuristic view of 'native' culture.

Coetzee lamented not only the absence of history, but that South Africa was constructed in the RWC ceremonies in the voice of the foreigner, in images and packaging more reminiscent of American hype than South African realities. He argued further that:

Now that rugby has fallen into the hands of an international cartel embracing a 'philosophy' of growth, we can expect the inherent intellectual muddle of the Rainbow Project to be compounded by floods of images of South Africa as an exotic sports-tourism destination, different certainly, but only in a piquant, easily digested way. (Coetzee, 1995)

Contemporary English-speaking post-colonial settler societies appear so similar that the primary way that difference can be expressed is through the selfing of the 'other', in a sense claiming aboriginal culture and peoples as integral parts of 'national' culture. South Africa differs in degree in that the aboriginal peoples are the majority, though the global marketing strategies are still largely shaped by whites and with a predominantly white Western audience in mind. Dean MacCannell (1992) argues that the global system and its dominant ideologies are the products of several centuries of development, particularly of 'white culture'. He argues further that within this white culture, 'ethnicity' is the only form that indigenous groups can assume in order to be a part of the totality of white culture. This can be seen readily in the emergence of ethno-tourism in the 1980s and 1990s. Even post-colonial societies like South Africa and Zimbabwe have used both the histories of their white minorities, and ethnic distinctions in order to attract white tourist expenditure.

As the evidence from South Africa suggests, the way that a global white culture of sport has been most totalizing is through its notions of apoliticality, and that participation can generate or demonstrate 'respectability', in other words mere participation in modern sporting forms is enough to demonstrate 'civilized' qualities. The post-colonial representations of exoticized 'others' has served to re-legitimate the hegemonic values surrounding Western sport. The role of rugby and other sports in the new South Africa demonstrates this clearly.

The ultimate success of events such as the RWC are not usually measured in precise economic terms, though figures spent by tourists and the revenue made at specific events are always produced. These so-called 'hallmark events' are part of contemporary development strategies in much of the Western world (Macintosh and Whitson, 1993), as the profiles generated by large sporting and other events are meant to produce a climate of tourist and business interest, to put a particular place 'on the map'. Indeed President Mandela in his welcoming message for the RWC stressed this point when he stated 'The 1995 Rugby World Cup Tournament represents one of the biggest ever sports events to be staged in Africa. We are determined to make it a resounding success, and prove to the world that Africa is also able to host major sporting events.' (Mandela, 1995.) Evident everywhere is the liberal ideology of inclusiveness, of 'we can do it too if we are only given the chance'.

Former colonized societies like South Africa continually draw on their different-ness from other western and white-dominated societies in promoting their uniqueness to the outside world. What is left in such representations are nations such as Canada that are represented by native Americans and Inuit (Eskimos), New Zealand represented by Maoris, Australia and its Aborigines, and South Africa with its Zulu and blanket-wearing Sotho. The Atlanta Olympic Games attempted to promote a diversity of the 'new South' through the use of many African-Americans in its ceremonies, but gone were the original inhabitants of Georgia, as were the San and Khoi in the RWC – in other words, representations that are readily recognizable by outsiders are used in packaging the nation to the 'global community'. Such representations, however, serve to legitimate the current global order and stress the exotic over the mundane. Thus, it is precisely at moments of advancement and change that those becoming less 'exotic' are re-exoticized to remind whites and 'the other' of their historic, though timeless, reality. Contemporary South Africa is replete with tourists seeking 'real Zulus', but only finding them in touricized villages where performances of 'authentic' African dance are presented. In the 1990s, this phenomenon has earned the appellation 'ethno-tourism' as first world urbanites span the globe in search of cultural difference.

In South Africa this phenomenon is presented in several tourist destinations such as Shakaland in Kwa Zulu-Natal, which is presented as a heritage site depicting Zulu life before white contact. About 70 per cent of the visitors to Shakaland in 1994 were from overseas and most of the remaining 30 per cent were white South Africans who paid R278 for a 24-hour stopover or R75 for a three-hour experience. Shakaland concentrates on attracting the international tourist rather than South Africans. More rare is the approach taken by the Basotho Cultural Centre which shows changes to Basotho culture over time (*Open Africa*, January 1995). Thus, while cultural tourist displays can serve the purpose of assisting in the imagining of a nation, many such destinations are purely for tourist consumption for foreigners who want to see real 'natives' and wild animals, as that is what Africa means for them.

The RWC imagery presented a 'real' Africa to its international audience, but also reinforced old apartheid concepts of separate nations and cultures within South Africa. Whites educated in this system readily understand such imagery and packaging, as a result white rugby fans can easily identify with their nation as presented at the stadium and via television, while the spectacle ignores the realities of the South Africa experienced by the majority of the population. In this context, even President Mandela could be viewed as an 'honourary white', or at least as transcending race, and temporary hero to those who were taught for years to treat the ANC as 'terrorists' and 'communists' through his wearing of the Springbok jersey, the most potent symbol of the old white South Africa. Thus any 'unity' generated by the RWC was illusory at best, and ignored problems that underlay the new South Africa in general and rugby in particular. Certainly post-World Cup events during 1996 bore this out.

International sporting competitions are some of the most significant locations of international contact and are sites for the generation of identities for local, regional and national consumption, while simultaneously being a locus for representing nations and communities to the global audience. This tension leads to the dual process of breaking down difference in generating readily recognizable packaging for global cultural consumption, while relying on recreated difference and ahistorical ethnic representations.

Along with such representations in sports, and the linking of sports and tourism, is a nostalgic underpinning of recreating an era of white cultural dominance, where everything legitimate was white (and nearly always male) and upper or middle class. In the face of rising immigration from the developing world, developed societies have relied on nostalgic representation, often in commodified forms to shore up white cultural identity and hegemony, and to entice 'others' into identifying with the world of the English public schools, elite universities, Hollywood, Nike and Disney World. In the new South Africa such cultural consumption is rampant as global cultural forms rapidly engulf the newly democratized nation. *Shosholoza* sung by white South African rugby fans, rather than migrant mineworkers, encapsulates the entire sanitation of the past. The 'It's the World in Union' RWC theme song bellowed out from a white South African woman, singing in African-American style in a ceremony replete with 'real' timeless 'Africans' and African wildlife, demonstrated the necessity of representations of 'otherness', while simultaneously promoting globality in search of the white tourist with hard currency in search of a 'real' encounter with another culture wherever it can be found. In this context, South Africa is caught up in the global trickle-down economic philosophy that suggests that major events and tourisized locations will bring investment that will ultimately benefit the local economy.

ONE OR MANY 'IMAGINED' SOUTH AFRICA(S)?

It is impossible to conclude that there is one national identity in South Africa or one that is culturally produced through activities such as sport. While identification with South African sporting success is strong, those white South Africans cheering their 'nation' to victory in rugby or cricket are not identifying with the mass of South Africans, nor are black South Africans who fanatically cheer on Bafana Bafana in soccer conceiving of South Africa in the same terms as many whites. While there is a long thread of non-racialism in the country (Fredrikse, 1992), it has not developed into a non-racial social cement that holds a unified 'imagining' of South Africa across all people. Additionally, dominant South African identities are still tied to patriarchy and exclude most women, and South African male sporting cultures have been particularly violent.

The position of women in relation to sports can be seen in many South African newspapers where advertisements for topless bars and strip shows appear in sports sections (for example see *Cape Times*, 8 December 1994: 39). A new black elite led by ANC officials readily endorse a masculinist sporting culture that has its roots in the imperial sporting experience. Steve Tshwete, in comparing rugby and soccer, has referred to the latter as a sissies game, though he actively supports Bafana Bafana. The transition to a new South Africa has not led to a new South African sporting culture, or one that is more inclusive of women on the field and positive towards women off the field.

'Unity' has, in fact, led to the demise of sports in some disadvantaged communities as former non-racial clubs were absorbed into the old sporting competitions. Unfortunately for non-racial clubs, there was not enough room for all the clubs, or at least white officialdom did not possess the political will to allow their competitions to be swamped by black-dominated teams. In June 1994, Casseim Jabaar, President of the historic Caledonian Roses Rugby Club in Cape Town, argued that rugby in the black areas of Cape Town was dying. The club even went so far as to ask permission of the Western Province Rugby Football Union to allow clubs to return to their old SARU structures so that composite senior teams could be selected for competition at higher levels (Behardien, 1994).

As with race and gender, there is a class element to the role in identification with a South African nation and with new sporting teams and structures. International rugby and cricket ticket prices put those sports out of the reach of the vast majority of South Africans. Ticket prices of R50 to R100, and more, serve to limit which South Africans can attend matches and form another way to segregate the population. In sport and in other areas of social life, those blacks who can afford to adopt the trappings of dominant white culture can buy their way into the establishment. In government blacks are the majority but in business, in some areas of culture and sports, whites still dominate and real social change has not occurred. The ANC has placed much faith in the ability of sport to break down old barriers in favour of a new national culture and identity in which it can draw all South Africans together. This is indeed an ambitious aim, but no different from the way that governments all over the world have used sport in an era of diminishing contrasts between nations.

'RAINBOW WARRIORS'? SPORTING HEROES AND THE NEW NATION

In the use of sport to generate national identities, sporting heroes are essential, and people must be able to identify with those who are supposedly representing them in the international arena. Although the success of Bafana Bafana in soccer in 1996 was important, the media has concentrated on rugby and cricket as the main nation-building team sports of the 1990s. In this context, some white heroes have been promoted, particularly team captains such as François Pienaar and Hansie Cronje, or flamboyant players such as James Small in rugby, or Jonty Rhodes and Fanie de Villiers in cricket. The media has gone further – searching for any white players at top level that have 'black' connections or who might be marketable to a multi-cultural audience.

In the January 1997 issue of *SA Sports Illustrated* an article entitled 'Zulu Warrior' on Natal and national team fast bowler Lance Klusener begins with a focus on his ability to speak Zulu and his background in rural Natal. The article states that Klusener, like well-known musician Johnny Clegg, is a 'white Zulu' since he learned to speak Zulu before English (Manthorp, 1997: 62). Klusener's potential as a Zulu spokesman for cricket has not been lost on Ali Bacher and other cricket authorities searching for those who can market the game to all South Africans.

Those few black players who have made it to the national cricket and rugby teams, so far all of them Coloured South Africans, are hailed as national heroes and nation builders. Chester Williams in rugby has been the only black Springbok since unity, while in 1995 and 1996 respectively Paul Adams and Herschelle Gibbs were the only 'black' cricketers in the national cricket team. Gibbs, educated at Bishop's in Cape Town and of very light skin colour, however, has not received the same treatment as a national non-racial hero as have Williams and Adams. President Mandela has referred to both Williams and Adams as 'nation builders', though ironically the same accolades are not given to white soccer players in the national team.

In rugby, particular players were used to market the game to different segments of the population. While Williams represented rugby to black communities and Pienaar became the overarching national hero, Joost van der Westhuizen reassured traditional Afrikaner Springbok supporters that the RWC 'Boks were their team, as well as the team for all South Africa'. Joel Stransky spoke to the English-speaking white population and Hennie Le Roux was used to reassure Afrikaners in the rural areas, or the platteland. Finally, James Small, represented as a rebel with a cause, sold the game to rebellious youth (Griffiths, 1996). Pienaar, Williams and Small in particular received much attention from all sections of the media. While the national press concentrates more evenly on the three major team sports, there is still an overwhelming focus on soccer in those newspapers targeted at a primarily black audience, while Afrikaans and English-language newspapers still concentrated mostly on rugby and cricket in 1997. The RWC only briefly transcended this trend.

A NATIONAL HANGOVER?
PUBLIC AND PRIVATE IN SOUTH AFRICAN TEAM SPORTS

Immediately after the RWC, rugby union became professional and the game's administrators narrowly averted an international revolt of the players. South African satellite channel M-Net then bought the broadcast rights for Super 12 and tests between South Africa and Australia and New Zealand, thus making those matches the preserve of the small handful of urban South Africans who can afford the service, most of whom are middle-class whites. The lack of major exposure on free-to-air television may halt rugby's attempts to be a truly national game in its tracks, as local soccer remains free-to-air and accessible to all who have access to a television. SARFU argues that the large television contracts, though, have provided more revenue to spend on the development of facilities in disadvantaged areas. Griffiths (1996: 201) argues that Luyt and his assistants at Ellis Park (son Louis Luyt Jr, son-in-law Oberholzer and Chris Dirks), were so secure in their own self-importance that the concept of rugby as a national game meant little – they were 'utterly detached'. Provincial unions squabbled with SARFU over who would pay for particular development projects and white SARFU officials remained unconcerned about development issues.

While rugby facilities are being built in some areas, the impetus from the 1995 RWC victories appeared to be fading in early 1996. In February Luyt fired Griffiths, who had at least pushed for development in the townships as a necessity if rugby was to improve its image and catch up with the progress made by other formerly white-dominated sports such as cricket. Mass participation in rugby had been encouraged at the time of the RWC through the strangely apartheid sounding 'Operation Rugby', a programme that aimed to construct or upgrade 42 rugby fields throughout the country using the 40 per cent of SARFU's RWC profits earmarked for development (Griffiths, 1996). With the dismissal of Griffiths and the other popular figures, the old Afrikaner establishment is in firm control of rugby and SARFU administration of rugby appears to be the same as it has been since at least 1956.

While the evidence about changes in rugby is depressing for the supporters of non-racial sport and social transformation in South Africa, other sports have progressed towards real development. Without defending the actions of sports officials, it must be remembered that real alterations in sports rarely happen quickly and take many years to accomplish. It was over fifteen years after independence before Henry Olonga became Zimbabwe's first black cricketer in the national team. The optimists voicing the virtues of sport in building the new nation predominate in public discourse in the mid-1990s, and government and business support weighed in heavily behind Cape Town's bid to host the Summer Olympic Games of 2004. Despite the bid's ultimate failure, it revealed South Africa's entrenchment in the global capitalist sports system.

THE GAMES FOR AFRICA: THE 2004 OLYMPIC BID

Along the drive into Cape Town and around the city, billboards supporting the Cape Town's 2004 Olympic Bid greeted passers by in 1997 with the faces of Archbishop Desmond Tutu or sporting heroes, such as Paul Adams, urging locals to support the bid and no doubt to demonstrate a sense of universal support to IOC members who vote on the selection of the host city. As with many other bids, Cape Town's concentrated on the development of local infrastructure, though the bid was more directly tied to the national policy of Reconstruction and Development than most bids have been. Organizers hoped that this factor would sway IOC officials, eager to see their influence on local and global affairs, to vote for a bid that was full of promise, but where many structural and economic difficulties would have to be overcome. By changing its logo from Table Mountain to an outline of Africa, the bid committee capitalized on the fact that no location in Africa has ever hosted the Olympics. As with Mexico City in 1968, bringing the Games to Africa will be full of risks, but many argue that if the Games are not held in South Africa soon, they may not be held in Africa for generations. While the bid helped to perpetuate a sense of national unity through sports, many local ratepayers in Cape Town were concerned about the effect the Games would have on their taxes and property values, particularly as the IOC now requires governments to underwrite any losses that the Games may incur.

CONCLUSION

South African sport has not been able to overcome the legacies of apartheid and the social divisions it, and the segregation system before it, generated over the past century. The RWC, cricket victories, a winning national soccer team and Olympic successes have all been important to many South Africans and have generated some momentary feelings of national identification. However, the overall conception of what South Africa is, or should be, is still being negotiated both through lived experiences and discursively through the media and other forms of public discourse. Some viewed the possible hosting of the world's largest sporting event in Cape Town in 2004 as the event that would galvanize the nation over the seven years from the IOC's decision in 1997 to the actual Games. Though that bid failed, others are sure to follow as the possible economic benefits of hosting major international events draw widespread capitalist and governmental support within South Africa. Sport is but one area where the South African nation can exist; however, the divisions that exist within sport and within wider South African society mean that it may be a long time before a truly 'national' identity is forged that takes account of race, class and gender differences.

The general societal difficulties that South Africa must overcome are best summed up by the great writer Breytan Bretyenbach:

Afternoon run in Pierre's car over hills and valleys deeper inland, taking us through what must be the plushest suburbs anywhere – riot of cultivated tropical vegetation in flower behind high security walls; then police outposts bristling with radio masts, enclosed within their safe perimeter by electrified wire fences; and suddenly cresting a hill, down through a patch of Kwazulu, abject poverty, pot-holed roads, burned-down schools and gutted houses, dilapidated shopfronts with glowering men shouldering a wall, scatter of fowl and goats and cattle. The killing fields. 'Only death in this place and this place we do not know': Anonymous. . . . I am looking to the future and it chills me to the bone. (Breytenbach, 1993: 201)

NOTES

1. Louis Luyt's last name is pronounced 'Late'.
2. This information was provided by members of staff at the University of Natal, Pietermaritzburg. Supplied by Christopher Merrett.

REFERENCES

Adams, R. (1992) 'Symbols of unity: apartheid and the Springbok emblem'. *SACOS*. Cape Town, p. 14.

African National Congress (1994) *Reconstruction and Development Programme*.

Altham, H. (1962) *A History of Cricket*. London: Allen and Unwin.

Altham, H. and Swanton, E. (1948) *A History of Cricket*. London: George Allen and Unwin. 4th edition.

Archer, R. and Bouillon, A. (1982) *The South African Game: Sport and Racism*. London: Zed Press.

Bale, J. (1994) *Landscapes of Modern Sport*. London: Leicester University Press.

Bale, J. and Maguire, J. (eds) (1994) *The Global Sports Arena: Athletic Talent Migration in an Interdependent World*. London: Frank Cass.

Bale, J. and Sang, J. (1996) *Kenyan Running: Movement, Culture, Geography and Global Change*. London: Frank Cass.

Bassano, B. (1979) *South Africa in International Cricket, 1888–1970*. East London: Chameleon.

Baxter, J. (1994) 'Towards a new sports dispensation in South Africa, 1985–1992', in R. Wilcox (ed.), *Sport in the Global Village*. Morgantown, WV: Fitness Information Technology.

Beattie, D. (1991) 'Craven dons Coat of Many Colours'. *Star*, 25 October.

Beckles, H. and Stoddart, B. (eds) (1994) *Liberation Cricket*. Manchester: Manchester University Press.

Behardien, R. (1994) 'Rugby dying on Cape Flats'. *Southeaster*, 24–28 June, p. 11.

Beinart, W. (1994) *Twentieth Century South Africa*. Oxford: Oxford University Press.

Benson, M. (1986) *No Easy Walk to Freedom: A Biography of Nelson Mandela*. Harmondsworth: Penguin.

Birley, D. (1979) *The Willow Wand*. London: Macdonald and Jane's.

Black, D. and Nauright, J. (forthcoming) *Rugby and the South African Nation*. Manchester: Manchester University Press.

Bonner, P. (1982) 'The Transvaal Native Congress, 1917–1920: the radicalisation of the black petty bourgeoisie on the Rand', in S. Marks and

R. Rathbone (eds), *Industrialisation and Social Change in South Africa*. London: Longman.

Bonner, P. (1988) 'Family, crime and political consciousness on the East Rand'. *Journal of South African Studies*, **14**(3), 393–420.

Bonner, P. (1990a) '"Desirable or undesirable Basotho women?": liquor, prostitution and the migration of Basotho women to the Rand, 1920–1945', in C. Walker (ed.) *Women and Gender in Southern Africa to 1945*. Cape Town: David Philip.

Bonner, P. (1990b) 'Squatter movements on the Rand, 1944–1952'. *Radical History Review*, **46/7**, 89–115.

Bonner, P., Hofmeyr, I., James, D. and Lodge, T. (1989) *Holding Their Ground*. Johannesburg: University of Witwatersrand Press.

Booth, D. (1990) 'South Africa's "Autonomous Sport" strategy: desegregation apartheid style'. *Sporting Traditions*, **6**(2), 156–77.

Booth, D. (1992) 'Accommodating race to play the game'. *Sporting Traditions*, **8**(2), 182–209.

Booth, D. (1995) 'United sport: an alternative hegemony in South Africa'. *International Journal of the History of Sport*, **12**(3), 105–24.

Bose, M. (1994) *Sporting Colours: Sport and Politics in South Africa*. London: Robson Books.

Bowen, R. (1970) *Cricket: A History of its Growth and Development Throughout the World*. London: Eyre and Spottiswoode.

Bozzoli, B. (ed.) (1979) *Labour, Townships and Protest*. Johannesburg: Ravan Press.

Bozzoli, B. (ed.) (1983) *Town and Countryside in the Transvaal: Capitalist Penetration and Popular Response*. Johannesburg: Ravan Press.

Bozzoli, B. (ed.) (1987) *Class, Community and Conflict*. Johannesburg: Ravan Press.

Bozzoli, B. and Delius, P. (1990) 'Radical history and South African society'. *Radical History Review*, **46/7**, 13–45.

Bozzoli, B. with Nkotsoe, M. (1991) *Women of Phokeng: Consciousness, Life Strategy and Migrancy in South Africa, 1900–1983*. Portsmouth, NH: Heinemann.

Bradley, J. (1992) 'The M.C.C., society and Empire: a portrait of cricket's ruling body', in J.A. Mangan (ed.), *The Cultural Bond*. London: Frank Cass.

Breytenbach, B. (1993) *Return to Paradise*. London and Boston: Faber & Faber.

Brickhill, J. (1976) *Race Against Race: South Africa's Multinational Sports Fraud*. London: International Defence and Aid Fund.

Callinicos, L. (1987) *Working Life: Factories, Townships, and Popular Culture on the Rand, 1886–1940*. Johannesburg: Ravan Press.

Cashman, R. (1988) 'Cricket and colonialism:colonial hegemony and indigenous subversion?', in J.A. Mangan (ed.) *Pleasure, Profit, Proselytism: British Culture at Home and Abroad 1700–1914*. London: Frank Cass.

Cashman, R. (1992) 'Symbols of unity: Anglo-Australian cricketers 1877–1900', in J.A. Mangan (ed.), *The Cultural Bond.* London: Frank Cass.

Cashman, R. (1995) *Paradise of Sport: The Rise of Organized Sport in Australia.* Melbourne: Oxford University Press.

Claassen, W. (1985) *More than Just Rugby.* Johannesburg: Hans Strydom.

Claassen, W. (1992) 'Is it worth being a Springbok?' *Rugby 15,* **2**(5), 4.

Clayton, K. and Greyvenstein, C. (1995) *The Craven Tapes: Doc Tells All.* Cape Town: Human and Rousseau.

Cobley, A. (1990) *Class and Consciousness: The Black Petty Bourgeoisie in South Africa, 1924–1950.* Westport, CT: Greenwood Press.

Cobley, A. (1994) 'A political history of playing fields: the provision of sporting facilities for Africans in the Johannesburg Area to 1948'. *International Journal of the History of Sport,* **11**(2), 212–30.

Connerton, P. (1989) *How Societies Remember.* Cambridge: Cambridge University Press.

Couzens, T. (1982) '"Moralizing leisure time": the transatlantic connection and black Johannesburg, 1918–1936', in S. Marks and R. Rathbone (eds), *Industrialisation and Social Change in South Africa: African Class Formation, Culture and Consciousness 1870–1930.* London: Longman.

Couzens, T. (1983) 'An introduction to the history of football in South Africa', in B. Bozzoli (ed.), *Town and Countryside in the Transvaal.* Johannesburg: Ravan Press.

Craig, P. G. and Rees, C. R. (1994) 'The Springbok trials: some critical reflections on South Africa's Unity Games', in R. Wilcox (ed.), *Sport in the Global Village.* Morgantown, WV: Fitness Information Technology.

Crapanzano, V. (1986) *Waiting: The Whites of South Africa.* New York: Vintage.

Cronin, M. (1994) 'Sport and a sense of Irishness'. *Irish Studies Review,* **9**, 12–16.

'Cypher', (1915) 'History of Natal cricket', in M.W. Luckin (ed.), *The History of South African Cricket.* Johannesburg: W.E. Horter.

DaSilva, F. and Faught, J. (1982) 'Nostalgia: a sphere and process of contemporary ideology'. *Qualitative Sociology,* **5**(1), 47–61.

Dassie, E. (1996) 'Moulded in the fire of history'. *Brazilians: The Official Magazine of Sundowns FC,* **1**, 6–7.

Davenport, T. R. H. (1969) 'African townsmen?: South African (urban areas) legislation through the years'. *African Affairs,* **68**(2), 95–109.

Davis, F. (1979) *Yearning for Yesterday: A Sociology of Nostalgia.* New York: The Free Press.

de Broglio, C. (1970) *South Africa: Racism in Sport.* London: International Defence and Aid Fund.

de Kiewiet, C.W. (1941) *A History of South Africa: Social and Economic.* London: Oxford University Press.

de Villiers, M. (1988) *White Tribe Dreaming.* New York: Viking.

Department of Foreign Affairs and Trade (Australia) (1988) 'Race and rugby in South Africa'. *Australian Foreign Affairs Review,* **59**(4).

Dobson, P. (1989) *Rugby in South Africa: A History, 1861–1988*. Cape Town: South African Rugby Board.

Dobson, P. (1990) *Bishop's Rugby*. Cape Town: Don Nelson.

Dobson, P. (1994) *Doc: The Life of Danie Craven*. Cape Town: Don Nelson.

Dobson, P. (1996) *Rugby's Greatest Rivalry: South Africa vs New Zealand*. Cape Town: Human and Rousseau.

D'Oliveira, B. (1969) *The D'Oliveira Affair*. London: Collins.

Donnelly, P. (1993) 'Subcultures in sport: resilience and transformation', in A. Ingham and J. Loy (eds), *Sport in Social Development: Traditions, Transitions and Transformations*. Champaign: Human Kinetics.

Dorey, H. (1912) *The Triangular Tests, 1878–1912*. London: Cricket and Sports Publishers.

Du Toit, B. (1991) 'The far right in current South African politics'. *Journal of Modern African Studies*, **29**(4), 627–67.

Duffus, L. (1947) *Cricketers of the Veld*. London: Swinfern.

Duffus, L. (1969) *Play Abandoned*. London: Bailey Brothers and Swinfern.

Duffus, L. (1980) 'South Africa', in E.W. Swanton and J. Woodcock (eds), *Barclay's World of Cricket: The Game From A–Z* (2nd edn). London: Barclay's.

Dyasi, A. (1983) 'Western Cape', in G. Thabe (comp.) *It's a Goal*. Johannesburg: Skotaville.

Etherington, N. (1988) 'Natal's black rape scare of the 1870s'. *Journal of Southern African Studies*, **15**(1).

Evans, G. (1989) 'Classrooms of war: the militarisation of white South African schooling', in J. Cock and L. Nathan (eds), *War and Society: The Militarisation of South Africa*. Cape Town: David Philip.

Evans, J. (1990) 'Time to kick compulsory rugby into touch?' *Personality*, 16 July.

Ferreira, A. (1995) Untitled South African Press Association/Reuter Report, 14 June.

Fortune, C. (1960) *Cricket Overthrown*. London: Bailey and Swinfern.

Frederikse, J. (1986) *South Africa: A Different Kind of War*. Boston: Beacon Press.

Frederikse, J. (1992) *The Threads of Non-Racialism in South Africa*. Bloomington: Indiana University Press.

Frederikse, J., Tomaselli, K., Muller, J. and Andersson, M. (1988) 'Culture and media: how we are made to see', in K. Tomaselli (ed.), *Rethinking Culture*. Bellville: Anthropos Publishers.

Fry, C. B. (1939) *A Life Worth Living: Some Phases of an Englishman*. London: Eyre and Spottiswode.

Gerhart, G. (1978) *Black Power in South Africa: The Evolution of an Ideology*. Berkeley: University of California Press.

Gleeson, M., 'Buck Up!' *Weekly Mail*, 14 August 1992.

Greyvenstein, C. (1989) *Great Springbok Rugby Tests: 100 Years of Headlines*. Cape Town: Don Nelson.

Greyvenstein, C. (1995) *Springbok Rugby: An Illustrated History*. London: New Holland.

Griffiths, E. (1991) 'Rugby League: new body to be launched tomorrow'. *Sunday Times* (Johannesburg), 25 August.

Griffiths, E. (1996) *One Team, One Country: The Greatest Year of Springbok Rugby*. London: Viking.

Grundlingh, A. (1996) 'Playing for power? Rugby, Afrikaner nationalism and masculinity in South Africa, *c.* 1900–*c.* 1970', in J. Nauright and T. Chandler (eds), *Making Men: Rugby and Masculine Identity*. London: Frank Cass.

Grundlingh, A. and Sapire, H. (1988) 'From feverish festival to repetitive ritual? The changing fortunes of Great Trek mythology in an industrialising South Africa, 1938–1988'. *South African Historical Journal*, **21**(1), 19–37.

Grundlingh, A., Odendaal, A. and Spies, B. (1995) *Beyond the Tryline: Rugby in South Africa*. Johannesburg: Ravan Press.

Gruneau, R. and Whitson, D. (1993) *Hockey Night in Canada*. Toronto: Garamond Press.

Guelke, A. (1986) 'The politicisation of South African sport', in L. Allison (ed.), *The Politics of Sport*. Manchester: Manchester University Press.

Guelke, A. (1993) 'Sport and the end of apartheid', in L. Allison (ed.), *The Changing Politics of Sport*. Manchester: Manchester University Press.

Guttmann, A. (1994) *Games and Empires*. New York: Columbia University Press.

Haigh, P. (1994) 'Viljoen looking good in the dominant role'. *Sunday Telegraph* (London), 13 November, p. 39.

Hain, P. (1971) *Don't Play with Apartheid: The Background to the Stop the Seventy Tour Campaign*. London: George Allen and Unwin.

Harris, S. (1972) *Political Football: The Springbok Tour of Australia, 1971*. Melbourne: Gold Star Publications.

Harrison, D. (1985) *The White Tribe of Africa*. London: BBC Books.

Hawke, M.B. (1924) *Recollections and Reminiscences*. London: Williams and Norgate.

Heilbuth, B. (1976) 'Do blacks want to wear the Springbok?: Craven and black rugby leaders have their say'. *Weekend Argus*, 21 August, p. 3.

Hellmann, E. (1934) *Rooiyard*. Cape Town: Oxford University Press.

Henderson, (1906) *South African Cricketers' Annual. 1905–1906*.

Hendricks, D. (1994) 'Sport and transformation: observations and projections on developments in South Africa from an "Eliasian" perspective', in R. Wilcox (ed.), *Sport in the Global Village*. Morgantown, WV: Fitness Information Technology.

Hirson, B. (1989) *Yours for the Union: Class and Community Struggles in South Africa, 1930–1947*. London: Zed Press.

Holt, R. (1982) *Sport and Society in Modern France*. London: Oxford University Press.

Holt, R. (1989) *Sport and the British*. London: Oxford University Press.

Huttenback, R. (1976) *Racism and Empire: White Settlers and Coloured Immigrants in the British Self-Governing Colonies, 1830–1910*. Ithaca, NY: Cornell University Press.

Iliffe, J. (1979) *A History of Modern Tanganyika*. Cambridge: Cambridge University Press.

James, C.L.R. (1984) *Beyond a Boundary*. New York: Pantheon.

Jarvie, G. (1985) *Class, Race and Sport in South Africa's Political Economy*. London: Routledge and Kegan Paul.

Jarvie, G. (ed.) (1991) *Sport, Racism and Ethnicity*. London: Falmer.

Jarvie, G. (1993) 'Sport, nationalism and cultural identity', in L. Allison (ed.), *The Changing Politics of Sport*. Manchester: Manchester University Press.

Jarvie, G. and Walker, G. (eds) (1994) *Ninety Minute Patriots? Sport in the Making of the Scottish Nation*. London: Leicester University Press.

Jeffrey, I. (1992) 'Street rivalry and patron-managers: football in Sharpeville, 1943–1985'. *African Studies*, 51(1), 69–94.

Jenkins, S. (1994) 'The sorry state of tennis'. *Sports Illustrated*, 9 May, pp. 78–86.

Joyce, P. (1981) *Reader's Digest South Africa's Yesterdays*. Cape Town: Reader's Digest.

Karis, T. and Carter, G. (1972–7) *From Protest to Challenge: A Documentary History of African Politics in South Africa 1882–1964* (4 vols). Palo Alto, CA: Stanford University.

Keegan, T. (1996) *Colonial South Africa and the Origins of the Racial Order*. Cape Town and Johannesburg: David Philip.

Kerr, A. (1968) *Fort Hare 1915–1968: The Evolution of an African College*. London: C. Hurst and Co.

Kidd, B. (1988) 'The campaign against sport in South Africa'. *International Journal*, 63(4), 643–64.

Kidd, B. (1991) 'From quarantine to cure: the new phase of the struggle against apartheid sport'. *Sociology of Sport Journal*, 8(1), 33–46.

Kidd, B. (1992) 'The campaign against sport in South Africa'. *International Journal*, 43(4), 643–64.

Kuper, L. (1965) *The African Bourgeoisie*. New Haven, CT: Yale University Press.

La Hausse, P. (1990) '"The cows of Nongaloza": youth, crime and Amalaita gangs, 1900–1936'. *Journal of South African Studies*, 16(1), 79–111.

Lapchick, R. (1975) *The Politics of Race and International Sport: The Case of South Africa*. Westport, CT: Greenwood Press.

Laubscher, L. and Nieman, G. (1990) *The Carolin Papers: A Diary of the 1906–07 Springbok Tour*. Pretoria: Rugbyana Publishers.

Leveson-Gower, H. (1953) *Off and on the Field*. London: S. Paul.

Lewis, D. (1992/3) 'Soccer and rugby: popular production of pleasure in South African culture'. *Southern African Political and Economic Monthly*, 6(3–4), 13–17.

Lewis, P. (1979) 'Axioms for reading the landscape', in D. Meinig (ed.), *The Interpretation of Ordinary Landscapes*. New York: Oxford University Press.

Lewson, P. (1954) 'A complete South African'. *Lantern*, January.

Lodge, T. (1983) *Black Politics in South Africa Since 1945*. London: Longman.

Louw, R. (1987) *For the Love of Rugby*. Johannesburg: Hans Strydom.

Lowenthal, D. (1985) *The Past is a Foreign Country*. Cambridge: Cambridge University Press.

Luckin, M. (1915) *The History of South African Cricket*. Johannesburg: W.E. Horter.

MacCannell, D. (1992) *Empty Meeting Grounds: The Tourist Papers*. London: Routledge.

McGlew, J. (1965) *Cricket in Crisis*. London: Hodder and Stoughton.

Macintosh, D., Cantelon, H. and McDermott, L. (1993) 'The IOC and South Africa: a lesson in transnational relations'. *International Review for the Sociology of Sport*, **28**(4), 373–93.

Macintosh, D., Greenhorn, D. and Black, D. (1992) 'Canadian diplomacy and the 1978 Edmonton Commonwealth Games', *Journal of Sport History*, **19**(1), 26–55.

McKay, J., Lawrence, G., Miller, T. and Rowe, D. (1993) 'Globalization and Australian sport'. *Sport Science Review*, **2**(1), 10–28.

Maguire, J. (1990) 'More than a sporting touchdown: the making of American football in England 1982–1990'. *Sociology of Sport Journal*, **7**(4), 213–37.

Maguire, J. (1994) 'Sport, identity, politics, and globalization'. *Sociology of Sport Journal*, **11**(4), 398–427.

Mandle, J. and Mandle, J. (1988) *Grass Roots Commitment: Basketball and Society in Trinidad and Tobago*. Parkersburg, IA: Caribbean Books.

Mandle, W. (1987) *The Gaelic Athletic Association and Irish Nationalist Politics 1884–1924*. London: Croom Helm.

Mangan, J.A. (ed.) (1992) *The Cultural Bond: Sport, Empire and Society*. London: Frank Cass.

Manthorp, N. (1997) 'Zulu warrior'. *SA Sports Illustrated*, 20 January, pp. 62–4.

Marks, S. (1970) *Reluctant Rebellion: The 1906–08 Disturbances in Natal*. Oxford: Clarendon Press.

Martin, P. (1991) 'Colonialism, youth and football in French Equatorial Africa'. *International Journal of the History of Sport*, **8**(1), 56–71.

Martin-Jenkins, C. (1980) *Who's Who in International Cricket*. London: Queen Anne Press.

Merrett, C. (1988) 'Problems of black sport in an apartheid city', in J. Laband and R. Haswell (eds), *Pietermaritzburg, 1838–1988: A New Portrait of an African City*. Pietermaritzburg: University of Natal Press.

Merrett, C. (1994a) 'Sport, racism and urban policy in South Africa: Pietermaritzburg, a case study'. *Sporting Traditions*, **10**(2), 97–122.

Merrett, C. (1994b) *A Culture of Censorship: Secrecy and Intellectual Repression in South Africa*. Pietermaritzburg: University of Natal Press and Cape Town: David Philip.

Merrett, C. (1995) 'Comrades of a particular type: an alternative history of the marathon, 1921–1983'. *Natalia*, **25**, 65–76.

Merrett, C. (1996) 'In nothing else are the deprivers so deprived'. *The International Journal of the History of Sport*, **13**(2), 146–65.

Metcalfe, A. (1987) *Canada Learns to Play: The Emergence of Organized Sport 1807–1914*. Toronto: McClelland and Stewart.

Mirwis, S. (1976) 'Potgieter calls for club level open athletics'. *Sunday Express*, 15 August, p. 9.

Mlokoti, C. (1996) 'Remembering the Glory Days'. *Amakhosi: Official Fan Magazine of Iwisa Kaizer Chiefs*, **4**, 16–17.

Moodie, D. (1975) *The Rise of Afrikanerdom: Power, Apartheid and the Afrikaner Civil Religion*. Berkeley, CA: University of California Press.

Morrell, R. (1996) 'Forging a ruling race: rugby and white masculinity in colonial Natal, *c*. 1870–1910', in J. Nauright and T. Chandler (eds), *Making Men: Rugby and Masculine Identity*. London: Frank Cass.

Motloung, M. (1994) 'Ungaged'. *New Nation*, 2 December, p. 31.

Muller. J. (1987) 'Cacophony of consent: the press in the struggle for educational reform', in K. Tomaselli, R. Tomaselli and J. Muller (eds), *Narrating the Crisis: Hegemony and the South African Press*. Johannesburg: Richard Lyon & Co.

Murray, B. (1994) *Football: A World History*. London: Scholar Press.

National Sports Congress (1991) 'The Sports Moratorium'. Policy Paper.

Nauright, J. (1991) 'Sport, race and empire: British responses to the 1905 New Zealand rugby tour'. *International Journal of the History of Sport*, **8**(2), 239–55.

Nauright, J. (1992) 'Sport and the image of colonial manhood in the British mind: British physical deterioration debates and colonial sporting tours, 1878–1906'. *Canadian Journal of History of Sport*, **23**(2), 54–71.

Nauright, J. (1993) '"Like fleas on a dog": emerging national and international conflict over New Zealand rugby ties with South Africa, 1965–74'. *Sporting Traditions*, **10**(1), 54–77.

Nauright, J. (1996a) 'A besieged tribe: nostalgia, white cultural identity and the role of rugby in a changing South Africa'. *International Review for the Sociology of Sport*, **31**(1), 63–77.

Nauright, J. (1996b) 'Colonial manhood and imperial race virility: British responses to post-Boer War colonial rugby tours', in J. Nauright and T. Chandler (eds), *Making Men: Rugby and Masculine Identity*. London: Frank Cass.

Nauright, J. (1996c) 'Sustaining masculine hegemony: rugby and the nostalgia of masculinity', in J. Nauright and T. Chandler (eds), *Making Men: Rugby and Masculine Identity*. London: Frank Cass.

Nauright, J. (1997) 'Muscular Islam, rugby and popular culture in the coloured community of Cape Town'. *International Journal of the History of Sport*, **14**(1), 184–90.

Nauright, J. and Black, D. (1994) 'It's rugby that really matters: New Zealand – South Africa rugby relations and the moves to isolate South Africa, 1956–1992', in R. Wilcox (ed.), *Sport in the Global Village*. Morgantown, WV: Fitness Information Technology.

Nauright, J. and Black, D. (1995) 'New Zealand and international sport: the case of All Black–Springbok rugby, sanctions and protest against apartheid 1959–1992', in J. Nauright (ed.) *Sport, Power and Society in New Zealand: Historical and Contemporary Perspectives.* Sydney: Australian Society for Sports History.

Nauright, J. and Black, D. (1996) 'Hitting them where it hurts: Springbok–All Black rugby, masculine national identity and counter-hegemonic struggle, 1959–1992', in J. Nauright and T. Chandler (eds), *Making Men: Rugby and Masculine Identity.* London: Frank Cass.

Nauright, J. and Chandler, T. J. L. (eds) (1996) *Making Men: Rugby and Masculine Identity.* London: Frank Cass.

Nauright, J. and White, P. (1996) '"Save Our Jets": professional sport, nostalgia, community and nation in Canada', *AVANTE,* **2**(3), 24–41.

Neame, L.E. (1929) *Some South African Politicians.* Cape Town: Maskew Miller.

Nepia, G. and McLean, T. (1963) *I, George Nepia.* Wellington: A.H. and A.W. Reed.

Newnham, T. (1975) *Apartheid is Not a Game.* Auckland: Graphic Publications.

Nixon, R. (1994) *Homelands, Harlem and Hollywood: South African Culture and the World Beyond.* New York and London: Routledge.

Norval, A. (1996) *Deconstructing Apartheid Discourse.* London: Verso.

Odendaal, A. (1977) *Cricket in Isolation: The Politics of Race and Sport in South Africa.* Cape Town: Self-published.

Odendaal, A. (1984) *Vukani Bantu! The Beginnings of Black Protest Politics in South Africa to 1912.* Cape Town: David Philip.

Odendaal, A. (1988) 'South Africa's black Victorians: sport and society in South Africa in the nineteenth century', in J.A. Mangan (ed.), *Pleasure, Profit, Proselytism: British Culture and Sport at Home and Abroad, 1700–1914.* London: Frank Cass.

Odendaal, A. (1995) '"The thing that is not round": the untold history of black rugby in South Africa', in A. Grundlingh, A. Odendaal and B. Spies, *Beyond the Tryline: Rugby and South African Society.* Johannesburg: Ravan Press.

O'Meara, D. (1983) *Volkapitalisme: Class, Capital and Ideology in the Development of Afrikaner Nationalism, 1934–1948.* Johannesburg: Raven Press.

Oriard, M. (1993) *Reading Football: How the Popular Press Created an American Sporting Spectacle.* Chapel Hill: University of North Carolina Press.

Pakenham, V. (1985) *The Noonday Sun: Edwardians in the Tropics.* London: Methuen.

Parker, G.A. (1897) *South African Sports: An Official Handbook.* London.

Partridge, T. (1991) *A Life in Rugby.* Halfway House: Southern Book Publishers.

Paton, A. (1964) *Hofmeyr.* London and Cape Town: Oxford University Press.

Patterson, S. (1953) *Colour and Culture in South Africa: A Study of the Status of the Cape Coloured People Within the Social Stucture of the Union of South Africa*. London: Routledge and Kegan Paul.

Payne, A. (1990) 'The international politics of the Gleneagles Agreement'. *Round Table*, **320**, 417–30.

Pearson, M. (1979) 'Heads in the sand: the 1956 Springbok tour to New Zealand in perspective', in R. Cashman and M. McKernan (eds), *Sport in History*. Brisbane: University of Queensland Press.

Phillips, J. (1987) *A Man's Country: The Image of the Pakeha Male*. Auckland: Penguin.

Phillips, R. (1930) *The Bantu Are Coming*. London: Student Christian Movement Press.

Phillips, R. (1936) *The Bantu in the City: A Study of Cultural Adjustment on the Witwatersrand*. Boston: AMS Press.

Pienaar, H. (1996) 'The Boere and the egg-shaped ball'. *Sidelines: South African Quarterly*, **8**, 6–19.

Pinnock, D. (1984) *The Brotherhoods: Street Gangs and State Control in Cape Town*. Cape Town: David Philip.

Pollock, W. (1941) *Talking About Cricket*. London: Victor Gollancz.

Posel, D. (1989) 'A "battlefield of perceptions": state discourses on political violence, 1985–1988', in J. Cock and L. Nathan (eds), *The Militarisation of South Africa*. Johannesburg: Ravan.

Quick, S. (1990) '"Black Knight Checks White King": The Conflict Between Avery Brundage and the African Nations over South African Membership in the IOC'. *Canadian Journal of History of Sport*, **21**(2), 20–32.

Ramokhoase, P. (1983) 'Transvaal Jumpers', in G. Thabe (comp.), *It's a Goal!* Johannesburg: Skotaville.

Ramsamy, S. (1982) *Apartheid: The Real Hurdle*. London: International Defence and Aid Fund.

Ranger, T. (1987) '"Pugilism and pathology": African boxing and the black urban experience in southern Rhodesia', in J.A. Mangan and W. Baker (eds), *Sport in Africa: Essays in Social History*. New York: African Publishing Company.

Rive, R. (1986) *Buckingham Palace, District Six*. London: Heinemann.

Roberts, C. (1988) *SACOS 1973–1988: 15 Years of Resistance*. Durban: Natal University.

Roberts, C. (1992) *Against the Grain: Women and Sport in South Africa*. Cape Town: Township Publishing Co-operative.

Roger, W. (1991) *Old Heroes: The 1956 Spingbok Tour and the Lives Beyond*. Auckland: Hodder and Stoughton.

Roux, E. (1948) *Time Longer Than Rope: A History of the Black Man's Struggle for Freedom in South Africa*. Madison: University of Wisconsin Press.

Ryan, G. (1993) *Forerunners of the All Blacks: The 1888–89 New Zealand Native Football Team in Britain, Australia and New Zealand*. Christchurch: University of Canterbury Press.

Schrire, R. (1991) *Adapt or Die: The End of White Politics in South Africa*. New York: The Ford Foundation and the Foreign Policy Association.

Simons, H. J. and Simons, R. (1969) *Class and Colour in South Africa 1850–1950*. London: International Defence and Aid Fund.

Smith, K. (1988) *The Changing Past: Trends in South African Historical Writing*. Johannesburg: Ravan Press.

Sorrenson, M.P.K. (1976) 'Uneasy bedfellows: a survey of New Zealand's relations with South Africa', in *New Zealand, South Africa and Sport: Background Papers*. Wellington: New Zealand Institute of International Affairs.

Stewart, K. (1988) 'Nostalgia – A Polemic'. *Cultural Anthropology*, **3**(3), 227–41.

Stoddart, B. (1988) 'Sport, cultural imperialism, and colonial response in the British Empire'. *Comparative Studies in Society and History*, **30**(4), 649–73.

Stoddart, B. and Sandiford, K. (eds) (forthcoming) *Cricket and Imperial Cultures*. Manchester: Manchester University Press.

Stuart, O. (1996) 'Players, workers, protesters: social change and soccer in colonial Zimbabwe', in J. MacClancy (ed.), *Sport, Identity and Ethnicity*. Oxford: Berg.

Sugden, J. and Bairner, A. (1993) *Sport, Sectarianism and Society in a Divided Ireland*. London: Leicester University Press.

Swaffer, H.P. (ed.) (1914) *South African Sport, 1914*. Johannesburg: Transvaal Reader.

Swanson, M. (1977) 'The "Sanitation Syndrome": Bubonic Plague and Urban Native Policy in the Cape Colony, 1900–09'. *Journal of African History*, **18**(3), 387–410.

Swanton, E.W. and Woodcock, J. (eds) (1980) *Barclay's World of Cricket: The Game From A–Z*. London: William Collins.

Sweet, R. (1989) 'Awakening the sleeping giant', in P. Dobson, *Rugby in South Africa: A History 1861–1988*. Cape Town: South African Rugby Board.

Taylor, H.W. (1925) 'South African cricket, 1910–1924', in Cape Times, *Sports and Sportsmen: South Africa*. Cape Town: Cape Times.

Tennyson, L. (1950) *Sticky Wickets*. London: Bailey and Swinfern.

Thabe, G. (comp.) (1983) *It's a Goal: 50 Years of Sweat, Tears and Drama in Black Soccer*. Johannesburg: Skotaville Publishers.

Thompson, L. (1985) *The Political Mythology of Apartheid*. New Haven: Yale University Press.

Thompson, R. (1964) *Race and Sport*. London: Oxford.

Tomaselli, K. (ed.) (1988) *Rethinking Culture*. Bellville: Anthropos Publishers.

Tomaselli, K. and Tomaselli, R. (1987) 'The political economy of the South African press', in K. Tomaselli, R. Tomaselli, and J. Muller (eds), *Narrating the Crisis: Hegemony and the South African Press*. Johannesburg: Richard Lyon & Co.

Tomaselli, K., Tomaselli, R. and Muller, J. (1987) *Narrating the Crisis: Hegemony and the South African Press*. Johannesburg: Richard Lyon & Co.

Tozer, M. (1992) 'A sacred trinity: cricket, school, Empire: E.W. Hornung and his young guard', in J.A. Mangan (ed.), *The Cultural Bond: Sport, Empire and Society*. London: Frank Cass.

Unterhalter, E. (1987) *Forced Removals*. London: International Defence and Aid Fund.

van der Merwe, F. (1991) 'L.S. Meintjes: his impact on South African sport history'. *Sporting Traditions*, 7(2), 192–205.

van Onselen, C. (1982a) *New Babylon: Studies in the Social and Economic History of the Witwatersrand 1886–1914, Vol. 1*. Johannesburg: Ravan.

van Onselen, C. (1982b) *New Ninevah: Studies in the Social and Economic History of the Witwatersrand, Vol. 2*. Johannesburg: Ravan.

van Wert, W. (1996) 'Disney World and posthistory'. *Cultural Critique*, 187–214.

van Zyl Slabbert, F. (1985) *The Last White Parliament*. London: Sidgwick and Jackson.

Walshe, P. (1971) *The Rise of African Nationalism in South Africa*. Berkeley: University of California Press.

Walvin, J. (1994) *The People's Game: The History of Football Revisited*. Edinburgh: Mainstream Publishing.

Warner, P. F. (1906) *The M.C.C. in South Africa*. London: Chapman and Hall.

Warner, P. F. (1951) *Long Innings: The Autobiography*. London: Harrap.

Webber, A.C. (1927) 'The control of cricket in South Africa', in M.W. Luckin (ed.), *South African Cricket, 1919–1927*, Johannesburg: W. E. Horter.

Wells, A.W. (1949) *South Africa: A Planned Tour of the Country Today*. London: J.M. Dent and Sons.

West, S. E. and Luker, W. J. (1965) *Century at Newlands, 1864–1964: A History of the Western Province Cricket Club*. Newlands: Western Province Cricket Club.

Wilkins, I. and Strydom, H. (1979) *The Broederbond*. New York: Paddington Press.

Willan, B. (1982) 'An African in Kimberley: Sol T. Plaatje, 1894–1898', in S. Marks and R. Rathbone (eds), *Industrialisation and Social Change: African Class Formation, Culture and Consciousness, 1870–1930*. London: Longman.

Willan, B. (1984) *Sol Plaatje: South African Nationalist 1876–1932*. Berkeley, CA: University of California Press.

Wilson, F. and Mafeje, A. (1963) *Langa: A Study of Social Groups in an African Township*. Cape Town: Oxford University Press.

Woods, D. (1981) *Black and White*. Dublin: Ward River Press.

Worger, W. (1987) *South Africa's City of Diamonds*. New Haven, CT: Yale University Press.

Wyatt, D. (1995) *Rugby Disunion*. London: Victor Gollancz.

Theses and unpublished papers

Badenhorst, C. (1992a) 'African boxing in Johannesburg'. Seminar paper presented to the African Studies Seminar, Queen's University, Kingston, Ontario, Canada.

Badenhorst, C. (1992b) 'Mines, missionaries and sport in black Johannesburg 1920–1950'. Unpublished PhD thesis, Queen's University, Kingston, Ontario, Canada.

Bonner, P. (1991) 'Backs to the fence: law, liquor and search for social control in an East Rand Town, 1929–1942'. Paper presented to the Association of African Studies Conference, York University, Toronto.

Goodhew, D. (1989) '"No easy walk to freedom": political organisation in the western areas of Johannesburg between the World Wars'. Seminar paper presented to the African Studies Institute, University of the Witwatersrand.

Jeffrey, I. (1990) 'Street rivalry and patron-managers: football in Sharpeville, 1940–1985'. Paper presented to the History Workshop Conference, University of the Witwatersrand.

Koch, E. (1983) 'Doornfontein and its African working class, 1914–1935: a study of popular culture in Johannesburg'. MA Thesis, University of the Witwatersrand.

Lebelo, M. J. (1990) 'Apartheid's chosen few: urban African middle classes from the slums of Sophiatown to the northern suburbs of Johannesburg, 1935–1985'. Unpublished paper presented to the History Workshop Conference, University of the Witwatersrand.

Magubane, B. (1963) 'Sports and politics in an urban African community: a case study of African voluntary organizations'. Unpublished BA Honours thesis, University of Natal.

Nauright, J. (1992) '"Black island in a white sea": black and white in the making of Alexandra Township, South Africa 1912–1948'. Unpublished PhD thesis, Queen's University, Kingston, Ontario, Canada.

Peires, J. (1981) 'Facta non verba: towards a history of black rugby in the Eastern Cape'. Unpublished paper, History Workshop Conference, University of the Witwatersrand.

Sapire, H. (1989) 'African urbanization and struggles against municipal controls in Brakpan, 1920–1958'. PhD thesis, University of the Witwatersrand.

van der Merwe, F. (1997) 'Rugby in the prisoner-of-war camps during the Anglo-Boer War, 1899–1902'. Paper presented at the Football and Identities International Conference, University of Queensland.

Interviews

Adams, Abdullah 'Meneer', Effendi, Meneer and Emeran, Goosain (1994) Interview by John Nauright, 16 December.

Benjamin, Rajab and members of Montrose Rugby Football Club (1994) Interview by John Nauright, 20 December.

Ebrahim, J. (1993) Interview by John Nauright, 8 February.
Effendi, M. (1994) Interview by John Nauright, 8 December.
Effendi, M. and Adams, A. (1994) Interview by John Nauright, 16 December.
Emeran, G. (1995) Interview by John Nauright, 30 January.
Hendricks, H. (1993) Interview by John Nauright, 4 February.

Internet resources

Mandela, N. (1995), 'Welcoming message from the State President of South Africa', January. RWC Home Page, http://www.rwc.95.org.za.
South African Press Association (1995) SAPA press reports on the Rugby World Cup available on the World Wide Web at http://www.rwc95.org.za.

Video resources

The 1981 Tour Ten Years After, Television New Zealand, 1991.

INDEX

ABOUT THE AUTHOR

JOHN NAURIGHT is a professor of sport management and the director of the Academy of International Sport at George Mason University in Virginia. He is also a visiting professor of sports studies at Aarhus University in Denmark and the University of the West Indies, Cave Hill in Barbados. He received his PhD from Queen's University in Kingston, Ontario, and his bachelor's and master's degrees from the University of South Carolina. He is author and editor of numerous books in sport management and sport studies including *The New Sport Management Reader; The Political Economy of Sport; Making the Rugby World: Race, Gender, Commerce;* and *Global Sport Management* (forthcoming). He has taught in Australia, Canada, Denmark, New Zealand, and the United Kingdom.